Visual Communication
PERCEPTION, RHETORIC, AND TECHNOLOGY

The Hampton Press Communication Series
VISUAL COMMUNICATION
Susan B. Barnes, supervisory editor

Visual Communication: Perception, Rhetoric, and Technology
Diane S. Hope (ed.)

FORTHCOMING

Visual Impact: The Power of Visual Persuasion
Susan B. Barnes (ed.)

Visual Communication
PERCEPTION, RHETORIC, AND TECHNOLOGY

Edited by Diane S. Hope

Papers from the William A. Kern
Conferences in Visual Communication
Rochester Institute of Technology

HAMPTON PRESS, INC.
CRESSKILL, NJ 07626

IN COLLABORATION WITH

RIT CARY
GRAPHIC ARTS
PRESS

Printed in the United States of America.

Cover photograph by Kevin Langton.

Library of Congress Cataloging-in-Publication Data

Visual communication: perception, rhetoric, and technology / edited by Diane S. Hope.
    p. cm. -- (The Hampton Press communications series. Visual communication)
    "Papers from the William A. Kern conferences in visual communication, Rochester Institute of Technology."
    Includes bibliographical references.
    ISBN 1-57273-668-2 -- ISBN 1-57273-669-0 (pbk).
    1. Visual communication. 2. Visual perception. 3. Communication and technology. I. Hope, Diane S. II. Rochester Institute of Technology. III. Series.

P93.5.V565 2006
302.23--dc22
    2005055045

Hampton Press, Inc.
23 Broadway
Cresskill, NJ 07626

Dedicated to my mother
Angelina DeFabio DiPasquale
(1920–2004)
who taught me to see

Contents

Acknowledgments

THE COLLECTION OF PAPERS IN THIS VOLUME and the conferences in which they were presented would not have been possible without the support of a number of people. I am especially grateful for the endowment of the Rochester Telephone Company in the name of former company president and Rochester Institute of Technology trustee, William A. Kern. The Kern Professorship, established to provide instruction and research in contemporary communication issues and residing in the Department of Communication, College of Liberal Arts, enables the RIT conferences in *Visual Communication: Rhetorics and Technologies* to bring together a variety of interdisciplinary scholars in productive exchange.

I wish to thank RIT President Albert J. Simone, and especially Provost Stanley D. McKenzie and Dean Andrew A. Moore for their trust and encouragement during my tenure as Kern Professor in Communications. Thanks to my department colleagues, Bruce Austin (Chair), Sue Barnes, Keith Jenkins, Michael Mazanec, David Neumann, Rudy Pugliese, and Patrick Scanlon for their collegiality and their help in making the 2001 and 2003 conferences successful.

A special thank you to Barbara Bernstein of Hampton Press and David Pankow, Curator, Cary Library and Director, Cary Graphic Arts Press, for their willingness to experiment with collaboration for this volume. They turned a wish into a productive publication experience. Thank you to Sue Barnes, Visual Communication Series editor for Hampton Press, for her encouragement of this project from the beginning, and to Amelia Hugill-Fontanel, Production Editor, and Marnie Soom, Design and Marketing Specialist, Cary Press, for their creative and efficient work. They have been a special pleasure to work with.

Special thanks to Tom Benson, Bruce Austin, Stan McKenzie and Pat Scanlon for their helpful comments on early drafts of the introductory chapter to this volume of papers. Their suggestions and insights helped to focus and refine the broad review presented here.

Thanks too to RIT colleagues, Therese Mulligan, former curator of Photography, George Eastman International Museum of Photography and Film, and to Robert Croog, former director of Trademark, Advertising and Copyright Legal Staff, Eastman Kodak, for delightful conversations about the Kodak Colorama and for their encouragement and help in continuing my exploration of that topic. Thank you to Phil Huge and his staff at Eastman Kodak Company's KRESS Imaging Services for their work in restoring the Colorama images and for making the images available.

The library and archival staff at the Eastman House, were, as always, gracious, helpful and kind—a special thanks to David Wooters, Photo Archivist, who turned me on to the Colorama in the first place and to Rachel Stahlman, librarian, and Barbara Galasso, photographer, for their assistance. Kari Horowicz, RIT photography reference librarian, and Rebecca Simmons, RIT archivist, were always available and I appreciate their enthusiasm and support.

Thanks to the many former student assistants who worked on the conferences, especially to Valerie (Dilliplane) Welch, Shira E. Katsir, Verda Duygun and Colleen McCarthy. Alexa Castle's work in building and maintaining the website for the first two conferences was creative and efficient. A special thanks to former graduate assistant Eileen Shannon for her diligent organization, editorial work, and research relating to this collection. My grateful thanks to Elizabeth Reeves, former student and colleague, who has been a remarkable professional editor of my work.

It is impossible to adequately acknowledge the exemplary work and skill of Cassandra Shellman, administrative assistant to the endowed chairs, College of Liberal Arts. Her calm and efficient organization during the conferences and in the production of this volume ensured the success of this project.

And a warm thanks for all the participants in the William A. Kern Conferences on Visual Communication. It is your work that inspired this collection.

Finally, my loving thanks to Warren Schaich, whose patient readings of many drafts of my papers consistently provide and provoke new insights. His unconditional support of my work is a source of energy and renewal.

Identity and Visual Communication

DIANE S. HOPE

THE CHAPTERS COLLECTED IN THIS VOLUME add to the extensive body of published research on visual communication as a source of meaning, knowledge, and behavior in contemporary culture. Selected from presentations at the Rochester Institute of Technology's William A. Kern conferences in visual communication,[1] the chapters reflect the increasing interest in visual communication from within and without the discipline. Visual images have been a focus in the communication discipline for three decades.[2] The production, influence, uses, and ubiquity of visual images has generated a wide variety of questions, theoretical approaches, and research methods (Barbastis, 2002; Benson, 1980; Gross, 1985; Moriarty, 2002; Smith et al.,

---

1. The William A. Kern Professorship in Communications at the Rochester Institute of Technology was established as an endowment by the Rochester Telephone Company to commemorate the 100 year anniversary of the company and to provide a memorial for a former company president who served as an RIT trustee from 1959 to 1964. The purpose of the endowment is to provide instruction and research into contemporary communication issues. The chapters collected here were presented at one of two Kern Conferences on Visual Communication, held in March 2001 and April 2003. A third conference is planned for 2006. In 1977-1978 the Kern endowment sponsored a year long Kern Program/Institute Forum on the moving image, under the coordination of Robert E. Golden. Three Kern conferences directed by Bruce Austin, former William A. Kern Professor in Communications, titled "Fast Rewind," focused on "the archeology of film" and occurred in 1989, 1991, and 1993.

2. See especially the work of Thomas W. Benson and that of Sol Worth and Larry Gross. For example, the early Science Research Associates module on nonverbal communication (Benson & Frandson, 1976) included an examination of photo

1

2005; Zettl, 1999). Both the National Communication Association (NCA) and the International Communication Association (ICA) recognize a visual communication division. Member lists include rhetorical critics; communication theorists; photojournalists; film, television, and Internet scholars; and researchers who investigate the processes of vision. Professional associations and nonaffiliated groups of communication scholars and departments sponsor conferences, seminars, and workshops devoted to visual communication and/or visual rhetoric with increasing regularity, testimony to the liveliness of research interest in visuality and visual artifacts as significant aspects of communication.[3]

The breadth of disciplinary interest in visual communication is reflected in the topic range of monographs and anthologies. Examples come from photojournalism (Barnhurst & Nerone, 2003; Newton, 2001), technical communication (Kostelnick & Roberts, 1998), perception and cognition (Barry, 1997), and numerous books on various aspects of the rhetoric of visuals; in social movements and environmental activism (DeLuca, 1999), print culture and circulation of FSA photographs (Finnegan, 2003), rhetorical iconography in American history (Olson, 1991, 2004); cartoons (Edwards, 1997; McAllister, Sewell, & Gordon, 2001); and an anthology of readings defining visual rhetoric (Hill & Helmers, 2004). A number of studies focused on some aspect of visual images are published in communication journals, and although rhetorical studies dominate, a variety of approaches and subjects are presented in the literature.

Interest in visual communication within the discipline is keen and substantial, and it is not difficult to predict an accelerated pace of research into modes of communication in which the visual is privileged. Yet, despite the profusion of research in visual communication, and periodic calls for visual communication in the basic course (Foss, 1982; Foss & Kanengieter, 1992), the inclusion of visual communication as an integrated component

---

graphic practices as rhetorical strategies. Rhetorical studies of "nondiscursive" forms, including visual modes, increased dramatically after the Wingspread conference on rhetoric in 1970 (Ehninger et al., 1971). Worth and Gross published "Symbolic Strategies" in 1974, which asked the basic question, "What can we know from these images and how can we know it?" (see also Gross, 1985).

3. Other conferences have included the Visual Rhetoric Conference (2001, Bloomington, IN) sponsored by Indiana University and the University of Iowa and the nonaffiliated interdisciplinary Visual Communication conference (sometimes called Rocky Mountain Conferences) now in its 20th year.

of the discipline is haphazard, and an integrated disciplinary approach remains in flux.

Three approaches to visual communication research were found to be prevalent in a recent review of the visual communication literature:

> Studies that take primarily a rhetorical approach consider images and designs key occasions of persuasion. . . . Studies that take primarily a semantic approach consider the visual as text in much the way that linguists look at language. . . . Studies that take primarily a pragmatic approach consider the visual a practice. (Barnhurst, Vari, & Rodríguez, 2004, pp. 629-630)

Rhetorical approaches to visuality were found to be dominant, and the fastest growth in research papers was in studies of new technology. "Rhetoric dominated in books on theory and on mass and popular media, in visual articles from communication journals, and in ICA papers" (p. 632).[4] Photographs, film, advertising, cartoons, television, photojournalism, monuments, and other visual artifacts were the subject of rhetorical critique in studies of cultural or collective memory, the social influence of technologies, and representations of gender, race, class and national identities. Each of these research areas contributes to understanding the influence of visual communication in an image-based society. The authors conclude, "[The studies] attempt to understand how the visual persuades or narrates, in most cases preferring rhetoric as an approach, rather than the pragmatics of image production and reception" (p. 621). The dominance of rhetoric in visual communication points to the significance of identity and identifications in the study of images.

"Visual studies," an interdisciplinary project spawned in the early 1990s by scholars and practitioners from a number of disciplines, engendered an ongoing debate about academic disciplinarity,[5] and established a theoretical canon, a number of scholarly journals and anthologies, and an

---

4. NCA presentations reflect a wide range of research interests as well. In 2004, in addition to the scores of presentations that addressed questions of visuality sponsored by other divisions, the NCA division of visual communication sponsored 14 programs of 42 papers reporting on topics as diverse as imagery in cyberspace, rhetorics of identity and ideology in the American West, science discourse, and a traditional campaign-year workshop on political advertising

5. W. J. T. Mitchell (1994) developed the term "indiscipline" to describe the connections in fields. According to Elkins (2003), "visual studies" overlaps with two other interdisciplinary areas of research: "cultural studies," a U.K.-based

extensive body of literature (Elkins, 2003). Although researchers debate the historical moment and circumstances that account for theorizing a "visual culture,"[6] there is wide agreement that the postmodern era is marked by the omnipresence of images: "It is beyond question that the number of images in circulation is greater than 100, 50, or even 10 years ago. The production, distribution and availability of images has increased radically, thanks to technological developments" (Gierstberg & Oosterbaan, 2002, p. 14). Although cave paintings and early carvings have long provided evidence of the significance of images and image-making as one of the earliest signs of communication in human culture (Baldwin, 1970; Benford, 1999; Flood, 1997; Schramm, 1988), the technologies of print, photography, film, video, digital display, and imaging have multiplied access to and uses of visuals as a way of knowing and ordering the world.

> Visual Studies is poised to become one of the most interesting and conceptually challenging subjects that has emerged in academic life in the last several decades. It can be the place where questions of visuality are discussed—where people from different disciplines come to discover new ways of understanding images. (Elkins, 2003 p. vii)

The discipline of communication is commonly referenced as central to visual studies,[7] and interdisciplinary scholarship in visual studies likewise enlarged the scope and direction of research in the communication discipline. Interdisciplinary interest in the visual corresponds to the increasing use of images in societies connected by image-rich electronic global networks. Visual artifacts are the material products of technologies; their production, reproduction, circulation, and consumption constitute major economic and social activities for individuals and collectivities. Most of the chapters in this volume focus on the prevalence of representational images circulated in cultural artifacts and communication media. Other important uses of images are peripheral to this collection but deserve mention as significant areas of research in visual communication. They include the use of visualization

---

approach started in the late 1950s, and "visual culture," emergent in the early 1990s in the United States.

6. See Elkins' (2004) discussion of visual culture as a "preeminently" an "American movement" (pp. 2-4).

7. Communication or media studies are cited as significant disciplines in the purpose statements of the following journals: *Journal of Visual Literacy, Visual Studies, Journal of Visual Culture,* and *Visual Communication.*

in informational displays and technical communication (Kostlenick, 1996; Kostlenick & Roberts, 1998; Robinson & Schraw, 1994; Tufte, 2001, 2003), ethics (Allen, 1996; Katz, 2001), conventions in visual graphics and computer displays (Barton & Barton, 1985; Tovey, 1996); education and training (Condon, 1986; Davis, Bathhurst, & Bathurst, 1990); scientific research (Calcagno-Tristant, 2003; Frankel, 2002; Van Buren, 2004), health (Coxall, Skelton, & Fletcher, 2003; Tanner, 2004; Thorson & Beaudoin, 2004), medical diagnosis and treatment (Mitchell, 2001) and environmental communication (DeLuca, 1999; DeLuca & Demo, 2000; Parkinson, 2002).

My purpose in these introductory notes is, first, to review briefly the history of visual communication studies and, second, to introduce the chapters by highlighting "identity" as a key conceptual term that links visual perception, rhetoric, and the technologies of symbolic structures, the major areas of research represented in this volume. The discussion seeks to position visual communication as a foundational core within the discipline of communication. Visual artifacts provoke intended and unintended meanings for individual and collective identity, and they begin with processes of perception. The research gathered here variously addresses questions of visuality as communication, yet, directly or indirectly, each chapter reveals the significance of *identity* as a key concept in visual communication research and as fundamental to understanding human communication.

A note about the structure of this book: Section One, *Visual Intelligence and Visual Perception* is comprised of two chapters: Rick Williams' keynote presentation, "Theorizing Visual Intelligence: Practices, Development, and Methodologies for Visual Communication," and Ann Marie Barry's "Media Memories, Videogame Lies," which focuses on visual intelligence, perception, memory, and cognition. These chapters were selected to open the book as an initial frame for understanding the connections among vision, meaning-making, and development of self. Section II, *Collective Identities, Visual Rhetoric and Public Space*, opens with a critique of visual rhetoric by Kevin Michael DeLuca. "The Speed Of Immanent Images: The Dangers Of Reading Photographs" raises theoretical questions and is followed by chapters that focus on methods, practices, and theories of visual rhetoric. Lester Olson's chapter, "Visual Rhetoric as Indices of Political Change: A Sketch of a Conceptual, Technical Approach to Benjamin Franklin's Pictorial Representations Portraying British America" opens Section III, *Visual Innovators, Structures, and Techniques,* which presents a group of chapters that examine the work and structure of individuals, notable for their production of visual artifacts.

Verbal and numeric literacy have structured education for centuries, and computer literacy has become a standard expectation, yet the study and teaching of visual literacy, outside of art-related disciplines, has had an indifferent reception in the academy. Traditionally, visual literacy courses acquainted students with elements of artistic production such as balance, design, proportion, shape, color, and perspective in canonical works of fine art. Such courses provided "a reference and guide for all studio, art history and art appreciation students" (Curtiss, 1987, p. vii), while slighting uses of visuals in the social sciences, science, education, history, and popular culture. The use of images in political propaganda and pornography historically cast them in a suspicious light; likewise the predominant use of images in advertising, entertainment media (especially television) perceived to be "low-culture," and in popular decorative arts diminished images as an appropriate subject of study for some faculty. Anthropologist Marcus Banks (2001) wrote, "It is almost as though the disembedding of visual culture, and its containment in a discourse of 'art', has caused a suspicion of images in other contexts, and a consequent need to constrain and limit the work that they do" (p. 9). Lingering academic resistance to the study of visual modes is most prominent in discourse-centered disciplines and is usually justified as a defense of rational thinking and learning, especially in philosophy, discourse studies, argumentation, and history, but attitudes and practices are changing.

English studies are investigating the use of images in argument and rhetoric and have revived the "sister arts" tradition as a way to approach the aesthetics of images (Allen, 2002; Blair, 2004; Helmers, 2004; Varga, 1989), and literature scholars use images to investigate cultural constructs of class, ethnicity, race, and gender (hooks, 1992; Zandy, 2004). Bruner and Oelschaeger (1994) lament the "linguistic turn" in philosophy and the "arcane discussions" that exclude public understanding of environmental ethics in their call for an "architectonic" rhetoric that might begin "with a symbol (or even an image)" (p. 395). Whereas the traditional use of images in history texts was "largely decorative" (Maimsheimer, 1985, p. 54), recent directions in history generate "a broader range of evidence, in which images have their place alongside literary texts and oral testimonies" (Burke, 2001, p. 9). *Visual Sociology* continues for the 19th year as the journal of the International Visual Sociology Association. Visual Anthropology is a thriving subdiscipline (Hockings, 1995). The Society for Visual Anthropology, founded in 1984, has published the *Visual Anthropology Review* for 20 years, and, according to Banks (2001), "Visual anthropology has never seemed more popular" (p. 2).

Although the use of images to arouse strong emotions remains somewhat suspect, there has been a rapid increase in the production of knowledge about the physiological and psychological processes of seeing and responding cognitively to images. Hill (2004) described how accumulated research has begun to alter academic iconophobia and legitimize study of the emotional impact of images as a significant aspect of meaning-making:

> Only recently, now that simple binary distinctions such as "emotional vs. rational" have been problematized in the theoretical literature and demonstrated as invalid by much of the empirical research into cognitive and neurological processes, has it become acceptable to treat rhetorical images as objects worthy of serious study without feeling the need to deny their largely emotional nature. (p. 27)

Research in perceptual psychology, cognition, and neurology has increased understanding of the primacy of visual perception in meaning-making and cognition, emotion, and memory (Barry, 1997, 2002; Cooper & Hochberg, 1994; Daw, 1995; Rosinski, 1977; Streri, 1993). As scientific research has accumulated, calls for pedagogies that explore the place of images in individual behavior and social life have been reinvigorated. Additionally, the development of visual technologies in the production, circulation, and accessibility of information and the steady rise in the cultural consumption of images and artifacts has weakened resistance to the study of visual presentations in educational institutions.

Calls for *visual* literacy have merged with calls for *media* literacy generated primarily by the extensive use of image-based television and the image-rich computer screen as primary sources of information, news, and entertainment (Stephens, 1998). Corresponding concerns from lay publics and researchers motivate examination of possible connections between violence and mediated images of violence (DeLuca & Peeples, 2002; Gerbner, 1994, 1996; Kamalipour & Rampal, 2001; Meyers, 2004; Surette, 1998), eating disorders and advertising (Kilbourne, 1994; Wolfe, 2002), overconsumption and advertising (Angus & Jhally, 1989; DeGraaf, Wann, & Naylor 2001; Ewen, 1976; Hope, 2002, 2004), civic disengagement (Bertman, 2000; McAllister, 1996; Postman, 1985), and racial, gender, and ethnic stereotyping in television, magazine, film, and news image (Calafell & Delgado, 2004; Davis, 2000; Dijkstra, 1996; Frith, 1997; Meyers, 1999; Scanlon, 2000).

Proponents of media literacy have long argued that visual communication skills should be formally taught, as children are especially vulnerable to misunderstanding visual images and indulging risky emotional responses (Dondis, 1973, 1981); research in cognitive development supports the claim (Daw, 1995). The Center for Media Literacy Web site (2004) offers curricular material, resources, and exercises for all grade levels. Other media scholars argue that corporate control of communication media marginalizes whole populations of viewer-citizens and mandates the teaching of critical media literacy: "Critical media literacy is necessary in the struggle to construct counter-hegemonic practices that are grounded in a recognition of the complex workings of power in a 'democratic' state" (Steinberg & Kincheloe, 1995, p. 3). Visual communication encompasses both visual and media literacy and broadens the focus to include professional career demands on communication practitioners to produce, manage, and promote effective visual images (Barnhurst et al., 2004; Davies et al., 1990). Visual communication courses are emergent in some communication departments at both the undergraduate and graduate levels. In some courses, rudimentary exercises in creating visuals are included; others instruct students in the use of technologies designed to produce visual presentations (Barnhurst et al., 2004).

Introductory courses in visual communication generally include some attention to shape, form, color, line, and design, but focus on visual perception, communication theories and models, media, graphics, ethics, and stereotyping. Texts typically revolve around the material culture of visual artifacts and their influences on society and include discussions of television, photography, film, cartoons, advertising, and computers (Berger, 1998; Lester, 2003; Morgan & Welton, 1986). Lester's (2003) *Visual Communication: Images with Messages,* in a third edition, is an example of a popular undergraduate text. Lester asserts that new knowledge about visual perception, new technologies of visual production, and the ubiquity of visual messages "all demand that we become more visually literate" (p. vii). He includes chapters on light, the brain and the retina, and sensual and perceptual theories of vision before examining the major modes of visual communication. Lester's textbook emphasizes ethics, social influence, stereotypes, and criticism of visual forms. The text provides an introduction to the major modes of visual communication and rhetorical artifacts that have become common examples in the literature, for example, Benetton's shock ads, Dorothea Lange's *Migrant Mother,* and Orson Welles' *Citizen Kane.*

Investigation of the relationship between visuals and meaning is at the center of visual communication and ranges across the discipline. Communication scholars are concerned with visual communication in and between individuals and small groups; media scholars focus on the history, functions, organizations, uses, and effects of a variety of visual technologies; and rhetorical scholars investigate the influence of visuals at work in the public sphere. Researchers use a variety of disciplinary theories, some adapted from psychology, sociology, semiotics, semantics, art, and design. Barnhurst et al. (2004) cite theories of rhetoric, persuasion, semiotics, symbolic interaction, feminist theory, and critical theory in their review of visual studies in communication. Visual communication scholars argue that the process of making meaning from visual images involves developmental patterns, unconscious associations, emotional responses, rational decisions, and technological competencies that cannot be explained by transmission theories of communication (DeLuca, 1999; Sholle & Denski, 1995). As early as 1944, noted theorist and designer Gregory Kepes described "visual language" as the "most powerful" and "effective" form of communication because of its integrative process in making meaning. "The experiencing of every image is the result of an interaction between external physical forces and internal forces of the individual as he assimilates, orders, and molds external forces to his own measure" (p. 16). Making meaning through visual images indicates a process that points to the centrality of self, identity, and identification.

VISUAL INTELLIGENCE, PERCEPTION, MEMORY, AND COGNITION

Neurological information about visual perception and physiological studies of cognition inform contemporary approaches to visual communication that recognize "engagement with the visual" begins with the act of seeing.[8] Cognitive processes resulting from visual perception are markedly different from the symbolic manipulations necessary to make meaning from words heard as speech or read as text. Images and pictures are meaningful to the youngest sighted child and the least educated citizen, making images extremely useful as modes of communication. For instance, the easy accessibility of images explains the dominant use of the pictorial in global advertising (Mueller, 1996), early education, and international icons when language barriers may present problems in maneuvering the basic tasks of every day life (Davies et al., 1990). Such uses assume functional visual literacy, and the common-sense assumption is supported by research in perception.

---

8. The phrase is borrowed from the *Journal of Visual Culture*. The journal describes itself as "a site for astute, informative and dynamic thought on the visual . . . and as essential reading for [those] engaged with the visual" (n.p., 2003).

In normal development, children need little formal training to make some kind of sense from what they see. At a young age they express themselves in drawing and can recognize themselves and others in photographs, in spite of anomalies of scale and dimension. "The ability to perceive objects and space based on photographic representations does not take specific training and follows a course of development similar to that of nonmediated perception" (Rosinski, 1977, p. 178). This is in obvious contrast to the skills of reading and writing, which take an average of 4-5 years of learning to develop. Contemporary research documents that in the first few years of life, vision is the major source of information (Davies et al., 1990). Yet, cultural conventions structure particular kinds of visual communication that, akin to verbal literacy, must be learned (Hoffman, 1998; Kostlenick & Roberts, 1998). Research in perception documents both developmental and learned modes of visual processing. Further complexity is indicated by evidence that in the chemical paths of the brain, visualization of objects and visualization of *images of objects* "fire" the same neurons, indicating that the mental processing of visual information does not discriminate between "reality" and mediated images (Barry, 1997; Cooper & Hochberg, 1994). The multiple processes of visual functions make evident the power of images to communicate and confuse. As Barry documents in her chapter, "Media Memories, Videogame Lies" in this volume, children frequently assume reality in fictional images and easily confuse mediated visual memories and memories of actual events.

Vision, the most sophisticated of the senses, is the major source of information for human mobility in space and for responding to external stimuli (Daw, 1995). Perceived patterns of illumination, color, shape, and movement are instantaneously "scanned" and compared with patterns learned in infancy. The immediacy of human response to visuals informs cognition with emotional complexity as well as data, making visual communication primary in the development of sentient consciousness. Additionally, the development of vision in infants is closely connected to touch and coordinated with the development of physical manipulations and reach (Streri, 1993). Although differing developmental theories and research studies are inconclusive about the precise neurological relationship among vision, orality, and the reach of arm and hand, the connections between sight and touch are established as the major way that infants "organize their knowledge about themselves and about the world at large" (Steri, 1993, p. xi). The infant develops consciousness by physically testing the boundaries of self and world through combined behaviors of vision and touch. At 3 to 4 months, babies begin to differentiate themselves from the objects they can see, reach for, and grasp. As visual perception continues to mature, children can imagine themselves in relationship to spatial environments, and they literally move into the world as cognition develops. "The way we picture the world and ourselves in relation to it is at the very core of our identity and is absolutely key in the process of communication" (Barry, 1997, p. 102). These earliest stages in the development of self suggest that visual perception and cognition are essential to identity formation, a starting place for human communication.

The lead chapters in this volume address directly visual perception, cognition, and intelligence. Rick Williams and Ann Marie Barry reference contemporary research in the psychological and neurological sciences; together, their chapters issue an urgent call for pedagogical attention to visual perception and cognition in constructions of a meaningful reality and, consequently, to communication. In "Theorizing Visual Intelligence," Rick Williams applies theories of visual perception to creative intelligence and the process of communication: "The power of visual images to communicate directly and instantaneously to the whole mind and to produce significant effects on perceptions of reality and on behavior has resisted theorizing and standardized methodologies" (p. 32). Williams believes that the study of visuals (outside of art) has been avoided precisely because much of the work of images is connected to unconscious emotional responses rather than "rational" cognitive processes; he argues that theories in visual communication must include explication of links among creativity, emotion, and identity. Williams provides pedagogical exercises developed to guide students toward understanding their own creativity and visual intelligence as a resource for visual literacy. Using his experience as a professional photographer, Williams' theories and practices demonstrate the links among self-identity, image-making, and values in an image-saturated world.

Ann Marie Barry's application of perceptual and cognitive research findings to the processes of human communication helped establish visual intelligence as a significant area for media research. Barry's seminal book, *Visual Intelligence* (1997), made an especially strong argument that visual perception and mediated images are joined in visual communication theory. For this volume, Barry continues to explore the connections among visual perception, meaning-making, and media. In her chapter, "Media Memories, Videogame Lies," Barry examines "how media experience becomes memory" in a discussion of video games and the fallibility of memory. Barry reviews the physiological processes connecting memory to self-development and urges communication scholars to probe connections among visual perception, memory, and communication media in the behaviors and attitudes of adolescents. In addition to the work of individual memory, visuals are significant in the construction of cultural collective memory (Blair, Jeppeson, & Pucci, 1991; Edwards, 2004). Together, these studies support the thesis that development of visual perception and cognition is closely associated with differentiating the self from the other and constructing memory of the self in the perceived world. The ambiguities of shifting visual perceptions, and the emotional stratum of visual cognition, establish visual intelligence as a complex process of meaning-making that, in turn, invites examination of the rhetorical dimensions of visual images.

VISUAL RHETORIC AND COLLECTIVE IDENTITY

The conflation of rhetoric, persuasion, and identification is the second consideration in tracing a conceptual link between studies of visual perception and visual rhetoric. Burke's expansion of rhetoric into forms of identification has had a sustained influence on what kinds of communicative events can be considered as rhetorical acts and what terms of analysis are available to the rhetorical critic (Burke, 1969). He summarizes,

> So, there is no chance of our keeping apart the meanings of persuasion, identification ("consubstantiality") and communication (the nature of rhetoric as "addressed"). But, in given instances, one or another of these elements may serve best for extending a line of analysis in some particular direction. (p. 46)

Advertising offers an obvious paradigm in explicating connections among constructs of self, identification, and visual images as rhetorical artifacts in the spaces of public discourse. The ubiquity of ads, their influence on consumer habits, cultural fantasy, and their symbolic appeals to identity have generated hundreds of research studies of which I cite only a few in this general overview.

Market researchers and advertising practitioners have contributed much to our understanding of how the process of identification in visual artifacts is exploited by advertisers (Klassen, Jasper & Schwartz, 1993; McQuarrie, 1996; McQuarrie & Mick, 1999; Schroeder, 1998, 2003). In a chapter for an anthology titled *Representing Consumers* (Stern, 1998), Schroeder "develops a framework for incorporating photography into consumer research that bears on questions of consumption, identity, and representation" (p. 194). He analyzes "interactions between photography and identity—personal identity, gender identity, ethnic identity," and notes that "photography is a critical medium that consumers use to represent themselves" (p. 195). Advertising's intentional manipulation of the photographic image as a source of identity formation substantiates theories of symbolic interactionism as well as persuasion and rhetoric (Goffman, 1979). Advertising's persuasive appeals to gender, racial, ethnic, national, and class/status identities have been studied from a variety of disciplinary approaches, and a large body of research documents the wide-reaching influence of advertising in constructing identities beyond that of consumer (Belknap & Leonard, 1991; Busby & Leichty, 1993; Hope, 2004; Kang, 1997; Marchand, 1985; McLaughlin & Goulet, 1999). Advertising, it can be concluded, markets identities along with products primarily by using photographic images framed and designed to appeal to fantasies of imagined selves.

The rhetorical strategy that pictures an association between desirable identities and products, services, or brands relies on the idea of *presence* in representational likeness. Rhetorical presence was explicated in *The New Rhetoric: A Treatise on Argumentation* (Perelman & Olbrechts-Tyteca, 1971), and the concept has been revived in studies of visual rhetoric. "*Presence*, as the term is used by Perelman and Olbrechts-Tyteca, refers to the extent to which an object or concept is foremost in the consciousness of the audience members" (Hill, 2004, p. 28, italics in original). Hill's discussion of presence in the psychological response to visuals connects the power of presence to the immediacy of visual perception and is further extended by a variety of argumentation scholars (Chryslee, Foss, & Ranney, 1996; Palczewski, 2002). Blair (2004) concluded, "The visual has an immediacy, a verisimilitude, and a concreteness that help influence acceptance and that are not available to the verbal" (p. 59). Palczewski (2002) offered one of the most complete reviews of visual presence in argumentation, and established the significance of visuals for argumentation theory in claims of identity.

The symbolic ambiguity of images combined with presence makes them a particularly powerful source of free-floating appropriations that can translate as iconic appeals to individual and collective identities beyond the blatant strategies of advertising (Edwards, 2004; Hariman & Lucaites, 2002, 2003; Lucaites, 1997; Olson, 1983; Reynolds, 2000). Multiple meanings are at the heart of the rhetoric of identification in various uses of visual images. In his discussion of "image and idea," Burke described how a "concrete" image of a mother, designed to "place it before our very eyes," can appropriate and accrue emotional associations that invite identification with any one of a number of ideas or ideologies. Burke listed the ideas of "security, affection, tradition, 'naturalness,' [and] communion" and uses the idea of "security" to exemplify his meaning (p. 87). Yet, the mother-image can indicate, as well, an absence of security, as in Dorothea Lange's image *Migrant Mother*. The familiar Lange image provides a useful example for our discussion of the multiple ways identification as rhetoric occurs in the production, circulation, and uses of a visual artifact.

The history and use of Lange's photograph figures prominently in various discussions of the symbolic power of visual images as persuasive appeal, iconic representation, compelling aesthetic, and historical document. The image, made in 1936, gained popular appeal through identification with the worried mother in the image; in the context of the Depression the image also confirmed a collective identity for a public that saw itself in sympathy with dispossessed citizens. Still, the image has many other interpretations: "To write about the *Migrant Mother* is not only an individual critical act, but an act that necessitates engagement with an ongoing interpretive controversy over the social, political, and ethical meanings of this image" (Finnegan, 2003, p. 99). Critical controversy regarding *Migrant Mother* revolves around interpretations of the identities read in the image. Finnegan references interpretations of the image as stereotype in overidentifying women with motherhood (Fisher, 1987, cited in Finnegan, 2003) and as a universal icon identifying the Depression era poor (Coles, 1997; Lucaites & Hariman, 2001; Meltzer, 1978, cited in Finnegan, 2003). Other interpreters include Shindo (1997), who examined Lange's photographs, along with John Ford's film, *The Grapes of Wrath,* John Steinbeck's novel of the same title, the songs of Woody Guthrie, and the lives of all four artists, and argued that the migrants' personal identities were appropriated by image-makers. He wrote:

> The various representations of the migrants' place in a democratic America relied on the attitude each producer had toward the migrants' culture and their understanding of it. Appropriation of the migrant experience resulted in an image of the migrant quite separate from expression of the migrant experience by the migrants themselves and these representations have had a more lasting impression on the American imagination than the migrants' own expressions. (p. 210)

Lester (2003) recounted the fate of Florence Thompson (never named in the early reproductions) and constructs her identity as a victim; he quotes her as saying, "That's my picture hanging all over the world, and I can't get a penny out of it" (p. 228). Thompson's grandson, Roger Sprague, supports this reading and maintains a Web site devoted to the saga of his grandmother and her highly publicized illness from cancer. Sprague offers a lecture series in which he is "prepared to impart the true story of his grandmother, including a discussion of the 'myths' and 'falsehoods' that have surrounded the photograph since it was taken" (Sprague, 2004). Bezner (1999) traced the history and practice of social documentary photographers from the depression (exemplified by Lange and the *Migrant Mother*), through the years of the McCarthy era, and relates how image makers, whose work documented the social ills of poverty, racial tension, discrimination, and violence were subject to suspicion as their patriotic identity was questioned. Frequently identified as "propagandists," Communists, and "anti-Americans," some image makers were blacklisted. Bezner frames this narrative of suspect identities as the victory of "American Photographic Expressionism" and a loss of photography as a tool for social change (pp. 219-226). Photographers, once identified as social activists, redefined themselves as artists, a less politically charged calling. *Migrant Mother* moved quickly from social document to art object and finally to commodity. The photograph was exhibited in the Museum of Modern Art only five years after it was made. In 1998 the signed portrait sold for $244,500 at Sotheby's auction house and was immediately resold to the Getty museum for an undisclosed amount of money (Lester, 2003).

In sum, the rhetorical history of one image reveals multiple uses of identification: identification appears as a strategy used to gain assent for public programs from viewers, unforeseen identifications challenge persuasive intentions, universal identities constitute cultural icons, and restricted identities reinforce social stereotypes. In addition, identities can be appropriated for diverse ambitions, self-identifies can be redefined, and narratives of division can transform identities. The multiple interpretations available in any image support Kevin Michael DeLuca's argument presented in his chapter, "The Speed Of Immanent Images: The Dangers Of Reading Photographs." DeLuca worries "about how we as a field use context, morality, and transcendent theory to reduce the rhetorical force of images to meaning, domesticating them for our studies." In order to situate the meaning of an image in a collective rhetoric, we can easily "obscure" the impact of its individual "singularity." DeLuca's theoretical challenge haunts the chapters in this volume and reminds us to return always and often to the image itself. Visual rhetoric attempts to influence publics and individuals through multiple strategies of identification present in individual images. A number of chapters in this volume focus on visual rhetorics that promote collective identities in the public sphere.

In "Memorializing Affluence in the Post-War Family: Kodak's Colorama in Grand Central Terminal (1950-1990)," Hope argues that the advertising images displayed by Kodak for 40 years helped solidify a post-war American family identity as a collective of consumers. Kodak produced a series of images portraying a fantasized vision of "family" life that excluded minorities, reinforced traditional gender roles, and valorized affluence in domestic family scenes. Additionally the enormous size of the display and its location in New York's Grand Central Terminal helped establish the legitimacy of commercial advertising in the public commons and magnified the impact of the images. Five additional chapters in Section II focus on the construction of collective identities in the spaces of public discourse.

Two chapters discuss how visual rhetoric can be used to shift identifications. Susan J. Balter-Reitz and Karen A. Stewart study the images accompanying news coverage of the murder of Matthew Shepard in "Looking for Matthew Shepard: A Study in Visual Argument Field." In the public spaces of magazines and magazine covers, they find reoccurring images focused on the *fence* in Laramie, Wyoming, where Shepard's body was found. Balter-Reitz and Stewart conclude that the images work to argue that the scene of the murder was most important and that the visual narrative "erased" Shepard's identity as a student and murder victim. The images "limited the range of discourse about this event," because they "directed the narrative to the Western landscape." The transformation of collective identity is also the subject of Julie Borkin's chapter "Amber Alert: The Subject Citizen and Technologies in Transformation." Borkin explores the electronic display system used to garner assistance from citizens in cases of child abduction and posits that the "widely disseminated, well-publicized and highly vaunted technology" transforms the identity of a "good citizen" into an illusionary agent of the law expected to monitor fellow citizens.

Gender is the identity focus of the last two chapters in Section II. Yana van der Meulen Rodgers and Jing Ying Zhang conduct a content analysis of international news magazines to evaluate the presence of sexually explicit images of women in *Business Week, The Economist, Far Eastern Economic Review, Newsweek* and *Time.* They argue that the circulation of such magazines in classroom settings contributes to gender bias in education by identifying women as sexual objects and men as agents of commerce. Leanne Stuart Pupchek's chapter "Woman's Public Image at a Crossroads: Negotiating Pieties and Paganism in a Southern City," traces a controversy created by the visualization of Hecate, Roman goddess of the crossroads, as the central figure in a commissioned fresco chosen to help "brand" Statesville, NC. Members of the community saw in the figure of Hecate a symbol of paganism and objected to her image as representative of the identities of southern

(Christian) womanhood. Pupcheck's analysis considers the controversy a negotiation of the conflicting artistic, historical, religious, and cultural identity of a southern city in transformation.

The significance of media technologies in the formation of social identity has been an ongoing focus of study for decades. In 1989, Angus and Jhally sketched the scope and direction of media influence on cultural identity:

> In contemporary culture the media have become central to the constitution of social identity. It is not just that media messages have become important forms of influence on *individuals*. We also identify and construct ourselves as *social beings* through the mediation of images. This is not simply a case of people being dominated by images, but of people seeking and obtaining pleasure through the experience of the consumption of these images. (p. 2, italics in original)

Together the chapters in Section II provide a multifaceted examination of rhetoric and collective identity in visual artifacts that predominate in the public sphere. The symbolic structuring of visual media invites study of the projected identities of visual producers, the subject of Section III of this book.

VISUAL INNOVATORS AND SYMBOLIC STRUCTURES

The structure of symbolic forms is a major component in theories of media, culture, rhetoric, symbolic interaction, communication, and art. Producers of visual messages invite identifications through the structuring of symbolic forms in various media technologies. Within the constraints of individual technologies, creator/producers appeal to audiences to construct specific identities by limiting choices, through specific structuring strategies. "The meaningfulness of treating technologies as communication systems begins with the recognition that form itself is rhetorical" (Chesebro, 2000, p. 9). Visual technologies structure images of reality; what viewers see, what they do not see, and how they contextualize images depends on structural choices made by producers, and include editing, framing, sequencing, contrast, focus, illumination, and grounding. The chapters in Section III focus on innovators who structure symbolic forms for various audiences. But viewing audiences are not necessarily passive. Viewers select, choose, and perceive images according to the context, knowledge, and life experience they bring to the act of viewing. Interactive media allow some manipulation in the production of messages and consumption of images to occur in the same event.[9]

Symbolic structuring in all media technologies can occur at each stage of production, circulation, and use.

Identifications presented in media images are shaped initially by structural choices made by producers. The significance of structure in film and video provides a model of how to think about structure in other forms of visual modes as well. Medhurst and Benson (1984/1991) collected several studies that use a structural analysis in their anthology *Rhetorical Dimensions in Media*. In their 1981 study of the documentary film *The City*, reproduced in the book, they wrote, "[T]he meaning of an image in the film is constructed by the viewer not only from the 'content' of the shot but also from the situation, the structural relation of shots to one another and to other dimensions of the film, and from the rhythm of the cutting" (p. 449). Gregg (1984) explored Benson's (1980) study of Frederick Weisman's *High School* to discuss thematic structures that inform "symbolic inducement" in visual media: "Benson's critical thesis is that *High School* invites viewers to experience the structural relations of the themes of power and sexuality . . . and the subordinate manifestations of these themes that appear in the . . . confused identities" which are apparent in the documentary (p. 146). Thus frames, sequence, and arrangement of visual images are ways that producers present themes and structure arguments with film and video. Production of video and film is increasingly accessible through digital technologies for those with funds and skill.

Although film provides a clear example of how structure invites response from viewers, we cannot treat all visual technologies the same; each has its own form, each its own symbolic structure. DeLuca (1999) "reads" television news coverage of the arrest of Earth First! activists as two structures in conflict. The news anchor's verbal narrative identifies the Earth First! protesters as "terrorists," but DeLuca argues that the images structure a positive narrative of peaceful nonviolent protestors in the minds of audiences. Furthermore, DeLuca insists that in a "mass-mediated public sphere" the images resonate more powerfully than the words and invite viewers to create their own narrative in ways not accounted for by the transmission model of communication (p. 138). The technologies of print

---

9. Chesebro theorized that the absence of nonverbal (visual) information in virtual reality chat rooms and in email exchanges affects presentations of the self and significantly alters the ways we understand the sender-receiver model of communication processes: "During computer chats, it is also possible to imply or actually lie about one's sociological characteristics," turning the "unreal" into the "real" (p. 12).

formats structure through page frames and sequences, but readers can flip through a magazine backwards as well as haphazardly, creating individual sequencing of images and ideas. Although producers present intentional structures, consumers of image-rich books are open to individualized patterns of looking and gazing.

A number of chapters in this collection investigate the rhetorical structuring of visual innovators. Lester Olson's chapter describes the methodology used in his extensive ongoing research of the emblems produced and circulated in revolutionary America (1991, 2004). In Olson's contribution to this volume, "Visual Rhetoric as Indices of Political Change: A Sketch of a Conceptual, Technical Approach to Benjamin Franklin's Pictorial Representations Portraying British America," he outlines the conceptual and technical approach used in his latest book to trace Franklin's changing political identity through his pictorial representations of British America. Olson's work is an outstanding demonstration of a methodology that traces the production and circulation of images. His work reveals how meanings and uses of visual icons can indicate changes in identity over time, geography, and audience. The symbolic structures created by six additional innovators complete Section III of this volume.

The visual rhetoric of film, illustration, posters, photojournalism, and documentary are examined in the works of Michael Moore, William Joyce, Lester Beall, and Mark Riboud, respectively. In his analysis "Free Guns and Speech Control: The Structural and Thematic Rhetoric of Michael Moore's *Bowling for Columbine*," Brian Snee examines the film's arguments through a lens of structural themes. He argues that Moore's film presents two competing arguments "articulated in two very different modes of documentary representation" that seek to identify the source of violence in American identities. Symbolic structure is also used by Timothy Gleason to probe the rhetoric of Marc Riboud's photojournalistic books in the chapter, "The Rhetorical Structure of Marc Riboud's Photojournalistic Books: A Journalist's Changing Attitude in *Three Banners of China* (1966), *Visions of China* (1981), and *Marc Riboud in China: Forty Years of Photography* (1997)." Gleason argues that the juxtaposition of images, the positioning of color and black and white sequences, and the pairing of specific photographs reveal how the photojournalist's changing opinion of China can be discovered in the "necessity to structure a book as a complete technical artifact."

Susan B. Barnes and Joseph Stanton discuss a different kind of structure in their chapters; the structures of design, illustration, line, color, and shape. Barnes outlines the vocabulary of bold modernistic designs in

Lester Beall's posters commissioned to promote rural electrification from 1937–1941. Her chapter, "Rural Electrification Administration: A Rhetorical Analysis of the Lester Beall Posters, 1937-1941," examines the design structure as an integral component of the posters' messages and argues that Beall's posters helped to transform the identities of American farmers for the modern age. In "Dashing Heroes and Eccentric Families in William Joyce's Picture Books of our Common Culture," Joseph Stanton traces the cultural and personal sources of William Joyce's illustrations as the structural frame of Joyce's children's books. He examines the illustrations as evidence of our common culture—a culture that in Joyce's work melds popular media and fine art into joyful "playful gestures" of identity.

Gregg (1984) isolated the significance of structure in symbolic inducement by tracing cognitive structuring back to the significance of "patterning" in visual perception:

> An important part of the meaning of any symbolic structure or pattern derives from the larger context in which the structure is perceived and understood. At fundamental levels of symbolic processing "following patterns" of neuronal firings always accompany initial patterns of firing. At more sophisticated levels of processing perceptual models are constantly being compared with relevant portions of our larger cognitive "maps" of "reality." (p. 135)

So we have come full circle. The processes of visual perception and cognition depend on structural patterns identified early in human development and central to formation of self. Visual artifacts influence identifications through appeals in which the presence of representational likeness is a powerful persuasive force. Finally, it is innovators who use various communication technologies to symbolically structure appeals to mediated identities. Their work, the messages, and the rhetorical strategies they use constitute an exploration of visual communication, exemplified in the chapters that follow.

REFERENCES

Allen, N. (1996). Ethics and visual rhetorics: Seeing's not believing anymore. *Technical Communication Quarterly*, 5(1), 87-105.

Allen, N. (Ed.). (2002). *Working with words and images*. Westport, CT: Ablex.

Angus, I., & Jhally, S. (Eds). (1989). *Cultural politics in contemporary America*. New York: Routledge.

Baldwin, G. C. (1970). *Talking drums to written word*. New York: Norton.

Banks, M. (2001). *Visual methods in social research*. Thousand Oaks, CA: Sage.

Barbatsis, G. (2002). Toward a phenomenological understanding of visual communication. *Journal of Visual Literacy, 22*(1), 1-18.

Barnhurst, K. G., & Nerone, J. (2003). *The form of news, a history.* New York: Guilford Press.

Barnhurst, K. G., Vari, M., & Rodríguez, Í. (2004). Mapping visual studies in communication. Special Issue. The State of the Art in Communication Theory and Research (W. L. Benoit & M. Pfau, Eds.). *Journal of Communication, 54*(4), 616-644.

Barry, A.M. (1997). *Visual intelligence: Perception, image, and manipulation in visual communication.* Albany: SUNY Press.

Barry, A. M. (2002). Perception and visual communication theory. *Journal of Visual Literacy, 22*(1), 91-106.

Barton, B. F., & Barton, M. S., (1985). Toward a rhetoric of visuals for the computer era. *The Technical Writing Teacher,* 12(2), 126-145.

Belknap, P., & Leonard, W. M., II. (1991). A conceptual replication and extension of Erving Goffman's study of gender advertisements. *Sex Roles,* 25(3/4), 103-118.

Benford, G. (1999). *Deep time: How humanity communicates across millennia.* London: Avon Books.

Benson, T.W., & Frandson, K. (1976). *An orientation to nonverbal communication.* Palo Alto: Science Research Associates.

Benson, T. W. (1980). The rhetorical structure of Frederick Wisemen's *High School. Communication Monographs,* 47, 233-261.

Bezner, L. C. (1999). *Photography and politics in America: From the New Deal into the Cold War.* Baltimore: Johns Hopkins University Press.

Berger, A. A. (1998). *Seeing is believeing: An introduction to visual communication.* Moutainview, CA: Mayfield.

Berger, A. A. (1984/1989). *Signs in contemporary culture.* Salem, WI: Sheffield Publishing Company.

Bertman, S. (2000). *Cultural amnesia.* Westport, CT: Praeger.

Blair C., Jepperson, M. S., & Pucci, E., Jr. (1991). Public memorializing in postmodernity: The Vietnam Veterans Memorial as prototype. *Quarterly Journal of Speech,* 77, 263-288.

Blair, J. A. (2004). The rhetoric of visual arguments. In A. Hill & M. Helmers (Eds.), *Defining visual rhetorics* (pp. 41-62). Mahwah, NJ.: Erlbaum.

Bruner, M., & Oelschaeger, M. (1994). Rhetoric, environmentalism and environmental ethics. *Environmental Ethics,* 16, 377-396.

Burke, K. (1969). *A rhetoric of motives.* Berkeley: University of California Press.

Burke, P. (2001). *Eyewitnessing: The uses of images as historical evidence.* Ithaca, NY: Cornell University Press.

Busby, L. J., & Leichty, G. (1993). Feminism and advertising in traditional and nontraditional women's magazines 1950s-1980s. *Journalism Quarterly,* 70(2), 247-263.

Calcagno-Tristant, F. (2003). Image and science: Between rhetoric and ideology. *Visual Communication, 2*(3), 356-362.

Calafell, M. B., & Delgado, F. P. (2004). Reading Latina/o images: Interrogating *Americanos. Critical Studies in Media Communication, 21*(1), 1-21.

Center For Media Literacy. <http://www.medialit.org> Accessed, November 17, 2004.

Chesebro, J. W. (2000). Communication technologies as symbolic form: Cognitive transformations generated by the internet. *Qualitative Research Reports in Communication, 1*(1), 8-13.

Chryslee, G. J., Foss, S. K., & Ranney, A. L. (1996). An exploration; The construction of claims in visual argumentation. *News Photographer, 51*(4), 9-16.

Coles, R. (1997). *Doing documentary work.* New York: Oxford University Press.

Condon, J. (1986). Exploring intercultural communication through literature and film. *World Englishes, 5,* 153-161.

Cooper, L. A., & Hochberg, J. (1994). Objects of the mind: Mental representations in visual perception and cognition. In S. Ballesteros (Ed.), *Cognitive approaches to human perception* (pp. 223–239). Hillsdale, NJ: Erlbaum.

Coxall, H., Skelton, P., & Fletcher, T. (2003). The art of public health. *Journal of Visual Culture, 2*(1), 33-50.

Curtiss, D. (1987). *Introduction to visual literacy: A guide to the visual arts and communcation.* Englewood Cliffs, NJ: Prentice-Hall.

Davis, N. Z. (2002). *Slaves on screen: Film and historical vision.* Cambridge: Harvard University Press.

Davies, D., Bathhurst, D., & Bathhurst, R. (1990). *The telling image: The changing balance between pictures and words in a technological age.* Oxford: Clarendon Press.

Daw, N. W. (1995). *Visual development.* New York: Plenum Press.

DeGraaf, J., Wann, D., & Naylor, T. H. (2001/2002) *Affluenza: The all-consuming epidemic.* San Francisco: Barrett-Koehler Publishers.

DeLuca, K. M. (1999). *Image politics.* New York: Guilford Press.

DeLuca, K. M., & Demo, A. T. (2000). Imaging nature: Watkins, Yosemite, and the birth of environmentalism. *Critical Studies in Media Communication, 17*(3), 241-261.

DeLuca, K. M., & Peeples, J. (2002). From public sphere to public screen: Democracy, activism and the "violence" of Seattle. *Critical Studies in Media Communication, 19 (2),* 125-151.

Dijkstra, B. (1996). *Evil sisters: The threat of female sexuality and the cult of manhood.* New York: Knopf.

Dondis, D. A. (1973). *A primer in visual literacy.* Cambridge: MIT Press.

Dondis, D.A. (1981). *Television literacy.* Boston: Boston University School of Public Communication.

Edwards, J. L. (1997). *Political cartoons in the 1988 presidential campaign: Image, metaphor, and narrative.* New York: Garland Publishing.

Edwards, J.L. (2004). Echoes of camelot: How images construct cultural memory through rhetorical framing. In C. Hill & M. Helmers (Eds.), *Defining visual rhetorics* (pp. 179–194). Mahwah, NJ: Erlbaum.

Elkins, J. (2003). *Visual studies: A skeptical introduction.* New York: Routledge.

Ehninger, D., Benson, T. W., Ettlich, E. E., Fisher, W. R., Kerr, H. P., Larson, R., Nadeau, R. E., & Niles, L. A. (1971). Report of the committee on the scope of rhetoric and the place of rhetorical studies in higher education. In L. F. Bitzer & E. Black (Eds.), *The prospect of rhetoric: Report of the National Development Project* (pp. 208-219). Englewood Cliffs, NJ: Prentice-Hall.

Ewen, S. (1976). *Captains of consciousness: Advertising and the social roots of the consumer culture.* New York: McGraw-Hill.

Finnegan, C. A. (2003). *Picturing poverty: Print culture and FSA photographs.* Washington, DC: Smithsonian Books.

Fisher, A. (1987). *Let us now praise famous women: Women photographers for the U.S. Government, 1935-1944.* London: Pandora Press.

Flood, J. (1997). *Rock art of the dreamtime.* Sidney: Angus and Robertson.

Foss, S. K. (1982). Rhetoric and the visual image: A resource unit. *Communication Education, 31*(1), 55-67.

Foss, S.K., & Kanengieter, M. (1992). Visual communication in the basic course. *Communication Education, 41*(3), 312-324.

Frankel, F. (2002). *Envisioning science: The design and craft of the science image.* Cambridge: MIT Press.

Frith, K. T. (Ed.). (1997). *Undressing the ad: Reading culture in advertising.* New York: Peter Lang.

Gerbner, G. (1994). The killing screens: Media and the culture of violence [video] (R. Dinozzi, Prod. & Ed., S. Jhally, Executive Prod., Dir. & Ed.). Amherst, MA: Media Education Foundation.

Gerbner, G. (1996). TV violence and what to do about it. *Nieman Reports, 50*(3), 10-16.

Gierstberg, F., & Oosterbaan, W. (Eds). (2002). Introduction. In *The image society: Essays on visual culture.* Rotterdam: NAiPublishers.

Gregg, R. (1984). *Symbolic inducement and knowing: A study in the foundations of rhetoric.* Columbia: University of South Carolina Press.

Goffman, E. (1979). *Gender advertisements.* New York: Harper.

Gross, L. (1985). Life vs. art: the interpretation of visual narratives. *Studies in Visual Communication, 11*(4), 2-11.

Hariman, R., & Lucaites, J.L., (2002). Performing civic identity: The iconic photograph of the flag raising on Iwo Jima. *Quarterly Journal of Speech, 88*(4), 363-393.

Hariman, R., & Lucaites, J. L. (2003). Public identity and collective memory in U.S. iconic photography: The image of "accidental napalm". *Critical Studies in Media Communication, 20*(1), 35-66.

Helmers, M. (2004). Framing the fine arts through rhetoric. In C.A. Hill & M. Helmers (Eds), *Defining visual rhetorics* (pp. 63-86). Mahwah, NJ: Erlbaum.

Hill, C. A., & Helmers, M. (Eds). (2004). *Defining visual rhetorics*. Mahwah, NJ: Erlbaum.

Hill C. A. (2004). The psychology of rhetorical images. In C.A. Hill & M. Helmers (Eds.), *Defining visual rhetorics* (pp. 25-40). Mahwah, NJ: Erlbaum.

Hockings, P. (1995). *Principles of visual anthropology* (2nd ed). New York: Mouton de Gruyter.

Hoffman, D.D. (1998). *Visual intelligence*. New York: Norton.

hooks, b. (1992). *Black looks*. Boston: South End Press.

Hope, D. S. (2002). Environment as consumer icon in advertising fantasy. In M. Meister & P. M. Japp (Eds.), *Enviropop: Studies in environmental rhetoric and popular culture* (pp. 161–174). Westport CT: Praeger.

Hope, D.S. (2004). Gendered environments: Gender and the natural world in the rhetoric of advertising. In C.A. Hill & M. Helmers (Eds.), *Defining visual rhetorics* (pp. 155-178). Mahwah, NJ: Erlbaum.

Kamalipour, Y. R., & Rampal, K. R. (Eds.). (2001). *Media, sex, violence, and drugs in the global village*. New York: Rowman and Littlefield.

Kang, M. (1997). The portrayal of women's images in magazine advertisements: Goffman's gender analysis revisited. *Sex Roles, 37*(11/12), 979-996.

Katz, S. N. (2001). In information technology, don't mistake a tool for a goal. *Chronicle of Higher Education,* B7-9.

Kepes, G. (1944). *Language of vision*. Chicago: Paul Theobald.

Klassen, M. L., Jasper, C. R., & Schwartz, A. M. (1993). Men and women: Images of their relationships in magazine advertisements. *Journal of Advertising Research,* March/April, 30-39.

Kilbourne, J. (1999). *Deadly persuasion*. New York: Free Press.

Kostelnick, C. (1996). Supra-textual design: The visual rhetoric of whole documents. *Technical Communication Quarterly, 5*(1), 9-33.

Kostlenick, C., & Roberts, D. (1998). *Designing visual language*. Boston: Allyn and Bacon.

Lester, P. M. (2003). *Visual communication: Images with messages* (3rd ed.). Belmont CA: Wadsworth.

Lucaites, J. L. (1997). Visualizing "the people": Individualism vs. collectivism in *Let us now praise famous men*. *Quarterly Journal of Speech, 83*(3), 269-288.

Lucaites, J.L., & Hariman, R. (2001). Visual rhetoric, photojournalism and democratic public culture. *Rhetoric Review, 20,* 37-42.

Maimsheimer, L. A. (1985). Imitation white man. *Studies in Visual Communication, 11*(4), 54-75.

Marchand, R. (1985). *Advertising the American dream: Making way for modernity 1920-1940*. Berkeley: University of California Press.

McAllister, M. P. (1996). *The commercialization of American culture*. Beverly Hills, CA: Sage.

McAllister, M. P., Sewell Jr., E. H., & Gordon, I. (Eds.). (2001). *Comics & ideology*. New York: Peter Lang.

McLaughlin, T. L., & Goulet, N. (1999). Gender advertisements in magazines aimed at African Americans: A comparison to their occurrence in magazines aimed at caucasians. *Sex Roles, 40*(1/2), 61-71.

McQuarrie, E.F. (1996). Figures of rhetoric in advertising language. *Journal of Consumer Research, 22,* 424-438.

McQuarrie, E. F., & Mick, D. G. (1999). Visual rhetoric in advertising: Text-interpretive, experimental, and reader-response analyses. *Journal of Consumer Research. 26,* 37-54.

Medhurst, M. J., & Benson, T. W. (1984/1991). *Rhetorical dimensions in media.* Dubuque, IA: Kendall/Hunt.

Meltzer, M. (1978). *Dorothea Lange: A photographer's life.* New York: Farrar, Straus, and Giroux.

Meyers, M. (Ed.). (1999). *Mediated women: Representations in popular culture.* Cresskill, NJ: Hampton Press.

Meyers, M. (2004). African American women and violence: Gender, race, class in the news. *Critical Studies in Media Communication, 21*(2), 95-118.

Mitchell, L. M. (2001). *Baby's first picture: Ultrasound and the politics of fetal subjects.* Toronto: University of Toronto Press.

Mitchell, W.J.T. (1994). *Picture theory.* Chicago: University of Chicago Press.

Morgan, J., & Welton, P. (1986). *See what I mean: An introduction to visual communication.* New York: Edward Arnold.

Moriarty, S. E. (2002). The symbiotics of semiotics and visual communication. *Journal of Visual Literacy, 22*(1), 19-28.

Mueller, B. (1996). *International advertising.* New York: Wadsworth.

Newton, J. H. (2001). *The burden of visual truth.* Mahwah, NJ: Erlbaum.

Olson, L.C. (1983). Portrait in praise of a people: A rhetorical analysis of Norman Rockwell's icons in Franklin D. Roosevelt's four freedoms' campaign. *Quarterly Journal of Speech, 69*(1), 15-25.

Olson, L. C. (1991). *Emblems of American community in the revolutionary era.* Washington, DC: Smithsonian Institution Press.

Olson, L.C. (2004). *Benjamin Franklin's vision of American community: A study in rhetorical iconology.* Columbia: University of South Carolina Press.

Palczewski, C. H. (2002). Argument in an off-key. In T. Goodnight (Ed.), *Arguing communication and culture: Selected papers from the twelfth NCA/AFA conference on argumentation: 2001* (vol. I, pp. 1-23). Washington, DC: National Communication Association.

Parkinson, C. (2002). Satellite imagery for environment reporting: Journalists can use these images and data to report and illustrate stories. *Nieman Reports, 56*(4), 86-90.

Perelman, C., & Olbrechts-Tyteca, L. (1971). *The new rhetoric: A treatise on argumentation* (John Wilkinson & Purcell Weaver, Trans.). Notre Dame: University of Notre Dame Press.

Postman, N. (1985). *Amusing ourselves to death: Public discourse in the age of show business*. New York: Penguin Books.

Reynolds, L. J. (2000). American cultural iconography. In L. Reynolds & G. Hutner (Eds.), *National imaginaries, American identities* (pp. 3-28). Princeton: Princeton University Press.

Robinson, D. H., & Schraw, G. (1994). Computational efficiency through visual argument: Do graphic organizers communicate relations in text too effectively? *Contemporary Educational Psychology, 19,* 399-415.

Rosinski, R. (1977). *Development of visual perception*. Santa Monica, CA: Goodyear Publishing Company.

Scanlon, J. (Ed.). (2000). *The gender and consumer culture reader*. New York: New York University Press.

Schramm, W. (1988). *The story of human communication: Cave painting to microchip*. New York: Harper Collins.

Schroeder, J. E. (1998). Consuming representation: A visual approach to consumer research. In B. B. Stern (Ed.), *Representing consumers* (pp.193-230). New York: Routledge.

Schroeder, J.E. (2003). Building brands: Architectural expression in the electronic age. In L. M. Scott & R. Batra (Eds.), *Persuasive imagery: A consumer response perspective* (pp. 349-382). Mahwah, NJ: Erlbaum.

Shindo, C. J. (1997). *Dust Bowl migrants in the American imagination*. Lawrence: University Press of Kansas.

Sholle, D., & Denski, S. (1995). Critical media literacy: Reading, remapping, rewriting. In P. McLaren, R. Hammer, D. Sholle, & S. Reilly (Eds.), *Rethinking media literacy: A critical pedagogy of representation* (pp. 7-31). New York: Peter Lang.

Smith, K., Moriarty, S., Barbatsis, G., & Kenney, K. (2005). *Handbook of visual communication: Theory, methods, and media*. Mahwah, NJ: Erlbaum.

Sprague, R. (2004). Migrant Mother: The story as told by her grandson. www.migrantgrandson.com. Accessed September 1, 2004.

Steinberg, S., & Kincheloe, J. (1995). Introduction. In P. McLaren, R. Hammer, D. Sholle, & S. Reilly (Eds.), *Rethinking media literacy: A critical pedagogy of representation* (pp. 1-6). New York: Peter Lang.

Stern, B. B. (1998). *Representing consumers*. New York: Routledge.

Stephens, M. (1998). *The rise of the image, the fall of the word*. New York: Oxford University Press.

Streri, A. (1993). *Seeing, touching, reaching: The relations between vision and touch in infancy*. (Tim Pownall & Susan Kingerlee, Trans.). Cambridge, Mass: MIT Press.

Surette, R. (1998). *Media, crime, and criminal justice: Images and realities* (2nd ed.). Belmont, CA: Wadsworth.

Tanner, A. H. (2004). Communicating health information and making the news: Health reporters reveal the PR tactics that work. *Public Relations Quarterly, 49*(1), 24-28.

Thorson, E., & Beaudoin, C. (2004). The impact of a health campaign on health social capital. *Journal of Health Communication, 9*(3), 167-195.

Tovey, J. (1996). Computer interfaces and visual rhetoric: Looking at the technology. *Technical Communication Quarterly, 5*(1), 61-76.

Tufte, E. R. (2001*). The visual display of quantitative information* (2nd ed.). Chesire, CT: Graphic Press.

Tufte, E.R. (2003). *The cognitive style of powerpoint.* Chesire, CT: Graphic Press.

Van Buren, C. (2004). *Flesh-data-image: The visible humans as animated morph.* Paper presented at the National Communication Association Annual Meeting, Chicago.

Varga, A. K. (1989). Criteria for describing word and image relations. *Poetics Today, 10*(1), 31-53.

Wolfe, N. (2002). *The beauty myth.* New York: Perennial Press.

Worth, S., & Gross, L. (1974). Symbolic strategies. *Journal of Communication, 24*(4), 27–39.

Zandy, J. (2004). *Hands: Physical labor, class, and cultural work.* New Brunswick, NJ: Rutgers University Press.

Zettl, H. (1999). *Applied media aesthetics* (3rd ed.). Belmont, CA: Wadsworth.

SECTION I
VISUAL INTELLIGENCE,
VISUAL PERCEPTION

CHAPTER ONE

Theorizing Visual Intelligence
Practices, Development, and Methodologies for Visual Communication

RICK WILLIAMS
FROM THE KEYNOTE ADDRESS

I N THE LAST 20 YEARS, both academia and popular culture have experienced an explosion of visual communication technologies and applications that have changed both culture and the study of culture significantly. The concept of *visual culture* is now at the forefront of research and in common use in multiple disciplines, including visual communication, media ecology, anthropology, sociology, psychology, cognitive neuroscience, education, comparative literature, and art. Science curricula in mathematics, physics, engineering, computer technology, biology, and chemistry now use sophisticated visual techniques both as tools of scientific method, exploration, and evidence and to teach students to think and solve problems in new ways. In popular culture, visual communication techniques have replaced 20th-century logocentricity as the primary mode of communication through TV programming, computer technologies, the World Wide Web (WWW), films, advertising, and many print media. At the personal level, individuals acting within cultural frames, are objects, subjects, and creators of visual images with multiple layers of meaning and affect.

For scholars, teachers, and practitioners working in visual media, evidence of the significance of visual imagery has produced an array of new knowledge and practices. Especially challenging in emerging pedagogy has been the need to develop theoretical perspectives that account for visual perception, cognition, evaluation, and behaviors in the processes of human communication. Although theories of apprehension, representation, and creativity are central in disciplines such as fine arts and graphic design, rethinking common assumptions in communication studies confronts a traditional bias for modes of verbal expression and against visual images. The nonverbal image has long been suspect as irrational, illogical, and somewhat slippery as *a measurable* concept. The power of visual images to communicate directly and instantaneously to the whole mind and to produce significant effects on perceptions of reality and on behavior has resisted theorizing and standardized methodologies. Yet the basic principle that drives both cultural and academic interest in visual communication is the very principle that makes visual communication effective on so many levels. Images generated through the physical eye or the mind's eye or by metaphor influence cognitive and behavioral processes before and beyond the processes of reason. The integration of intuitive, visual knowing with rational cognitive processes generates expressions of whole-mind cognition that have the potential to foster greater creativity, more powerful problem-solving abilities, and balance between quantitative and qualitative analyses. As such, the necessity to theorize visual intelligence has generated diverse approaches from a cluster of fields in communication, including photojournalism, rhetoric, mass communication, advertising, digital media, and interpersonal and intrapersonal communication. The intuitive and unconscious cognitive nature of visual communication explains why significant aspects of visualization and visual meaning elude traditional semiotic, rhetorical, and other rational and logocentric measurement techniques. It also portends the need to develop new techniques to understand visual meaning and effect.

As a communication scholar and an advertising and documentary photographer, the development of theories of visual communication and cognition over the past 25 years is profoundly central to my work. My theoretical approach considers both cultural and personal influences as equally significant to visual cognitive processes and subsequent behavior. This chapter reports on the development of theoretical constructs as they have emerged through work on two separate projects. The first was the twenty year production process of my documentary/ethnographic book, *Working Hands* (2000). The second, in 1995, was the development of a visual theory of cognitive balance that generated a course in Visual Literacy, in which I evolved specific pedagogies that can be used effectively to teach and increase visual intelligence. I report here on the theoretical development and on one pedagogical exercise, the Personal Impact Assessment (PIA) instrument. In both projects, I began to note that certain *intuitive* practices in my work were signposts, pointing the way to theoretical perspectives for understanding how visual intelligence worked and enabling me to systematize methods for increasing visual intelligence. My work was guided and informed by a wealth of literature. Background and a brief review of the theory are presented here.

Since the Greek Golden Age of Reason, traditional approaches to knowing and understanding in education, science, and culture in general have become increasingly based in reason and highly biased against the development and use of intuitive modes of cognition. This is evident in the linear bias of our educational system, in which entrance evaluation tools, curricula, and progress are based predominantly on developing and testing mathematical and linguistic proficiencies (Gardner, 1985). It is evident in our industrial culture, in which quantity is the measure of success and numbers of the bottom line overwhelm qualitative concerns about life, the environment, and larger cultural concerns. It is evident in the U.S. government, in which the health and wealth of the few are valued over concerns for the poor and disenfranchised.

However, as rational science steadily advances into clear neurobiological explanations of our cognitive processes, it becomes clear that intuitive, visual modalities are not only primary sources of memory and cognitive learning, but also the primary motivators of behavior before and beyond reason and rational processes. Nevertheless, even the behavior motivated by our intuitive intelligences must operate within the laws and bounds imposed by cultural domains. When the culture is rationally biased, the intuitive processes are bound within that bias. However, as neuroscience, math, physics, and biological sciences begin to break through the rational bias and uncover and reveal the hidden significance of the intuitive mind to knowing and behaving, then integrative research, theories, and technologies advance in ways that have the potential to change cultural biases.

INTEGRATING QUALITATIVE AND QUANTITATIVE

Consider, for example, that our global culture has experienced far-ranging shifts toward merger and integration of cultures, technologies, economies, governments, and corporations in the last 50 years, just as science has advanced quantitative evidence of the significance of the unconscious, intuitive cognitive processes. At the same time, the theory and practice of research and academic innovation have begun to adopt an extraordinary interdisciplinary framework that embraces the concept of the integration of rational and intuitive processes.

Physics and mathematics look to visual theory and art to explore theoretical constructs expanding concepts of reality out to the 11th dimension via string theory. Communication and literature integrate research in psychology, neurobiology, cognitive science, and across the arts to explore creativity and the role of unconscious and visual cognition in communication and media. The social sciences and cultural studies are integrating psychology and cognitive neuroscience to understand the role of the unconscious mind and visualization as a motivator of behavior and shaper of culture. Researchers in business, engineering, and government integrate highly intuitive, visual media processes into their marketing and propaganda strategies to increase compliance, productivity, and profit.

One explanation of this integrative phenomenon is that, having played out a long, limiting, and often disastrous fascination with reason, science is rediscovering its origins in the creative, unconscious, intuitive aspects of cognition and whatever other forms of knowing and being lie beyond purely rational cognition. To a significant degree, it is this unconscious, intuitive order of thinking that generates and sustains the desire and ability to "break set" and reach out to explore beyond what we already know and to understand in ways that have not previously been considered primary cognitive functions. Of course these abilities have always been a part of human cognition and understanding, but the ability to fully use the creative faculties of our intuitive intelligences has been hindered, marginalized by the rational bias of our traditional linear, scientific perspective.

INTEGRATIVE COGNITIVE NEUROSCIENCE, VISION, AND INTELLIGENCE

When these cognitive concepts are applied to contemporary cognitive neuroscience and visual communication, a clear correlation evolves between the conscious and unconscious facets of visual cognition and the rational and intuitive characteristics of the primary cognitive modes and their respective intelligences (Barry, 1997; Damasio, 1994, 1999; Gardner, 1999; LeDoux, 1996; Williams, 1999, 2000; Winson, 2002). The complexities of visual communication are well documented in the literature of visual cognition, neurobiology, and communication theory. In 1986, Joseph LeDoux explained the prerational nature of visual cognitive processes from a neurobiological perspective. LeDoux clarified how "the sensory signals from the eye travel first to the thalamus and then, in a kind of short circuit, to the amygdala before a second signal is sent to the neocortex," the structure of the brain where rational thought is generated (pp. 237–248). Bechara and Damasio furthered this concept in 1997 with empirical evidence suggesting that the prefrontal lobes of the brain are the repository of the unconscious memory that generates " . . . nonconscious biases [that] guide behavior before conscious knowledge does," and that "rational behavior is dependent upon access to unconscious biases" (Bechara, Damasio, Tranel, & Damasio, 1997, pp. 1293–1295).

There is a clear correlation between LeDoux's and Bechara and Damasio's work which suggests the amygdala and prefrontal lobes mediate and create preconscious behavioral motivations using visual and other stimuli. In this scenario, the amygdala provides the more spontaneous, rudimentary response and the prefrontal lobes provide the more sophisticated, synthesistic response, both in preconscious formats before the rational, neocortex receives the neural impulse or understands the information.

Simply put, visual cognition operates on preconscious levels to process visual information into knowledge that motivates behavior before the conscious processes of the neocortex receive or understand the information. I call this prerational, predominately preconscious cognitive ability *intuitive intelligence* because intuitive means to attain to knowledge through cognition without the use of reason.

I believe that *visual intelligence* is the primary intuitive intelligence because the majority of information that the brain processes is visual and most other intelligences also employ significant visual cognition. This does not suggest that visual information cannot be used rationally, but that the initial, primary response to visual cognition is preconscious. Among the many researchers who contribute to this perspective, Winson (2002) further illustrated that nonocular visual information, such as that from dreams and meditations, is processed into memory in the same way that ocular information relating to the formation of strategies of survival is processed. Gardner (1993, 1999) defined eight primary intelligences of the human mind, only two of which are primary rational intelligences. On primary cognitive levels, the other six intelligences are intuitively based. All eight intelligences have significant visual components: visual/spatial intelligence is clearly visual; musical intelligence employs vision both to read and write music, and music often generates mind's eye imagery or dreamlike meditations; intrapersonal intelligence employs dream imagery, and both intra- and interpersonal intelligences employ sight as does bodily kinesthetic intelligence; linguistic and mathematical intelligences (the rational intelligences) use both physical sight and generate mind's eye imagery as in thinking about a geometric figure or imagining a scene from literature; and naturalistic intelligence is an integrating process that employs the other intelligences, often in visual ways, to understand the natural world.

The concept that all intelligences have significant visual components suggests that visual processes can be used to develop intelligence in multiple cognitive modes, including all intuitive modes and those that support rationally dominant processes, such as math, linguistics, and traditional science. Therefore, the development of processes and creative exercises that will help individuals value and use intuitive intelligence as a complement to rational intelligence will help ameliorate the rational bias and fulfill the need for balance in our cognitive modalities, our educational systems, and subsequently in our culture. The order of business now is to promote cognitive balance by learning to access and use our intuitive intelligences on sophisticated levels as cognitive modalities that are as equally significant to whole-mind processing and creativity as our rational intelligences. The following descriptions detail the discoveries of visual processes I have made through analysis of my own work.

WORKING HANDS: INTEGRATING DATA WITH VISUAL EXPRESSION

Working Hands is the result of my work as a documentary photographer and ethnographer. The potential to develop a deeper and fuller understanding of a subject by integrating the aesthetics of visual communication with traditional ethnographic research was key in my final decision to produce *Working Hands* (2000) as a photographic book with commentary, rather than an ethnography with pictures.

Originally conceived as an ethnographic study entitled, "Common Ground: The Effect of the Integration of Urban and Rural Communities on Traditional Values," I designed the project to explore the relationship between values and the evolving character of cultural transitions in Texas. I began by researching the history of ranching, oil, and the Texas economy. Between 1980 and 1986, I recorded and analyzed hundreds of hours of ethnographic interviews, values samplers, and t tests. I also produced thousands of negatives to supplement the commentary of my study. When the quantitative results of that study affirmed my initial hypothesis, but indicated that further study of value-based behavior over three generations was needed to take a subsequent hypothesis to its conclusion, I found that I had lost my passion for the project. Somewhere in my efforts to quantify the qualitative and explain in words things that were more fully expressed visually, I lost interest. For me the search for the answer to the question of what the evolving character of our cultural transitions has to do with values, and how values affect behavior, was not to be found exclusively in systematic, rational research. For me insights were generated from the integration of that traditional research with the more intuitive recording of daily life and work through the images I made as artistic experience and visual expression. Indeed, when Texas author Larry McMurtry reviewed an early draft of *Working Hands* for me, he commented that the images spoke for themselves, and suggested that I did not need so much text.

I did not abandon the quantitative data. The data was, by then, after 6 years of ethnographic work, such an integral part of my thinking that it permeated my image making and my writing. I adopted a method that extends the traditional, verbal ethnographic, and participant–observation approach to oral interviews by using the meaning of those data to generate creative writing and personal reflection and by integrating that data with photographs of the subjects.

I believe that this approach recognizes and utilizes both the semiobjective aspects of data collection and the personal, subjective aspects of information gathering and reportage in ways that add depth of knowledge to the verbal stories. It also visually explores and documents the cultural transitions in ways that data and words alone cannot do. *Working Hands* expands traditional documentary methodology by relying on visual methods to provide insight into abstract concepts, such as transitions in cultural traditions and community structure. It took me two decades to fully understand rationally what I knew intuitively all along—that visual communication operates cognitively without the need for reason or before the rational mind is activated. *Working Hands* was published 20 years after I shot the first image in 1980 and the same year that I shot the last image in 2000. The systematic practice of integrating data and visual expression is offered as a method for documenting sociocultural transitions.

The content and composition of the images in *Working Hands* are diverse and complex. The entire book is set up in triptychs—three images that follow one another, each representing one of three cultural groups—cowboys, roughnecks, or high-tech assembly line workers. The images are related by concept, content, aesthetics, or all three. Because I want to emphasize telling the story visually, the book begins and ends with pictures rather than text. The arrangement of the images on the pages is designed to emphasize the similarities and contrasts among the three groups and to suggest some of the transitions that are taking place in Texas culture. Through the integration of data and visual expression, the images throughout the text are the primary means of communicating about the three cultural groups. This method uses the visuals to explore and understand transitions in culture by documentation, but also through intuitive choices I made in selecting and arranging the images. For example, I believe that clear themes, which are recognized by most viewers, are expressed not only in each image, but also in my intentional juxtaposition of images. I am also certain that individuals will take different meanings from the individual images and the groupings than I intended. They will see things that I may have seen on intuitive, vi-

Conversation, Jones' Rig 1986

Road Talk, Green Ranch 1984

Outside Contact 1996

Figure 1.1. Williams, 2000, pp. 88-91

sual levels, but did not "see" and still have not "seen" on rational, verbal levels. I believe that the more readers/viewers put into the work by looking at the images and pondering their meaning, rather than simply reading data sets or what I have to say about them, the more they will be invested in the process and the more they will take away with them.

The images in the Figure 1.1 triptych pose questions for the curious and the visually literate that can lead to insights about cultural transitions, relationships, and values: What are the individuals doing? Who are they? What do their clothes, tools, and location tell you about them as individuals or as members of a particular workforce and a particular culture? What is their socioeconomic situation likely to be? How do they relate to each other? What is the nature of their work? How would you feel working in the same situation? How do they relate to the land and to each other? As a group, what stories do the three images tell? How are they related or isolated by location, land, work, culture, and personality? What do the three images tell about the individuals and about the similarities and differences in their work and culture? What do the images say about changes in cultures as we move from:

- Roughnecks who work on small, steel platforms above that same land to
- The cowboys who ride over huge expanses of land in trucks or on horseback to
- High-tech workers who work on the same land, but in complete isolation from it.

It was not until I had worked on the project for several years that I became acutely aware that the cowboys, roughnecks, and high-tech workers were all connected by land and that the land was a significant part of the story. The prominence of land was revealed in the images made to document the lives of the workers. The ranchers settled the land and now use its surface to grow crops and raise cattle. The oil companies both buy and lease the land from the ranchers and use it as a platform to drill for oil and gas below the surface and to store and transport oil on the surface. The high-tech industry buys the same type of ranch land on the outskirts of large cities and builds multiple-acre buildings designed to isolate their work and workers from the land. All three groups work on the same land, but use it in different ways for different purposes.

Accordingly, the way that each group of workers relates to the land influences how they relate or do not relate to each other and to others in the development of culture. By looking at these relationships, we not only can tell a great deal about transitions in Texas and other cultures, but we also better understand how those transitions and relationships feel. It is my intention that a series of visual stories, such as this one, suggest thought-provoking ideas about what kind of culture we have come from and what kind of culture we are creating in Texas and beyond. For example, one cultural question implied in these three images is: As one becomes more isolated from the land and those things associated with working on and with the land, does one also becomes more isolated from other workers, other individuals, or some part of themselves?

The images tell their stories in as least three different ways. They are representational, culturally symbolic, and intrapersonally symbolic. By *representational* I mean that the images visually describe real people and objects as I saw and experienced them in real time. Because I did not set these scenes up, but shot them in real time as they happened, in this representational mode the images give us a semi-objective, reasonably accurate window into the world of a specific person, object, or cultural setting. I say semi-objective because I assume that my presence influences the individuals, and I also choose the film, angle, composition, and moment, and, of course, I have my own point of view even when I am trying to report as objectively as possible. The images tell us what the people looked like, how they dressed, where and how they lived or worked, and where they were and what they were doing at specific times and places. For instance, in the triptych in Figure 1.2, you find a comparison of three types of bosses. Bob Green's family settled in Shackelford County, Texas, in the last part of the 19th century. Bob owns the land his family settled and oversees their large ranch near Albany, Texas. From the images, we can see him dressed in jeans, work shirt, jacket, cowboy hat, and boots and how he works directly with cowboys and cattle in the dirt and dung of the corral. A.V. Jones' family settled in Albany, Texas in the early part of the 20th century. A.V. owns and operates the family oil business with his brother, J.R. Jones. The image shows us that A.V. wears a white dress shirt and slacks, and works in an office with a cluttered desk and closed windows, and communicates with others via letter and phone. He is surrounded by expensive remnants of Texas history, including an antique gun. The only indication of his relationship to the land on which he drills for oil is an oil painting of the Texas landscape. The image of executives of Applied Materials include the CEO, the global communications manager, the vice president,

© Rick Williams, 2004   Bob Green, Green Ranch 1984

© Rick Williams, 2004   A.V. Jones, Jones Co. Ltd. 1982

© Rick Williams, 2004   The Executives 1996

Figure 1.2. Williams, 2000, pp. 100-103

and the plant manager of the Austin facility. All are first-generation Texans, except the CEO, who lives in California. The image shows us that they are well-heeled, fast-paced leaders who dress in formal business attire and work in a building that is all concrete, steel, and glass, and the landscape can only be viewed through the windows. There is no visible artwork in the building and no indication that the men are in Texas. The booties on their feet indicate that they work in a meticulously and necessarily *clean* environment absent of Texas dirt, dust, and land.

As cultural symbols, the images reveal relationships among individuals or groups from which we can infer information about a larger cultural topic. They allow us to compare and contrast aspects of one group with another. By placing the images together in tryptichs and as a book of visuals with text, we can look at the work, tools, dress, products, byproducts, and relationships and infer something that is personally, culturally, politically, economically, or ecologically significant. For instance, images throughout the book work individually and collectively to suggest that, as we move from the agrarian to the mechanical to the technological, we move away from a direct, caretaker relationship with the land and ecosystem, to a system that is basically exploitative in terms of its relationship with the land, to a high-tech system that shuts out the land and then refines caustic manufacturing materials before discarding them to the ecosystem.

One of the major themes of my work is the integration and balance of grace and power. I consciously discovered this intrapersonal perspective and put words to it, in part, from looking at and thinking about the images that I took for *Working Hands*. As intrapersonal representations of the artist or author, the images provide insights, as a revealing self-portrait, not only into my style and point of view or biases, but also into my psyche. This helps the visually literate reader know more about me as the storyteller, and thus more about the implications of the story as I tell it. We see these relationships between the balance of grace and power in Figure 1.3:

- In the first image, a human body flexes and bends powerfully, yet almost in dancelike movement, as the roughneck turns some 20,000 pounds of drilling pipe suspended gracefully in the air above him.
- The second image is, again, a sort of graceful ballet set in a sterile environment, as two anonymous, androgynous figures move a chrome, other-worldly, flying-saucer-like chamber lid in a high-tech lab.

Unloading Drilling Pipe 1985

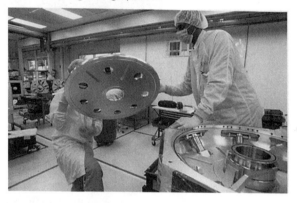

Loading Chamber Lid 1996

Bennie Roping 1981

Figure 1.3. Williams, 2000, pp. 54-57

- In the third image, a cowboy roping a horse throws a rope that flows through the frame in graceful loops that seem to embrace the power of both the man and horse.

Because *Working Hands* is about transitions in culture, this intrapersonal idea of the interplay and balance of grace and power becomes a visual metaphor that integrates the representational and cultural concepts of balancing industry and environment, human and machine and technology and human touch in the form of rope and steel, human and animal, and mud and chrome. "From the beginning," I write in this book, "long before I was consciously aware of this concept of balance, my images symbolically portrayed this integrative unity. It has taken me two decades to begin to understand rationally and write about what I have known intuitively all along" (Williams, 2000, p. 14).

Finding a sense of balance between grace and power has evolved in my own life and in my artistic expressions and permeates the imagery in *Working Hands*. Thus, the representational images I made serve as cultural and intrapersonal symbols of my intuitive perceptions. Intrapersonal insight is important to a reader/viewer because it underscores the idea that, as neuroscience tells us, the intuitive mind guides our perceptions of reality and our behavior before the rational mind is engaged. Our own deeply held values and perceptions critically influence the cultural studies in which we participate. We cannot be aware of all of these influences and cannot control for them completely even if we want to. *Working Hands* is about the integration and balance of contrasting concepts and behavior: integration of nature and science, integration of people and traditions, integration of diverse cultures, integration of quantitative and qualitative research, and integration of mind and spirit. My purpose in creating *Working Hands* was not to tell people what to think, but rather to help them become more aware of the cultural transitions that are taking place and that affect all of us. I wanted to present information in ways that stayed with readers/viewers and stimulated them to think more clearly and deeply about this transformational process and its effects. Images are more readily remembered than words—they influence us on deep, unconscious levels that shape our perceptions of reality and guide our behavior. Visual images allow expression of intuitive intelligence through presentation of our own intrapersonal symbols. The integration of data collection with the artistic expression of photography offers an approach to documentation that more closely represents the limited truth of what we can know about diverse cultural experiences. The approach, exemplified by *Working Hands,* invites viewers to make interpretations from a balance of their own rational and intuitive perspectives. The task for viewers of visual messages is to learn how to access and cultivate their own visual intelligence, which is the focus of my work in visual literacy.

OMNIPHASIC THEORY OF COGNITIVE BALANCE

In 1995, I introduced a new course in visual literacy that integrated my own work in photography and visual theory with historical and contemporary research in cognitive neuroscience, psychology, communications, literature, and art. The Omniphasic Theory of Cognitive Balance (Williams, 1999, 2000), which evolved from this integrative curricular initiative, characterizes the two primary cognitive modes of the human brain (Bogen, 1979; Homer, 600 B.C.E.; Jaynes, 1986, 1994; Sperry, 1973, 1979) as either rationally or intuitively dominant. It follows that the multiple intelligences (Gardner, 1993) that each of the cognitive modes employs in the process of knowing can also be characterized as rational or intuitive on primary cognitive levels. The dual visual pathways of LeDoux's and Bechara and Damasio's conscious and unconscious cognitive functions also flow into the intuitive model. Table 1.1 illustrates the Omniphasic integration of these theories and cognitive modalities.

My goal in developing this work has been to go beyond theory to create applications using integrative visual techniques to help individuals

Table 1.1. Omniphasism: Integrated Theories and Relative Cognitive Modalities

OMNIPHASISM	INTUITIVE	RATIONAL
Homer	Divine	Secular
Jaynes	Unconscious	Conscious
Bogen & Sperry	Right hemisphere	Left hemisphere
LeDoux	Thalamus	Visual cortex
Bechara/Damasio	Unconscious bias	Conscious awareness
Gardner	Nonlogical intelligences	Logical intelligences
Multiple intelligences	Visual/spatial	Linguistic/verbal
	Musical	Logical/math
	Intrapersonal	
	Interpersonal	
	Bodily kinesthetic	
	Naturalistic	

recognize, develop, and use all of their intuitive intelligences in conjunction with their rational cognitive abilities. I believe that the intentional development and integration of rational and intuitive cognitive processes has the potential to help solve critical problems in creative ways that balance quantitative and qualitative concerns toward an ecologically sound perspective. I have developed or adapted 14 exercises to contribute to this effort.

One of the primary exercises I have developed is called Personal Impact Assessment (PIA). PIA, adapted from a Jungian/Johnson dream interpretation process, is designed to help the individual assess and bring into consciousness the intrapersonal meaning of an image from a balanced cognitive perspective. Mass media are the most pervasive and effective system for delivering visual messages to the public and for shaping public opinion and behavior. Therefore, using PIA to analyze media images provides the individual with insights into the way media images are used to shape their own perceptions of reality and guide their behavior within a public forum. PIA helps anyone who uses it to reverse the persuasive and manipulative intent often embedded in media images. By using PIA, the individual gains personal insights that are useful tools for both overcoming the manipulative intent and learning to guide one's own behavior in constructive, balanced ways.

OMNIPHASIC PROCESSES AND CREATIVE EXERCISES

The techniques that modern media use to convey their messages of persuasion are visual, musical, and metaphorical flights of fantasy and magic, similar to our dreams. They are processed in the brain using the same intuitive cognitive processes, many of them unconscious, that are used to develop knowledge and memory. These stimuli follow neurological paths through the thalamus, amygdala, and prefrontal lobes to bypass reason and direct this great cultural concert from the powerful unconscious mind. Because the brain does not distinguish between mediated and real imagery as it encodes visual messages into memory, and because of our belief in the unassailable supremacy of reason, we often are not even aware that we have been seduced and manipulated.

Media imagery is similar to dreams in format, content, and the way the images become part of our unconscious memories. Therefore, it makes sense to adapt a classic process of dream interpretation to understand media images from an intuitive perspective that reveals their effects on one's unconscious memory, decision-making abilities, and behavior. PIA is an instrument that I adapted from a Jungian/Johnson (Johnson, 1986; Jung, 1961) dream interpretation technique to foster self-awareness and self-direction in its user.

The application of PIA that follows explores the influence of a media-delivered image on the unconscious, intuitive motivations of the self. Becoming aware or conscious of this influence is critical to understanding and guiding the effects of those motivations on one's own behavior in both intrapersonal and interpersonal relationships. This is significant on two levels.

First, if one is to guide one's own behavior in ways that are individually and culturally advantageous, it is critical that one understand what motivates one to behave in a particular way. As Jung might suggest, bringing one's own unconscious motivations into consciousness and integrating that understanding with reason allows a person to consider more fully and critically the outcome of a particular response to those motivations and to guide that response in ways that are consistent with personal values and beliefs. Using PIA to assess one's personal imagery, including dreams, meditations, drawings, paintings, photographs, and metaphorical writing, from an intuitive, synthesistic perspective, does make one more aware of the intrapersonal motivations that generated the work. Understanding these intuitive motivations is a direct way to integrate the unconscious and conscious toward greater self-awareness and balance.

Second, it is clear that most media images are permeated with messages of persuasion that are specifically designed to bypass reason. With symbolic, archetypal power beyond logic, they communicate to our interior feelings, values, needs, and desires in ways that shape our beliefs and direct our decision making and external actions. Similar to waking dreams, these media images speak to our whole minds instantaneously, leaving powerful memory suggestions in our unconscious memories and psyches. In today's visual culture, it is critical to the individual and society that we learn to recognize and develop those intelligences that provide a defense against media seductions and manipulations. In fact it is critical to our survival as self-aware, self-determining individuals, and to the survival of our planet, that we learn to reverse the effects of these messages of consumerism on the psyche and to reverse the subsequent, unbridled development of the consumer culture that is consuming our self-identities, our resources, and our environments.

To this end, any process that helps integrate the whole mind toward the goal of greater awareness of personal values, beliefs, and motivations and to apply that awareness to the development of a culture that balances quantity and quality is worth pursuing. I believe that PIA is such an instrument. With a minimum level of involvement, PIA can help an individual understand more about her or his own motivations and actions. With sustained application, individuals and groups can use PIA to reverse the manipulative impact of media messages. By using the information in those messages—messages specifically designed to manipulate a response—to gain intrapersonal insights, PIA can help the individual and group become more personally and socially aware and active in ways that cultivate more balanced and sustainable educational, scientific, economic, and cultural systems.

A list of the steps in PIA and an example of a completed PIA with commentary about the process follow. The example PIA is an individual's assessment of an advertising image. There are seven steps in the PIA process. Each step is numbered and titled. A brief explanation of the step follows each title. The steps may seem linear and tedious. However, remember, they trace a pathway to the unconscious through intuitive as well as rational means. Reaching the unconscious mind with a conscious process is not simple, but it is rewarding. Carl Jung suggested there were only two primary ways to access the unconscious mind—dreams and meditations. My hope is that PIA is a third path and one that is particularly relevant to our contemporary visual culture of mediated imagery.

THE SEVEN STEPS OF PERSONAL IMPACT ASSESSMENT[1]

1. **Choose and View the Image.** Select an image to assess. Spend at least 2 or 3 minutes just looking at the image and letting your eye and mind wander around the different parts. Notice the light, its direction, contrast, and feel. Notice the primary points of interest and where they are placed. Notice lines, curves, and basic design elements and how they help or hinder your eye movement. Notice the grain structure. Notice the range of tones and/or colors and how they affect your feelings. Notice how the image makes you feel. Does it draw you in or keep you out? Does it tell a clear story? Does it stimulate your imagination to develop your own ideas or stories?

2. **List Primary Words.** List a single word that describes each of the significant parts of the image that seem significant to you—characters, places, things, colors/tone, feelings, and so on—in a column on the left side of a blank sheet of paper. Leave enough space around each primary word on the list to write a number of other words.

3. **List Associative Words.** Look at each of the primary words you

---

1. Portions of this section were first published in *The Journal of Visual Literacy* (2000a), and *Explorations in Media Ecology* (2003).

have written, one at a time. Start with the first word and, beside or in a circle around that word, write other words (word associations that come into your mind as you think about the first word). Finish all of the associations for the first word before you move on to the next word. List at least three associative words for each primary word. Listing more words is fine.

4. **Select the Most Significant Associative Word.** When you have completed the list of word associations, go back to the first primary word and mull its associative words over in your mind. Again start with the first primary word and its associative words and go down the list. Try to intuit which is the most significant associative word for each primary word and draw a circle around it or underline it. Do not over think this; just say the associative words to yourself until one seems most significant. Do this for each group of associative words you have listed, one at a time. There are no right or wrong answers. Simply pick the word that seems most appropriate to you as you read the words. If more than one word seems correct, then circle both. Finally, make a separate list of the most significant associative words. Keep them in the order in which they appear on the primary word list.

5. **Relate Associative Words to an Inner Part of Yourself.** Look at each word in the "significant word association" list and consider what part of your inner self that word represents or symbolizes. Write that part of yourself to the right of the "significant word association." To identify the inner parts of yourself, it may be helpful to say, "My inner_____ self" (i.e., my inner *vulnerable* self, my inner *trusting* self, my inner *fantasy* self). Again, there are no right or wrong answers. This is your personal assessment.

6. **Review the Inner Symbols.** Look over the word symbols of your inner self and see if there is some clear connection or story that arises about yourself from the interaction of the inner symbols from the image. This story, connection, or meaning may be just a simple feeling or it may come to you in a flash or as an aha-type response. It will often reveal the inner conflicts, emotions, values, or feelings that are behind your personal, intuitive creation of or attraction to the image.

7. **Write Down The Story or Insight.** Think about how the story applies to your attraction to the image or how it offers insights about your own life. If you are using a media-generated image such as

an advertisement, consider how the association of the product with fulfillment of these inner desires and values might establish unconscious biases and motivations. Consider how these unconscious motivations might influence your desire for the product, lifestyle, or things the image associates with the product (i.e., sex, physical perfection, love, freedom, or luxury) and how this desire might influence you to adapt your behavior in some way.

EXAMPLE OF PERSONAL IMPACT ASSESSMENT OF A MEDIA IMAGE

This example was also published in the *Journal of Visual Literacy* (2000, 20(4), 219-242). The article, edited by Nancy Nelson Knupfer, was entitled "Beyond Visual Literacy: Part III: Omniphasism in the Classroom through Visual Literacy Toward a New Educational Model."

It includes the image of the perfume ad on which this example is based. Unfortunately, I was unable to obtain permission to use the image in this publication, but I describe it in detail below. The image is a very sensual black and white/brown tone close-up of a young man and woman kissing. The young woman fills the right side of the frame that includes her upper torso and her head. She faces left in profile and is wearing a shiny light-colored silk blouse that is pulled tight against her breast. She has long blond hair that flows back over her ear and spreads over the pillow upon which she slightly reclines. Her face is turned toward a young man with short dark hair who fills the left side of the frame, is shirtless and leans in, their bodies touching. We see his right profile and the moment is either an instant before their slightly open lips meet to kiss or just as the lips pull away from a kiss. This lack of clarity gives the moment a strong sense of spontaneity.

Steps 1, 2, 3 and 4: Viewing, Listing Primary Words, Word Associations, Significant Word Association are all done on one page as follows.

In this example of a Personal Impact Assessment of an advertising image (Part 1), the words in bold caps are the primary parts of the image (Part 2). The lower case words are the associations (Part 3). The underlined words represent the most significant associative words (Part 4).

	ROMANTIC				REVEALING	
<u>DARK</u>	**BLACK**	CONTRAST		LIGHT	**WHITE**	<u>CONTRAST</u>
	DREAM-LIKE				LONGING	
<u>FANTASY</u>	**GRAY**	SHADOW		<u>DESIRE</u>	**SEXY**	<u>BEAUTY</u>
	SOFT				WARMTH	
PASSIONATE	**KISSING**	<u>INTIMATE</u>		<u>NAKED</u>	**BODIES**	CLOSENESS
	WONDERFUL					

	SOFT				WARMTH	
LUSCIOUS	**LIPS**	TENDER		CONTENT	**SOFT**	SKIN
	BIG					

	CLOSENESS				DESIRE	
CONTENT	**PERSONAL**	PRIVATE	EXCITEMENT		**TOUCHING**	WARMTH
	TRUST				CLOSENESS	

	WARMTH				SOFT	
CARESS	**CLOSENESS**	LOVE		NAKED	**SKIN**	SMOOTH
	RELATIONSHIP					

	SEXY				PASSION	
MESSY	**HAIR**	LONG, FLOWING	LIPS		**TASTE**	DESIRE
	SOFT				TONGUE LOVE	

	HAPPY				CLOSENESS	
ANIMALISTIC	**SMELL**	DESIRE		DESIRE	**EMBRACE**	WARM
	SCENT CLOSENESS				LOVE	

Note that in some cases, two significant associative words were chosen for a single primary word. This is fine if they seem equally significant. It is also possible that some associative words will have the same inner-self association.

Steps 4 and 5: List of Significant Word Association and List of Inner-self Associations

SIGNIFICANT WORD	INNER SELF
DARK	inner self
CONTRAST	fantasy self
DREAMLIKE	fantasy self
FANTASY	make-believe self
BEAUTY	feminine self
DESIRE	wanting self
INTIMATE	vulnerable self
NAKED	vulnerable self
TENDER	maternalistic, loving self
SKIN	naked, exposed self
TRUST	trusting self
EXCITEMENT	wild, impulsive self

WARMTH	loving, content self
SMOOTH	extreme sensitive self
MESSY	impulsive self
FLOWING	feminine self
DESIRE	intimate, sexual self
TONGUES	highly sensitive self
ANIMALISTIC	sexual, wanting self
CLOSENESS	content, trusting self

Steps 6 and 7: Assessment and Story

I think this ad drew me in immediately because it had aspects that appealed to me. It looks like a <u>dream</u> or a <u>fantasy</u>, and I <u>wanted</u>, for a second, for that <u>fantasy</u> to be me. I envisioned myself in the bed with the handsome man kissing gently, then more <u>passionately</u>. It appealed to my <u>vulnerable</u>, <u>gentle</u>, <u>trusting</u>, <u>loving</u> self and to my <u>impulsive</u>, <u>wild</u>, <u>animal-like</u>, <u>desired</u> self. I felt all of those feelings at once. At the same time, the woman radiates <u>beauty</u>, <u>femininity</u>, and <u>sexiness</u> all at once. I would <u>love to look like her just for that one moment in my dream</u>.

COMMENTARY ON THE PIA PROCESS

In the student's assessment/story, I underlined all of the words that are also found in the student's Significant Associations and Inner-Self Associations lists. This comparison makes clear not only that something critical exists below the surface of the obvious sexual attraction implicit in the ad, but what that something is in terms of persuasive seduction for the particular individual assessing the image impact. I want to point out that this PIA is the work of one individual, but it does not stand alone. My own reviews of 3,000 PIA applications from my students, along with their self-reports about their experiences and anonymous evaluations of techniques they learned in my visual literacy courses, indicate that most find this technique useful in uncovering their own inner motivations and needs in ways that help them better understand themselves and the effects of mediated images on their lives.

Most individuals can take a quick look at the image and logically reject the idea that using the product will fulfill their needs in the way that is illustrated or suggested through some of the obvious associations in the ad. Through this rejection, a person may feel she or he has understood and countered the effect of the ad. This conscious reasoning process masks the full impact of the image, however. When they find themselves unwittingly wishing to shape their own lives in ways that fulfill the ad's fantasies or standing at the counter purchasing this or similar products over and over again, they must begin to consider that their rational evaluation and rejection, in fact, did not work and that something else was at play.

PIA is designed to help unmask and bring into consciousness a sophisticated intuitive messaging system that, on preconscious cognitive levels, associates product use with fulfillment of deeply held needs and desires that are both primal and personal in nature. For the student in this example, those promises of fulfillment included love, tenderness, contentment, beauty, trust, relationship, maternalism, sensitivity, and vulnerability, on the one hand, and passion, desire, fantasy, impulsiveness, animalistic nature, sexuality, and wildness, on the other. As these associations become part of our unconscious memory systems, they become part of our decision-making processes. Because the unconscious memory processes do not differentiate between mediated and real experiences, the associations made by these images are real to us and are powerful in their influence on our behavior. But there are alternatives.

Beyond the ability to reveal the persuasive aspects of media imagery and messages, PIA provides the opportunity for individuals to reverse the original manipulative intent of the message. By using PIA on the message to gain insights about one's own inner motivations and needs, the individual becomes more self-aware. This self-awareness establishes some defense against media seductions. It also provides the information needed for the individual to go further—to develop and guide his or her own intuitive experiences in ways that are productive and will fulfill his or her intrapersonal needs. This will sustain and enrich the individual and, through his or her personal development, will enrich our culture.

For instance, in the previous example, the individual revealed an inner dichotomy between her *wild, impulsive, animal-like,* and *sexual* self and her *loving, vulnerable, gentle,* and *trusting* self. There is also the suggestion that she "felt all of those things at once" and wanted to be with the man and look just like the woman in the image. I am drawing this directly from the student's list of "inner-self words" and her "story." As suggested in my own earlier work (Williams, 1999, 2000a, 2000b, 2003), there are any number of ways, in addition to PIA, to use self-directed techniques and one's energy to explore the inner self. Because the inner needs revealed in this PIA are specifically active suggesting wildness, impulsiveness, and animal-like behavior, this individual might look for things that fulfill those needs, such as outdoor physical activity, hiking, climbing, cycling, or sports, and delve into his or her fantasies with more creative work such as drawing or creative writing. The person might become more involved in understanding her own unique sexuality. Yet the PIA revealed needs for love, trust, gentleness, and care of the core or inner self. Here meditation, dream interpretation, reading, or involvement with groups of people who explore the nature of the self might be helpful. Of course the individual would have to determine how to meet these revealed needs her or himself. This is the point—that one develop self-directed, rather than media-directed, experiences that nurture and sustain the specific inner needs of the self. In this way, one begins to better fulfill and balance intrapersonal needs with external behaviors that nurture and sustain the self, rather than seek self-fulfillment through consumerism and empty promises that associate inner needs with unrealistic lifestyles, ownership, and use of products.

CONCLUSIONS

My work focuses on integrating and balancing intuitive and rational aspects of techniques for gathering and considering intrapersonal information by using the intelligences of our whole minds. We have moved so far into a culture dominated by sophisticated, visual media that these skills are requisite for even the most basic understanding of the communication processes that shape our lives. Unfortunately, our educational system has largely abdicated the teaching of intuitive intelligences, and the media have become the educators and exploiters of our intuitive, visual illiteracy. Students are taught that only artists can express themselves intuitively or creatively and that quantifiable data are the only source of true knowledge. The reality of this situation is the development of a culture of unaware consumers who walk blindly into a future dominated by corporate economic and political agenda. Within this cultural system, the logic of the bottom line directs behavior without regard for the resulting intrapersonal, interpersonal, and ecological devastation of individuals and culture.

As we educate the general public, ourselves, and our students at all levels to become expressive, self-aware, self-guided individuals, it is equally significant that we teach those who will become our journalists, mass communicators, leaders, and scholars the personal and social responsibilities of both applying those skills and consuming information in the mass communication media. It is important that they develop an awareness of and empathy for those with whom they communicate and whom they study. It is important that they develop personal integrity and personal, social, and ethical standards. To do this, it is imperative that future mass communicators and scholars learn more than how to push the buttons and make the words and images work together for the effective delivery of information. They must also understand how the construction and delivery of that information affects the reader/viewer/user. Without an Omniphasic understanding, both personal and social ethics are incomplete and unbalanced.

When it comes to creating intuitive communication messages; when the construction of those messages is controlled by the corporate elite who also control the mass communication systems of delivery; when those messages are designed by highly literate, intuitive communicators to merge commerce and art into a strategy of persuasion; when that strategy is to exploit the visual illiteracy of the populace by developing unconscious biases within the individual and the culture; and when those unconscious biases construct a perception of reality that reflects only the constructed reality of the corporate ethic, then the personal and social ethic is lost and all that counts is the quantity of the bottom line. Quantity has trumped quality. The advantages of balance within the self, and therefore within the community, are lost. This scenario, which is played out constantly in our visual consumer culture, emphasizes the need to develop alternative personal, economic, educational, and cultural strategies and techniques to help develop and balance the cognitive potential of the whole mind.

The transformation toward a more balanced culture begins with individuals. Encouraging artistic visual expression, and using PIA and other techniques developed by Newton (2000), Barry (1997), Lester (1995), Edwards (1989), others, and myself, one can learn to recognize and develop intuitive intelligences, side by side with rational intelligences, as equal and complementary aspects of whole-mind cognitive abilities. One can learn to overcome the rational bias and become a more self-determining, creative, and balanced individual in pursuit of more balanced and sustainable educational and cultural systems.

REFERENCES

Barry, A.M.S. (1997). *Visual intelligence: Perception, image, and manipulation in visual communication.* New York: State University of New York Press.

Bechara, A., Damasio, H., Tranel, D., & Damasio, A. (1997). Deciding advantageously before knowing the advantageous strategy. *Science, 275,* 1293–1295.

Bogen, J.E. (1969). The other side of the brain. *Bulletin of the Los Angeles Neurological Societies, 34,* 73-105.

Damasio, A. (1994). *Decartes' error*. New York: Putnam.

Damasio, A. (1999). *The feeling of what happens*. New York: Harcourt Brace & Company.

Gardner, H. (1985). *Frames of mind: The theory of multiple intelligences*. New York: HarperCollins.

Gardner, H. (1993). *Multiple intelligences: The theory in practice*. New York: HarperCollins.

Gardner, H. (1999). *Intelligence reframed: Multiple intelligences for the 21th century*. New York: Basic Books

Jaynes, J. (1976/1990). *The origin of consciousness in the breakdown of the bicameral mind*. Boston, MA: Houghton Mifflin.

Johnson, R. (1986). *Inner work*. San Francisco: Harper & Row.

Jung, C.J. (1961). *Memories, dreams, reflections*. New York: Random House.

LeDoux, J. (1986). Sensory systems and emotion. *Integrative Psychiatry, 4*, 237–243.

LeDoux, J. (1996). *The emotional brain*. New York: Simon & Schuster.

Lester, P. M. (1995). *Visual communication: Images with messages*. Belmont, CA: Wadsworth.

Newton, J. (2000). *The burden of visual truth: The role of photojournalism in mediating reality*. Mahwah, NJ: Erlbaum.

Sperry, R.W. (1968). Hemisphere disconnection and unity in conscious awareness. *American Psychologist, 23*, 723-733.

Sperry, R.W. (1973). Lateral specialization of cerebral function in the surgically separated hemispheres. In F.J. McGuigan & R.A. Schoonover (Eds.), *The psychophysiology of thinking* (pp. 209-229). New York: Academic Press.

Sperry, R.W., Gazzaniga, M.S., and Bogen, J.E. (1969). Interhemispheric relationships: The neocortical commissures; Syndromes of hemisphere disconnection. In P.J. Vinken & G.W. Bruyn (Eds.), *Handbook of clinical neurology* (pp. 273-89). Amsterdam: North-Holland.

Williams, R. (1999). Beyond visual literacy: Omniphasism, a theory of cognitive balance, Part I. *Journal of Visual Literacy, 19*(2), 159–178.

Williams, R. (2000a). Omniphasic visual-media literacy in the classroom, Part III. *Journal of Visual Literacy, 20*(2), 219–242.

Williams, R. (2000b). Visual illiteracy and intuitive visual persuasion, Part II. *Journal of Visual Literacy, 20*(1), 111–124.

Williams, R. (2000). *Working hands*. Bryan: Texas A&M University Press.

Williams, R, (2003). Transforming intuitive illiteracy: Understanding the effects of the unconscious mind on image meaning, image consumption, and behavior. *Explorations in Media Ecology, 2*(2), 119–134.

Winson, J. (2002). The meaning of dreams. *Scientific American: The Hidden Mind, 12*(1), 54–61.

CHAPTER TWO

Media Memories, Videogame Lies

ANN MARIE BARRY
BOSTON COLLEGE

O NE OF THE MOST SIGNIFICANT AREAS OF MEDIA INFLUENCE where unconscious emotional learning and procedural conditioning come together is videogames—an industry representing sales in computer and console
games exceeding $10 billion annually (Poole, 2000). Although videogame
research is still in its infancy, existing research shows a positive correlation
between real-life aggression and violent videogame play, and between violent
videogame play and delinquency, with a heightened response in youth already
predisposed to anger and violence (Anderson & Dill, 2000; Anderson & Ford,
1986; Ballard & Weist, 1996; Dill & Dill, 1998; Emes, 1997; Huesmann,
1986; Huesmann & Miller, 1994; Irwin & Gross, 1995; Lynch, 1994, 1999;
Matthews, 2002; Van Schie & Weigman, 1997; Winkel et al., 1987).

As a source of vicarious experience, media work on both rational and
emotional levels in the user, and both of these levels have their own memory
systems and functions. To understand the full impact of media in general
and videogames in particular, we must first understand something of the
fallibility of memory, as well as how media experience becomes memory,
mixes with other memories, and emotionally sets us up for dealing with
reality. This reality, too, is not absolute in itself, but is always a conclusion
drawn as a result of perceptual processes.

Certainly considerable research has shown the fragility—and fallibility—of
memories that seem highly detailed and realistic. However, unconscious
emotional memories of trauma can affect people who have no conscious understanding of what is going on. The mere sight of the person or the instrument that was used in the trauma—a belt used in a beating, say—can activate
the emotional system, causing panic attacks and fear responses that can be
generalized to leather, animals, and many other things. Unconscious emo-

tional memories can therefore have widespread, long-lasting effects without our having any understanding of what is triggering certain responses or feelings. (LeDoux, 1999, p. 143)

A neuroscientist who has done research on brain functioning, particularly in the relationship between emotion and reason, Joseph LeDoux is one of many medical and social scientists concerned with traumatic memory. What they tell us is that, although we tend to take for granted the essential truth of memory, memory is in fact a complex and highly fragile process susceptible to error not only at every stage of encoding, but also to revision after the fact. Memory—both hippocampal (conscious) and amygdalal (emotional)—is essentially a reactivation of the same pattern of neurons activated at the time of the original experience.

When we see, signals are sent by the eye via the optic nerve to the thalamus. Then the message is split, with one signal sent directly to the amygdala, the seat of our emotions, and another to the cortex, the seat of conscious processing. The signal sent through the thalamo-amygdala pathway is shorter and less complex than the signal sent through the cortical pathway. Therefore, emotional reactions are faster than conscious ones, and emotional memory frames all conscious responses. The cortex also sends a second signal to the amygdala, adding conscious input to emotional reaction and emotional response to thought. Emotional reaction and the memory of past experience on which it is based is a survival-oriented unconscious response that can bypass conscious thought altogether (see Figures 2.1 and 2.2).

When the memory stimulus comes from vicarious media experience, the senses still respond as if to actual experience, further confusing media experience with actual experience, not in the conscious mind initially (although later source amnesia may occur as well), but rather in the emotional system that sets up the way we perceive reality and habitually act on it. Each repeat activation of a particular neuronal circuit facilitates the next activation of the same circuit. Habitual action or thought patterns develop at the cellular level through repetition of the same firing patterns, and the emotional system is automatically trained through this repetition. Eventually, the activation of a single part of the circuit serves to stimulate the whole circuit, and we develop a kind of conditioned response that operates on an unconscious level.

In vicarious media experience, this effect is further enhanced by the fact that millions of other children and adolescents are similarly exposed, and the experience is mutually reinforced and normalized on a conscious level as well. Not only do violent media serve to mainstream various be-

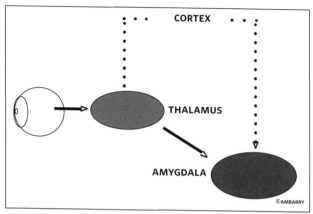

Figure 2.1. Signals received by the eye are sent from the thalamus to the amygdala and to the cortex. The thalamo-amygdala pathway is shorter and less complex than the the cortical pathway, which also sends a post-processing signal to the amygdala. Emotion thus frames all perceptual processing.

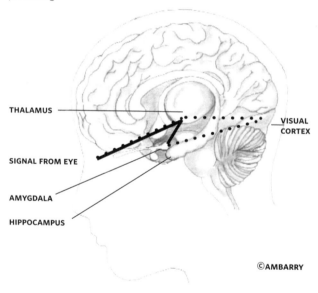

CORTICAL PATHWAY • • • • • •
AMYGDALA PATHWAY ━━━━━

Figure 2.2. Visual Processing involves both cortical and amygdala pathways. The amygdala pathway—older, immediate, and strong—functions independently of cortical reasoning and can, at least for the short term, overwhelm reason in reacting to any given stimulus.

liefs (i.e., diminish cultural, sociological, and individual differences in attitudes and thinking), but they also reinforce conscious negative patterns of thought and behavior and can substitute for positive parenting in emotionally deprived children. Thus, it is a false dichotomy to separate media violence in programming from arguments based on positive parenting as a response to violence. All visual media educate emotionally, and in children this can have devastating effects, particularly but not exclusively, when positive parenting is absent. This is particularly problematic because, according to the Society for Adolescent Medicine, American youth devote more time to media than to any other waking activity—up to one third of each day (Roberts, 2000).

In a cyclical fashion, emotional memory—which is independent of conscious thought and motivation—sets up a map for perception, anticipating both what is important and how to proceed by drawing from past experience. Rational memory can then either confirm or revise the perceptual map, but emotional memory begins and ends the process of perception, playing a key role in how we come to see the world and act in it.

Although they normally work together and fuse so immediately that we cannot separate the different kinds of memory, hippocampal memory and amygdalal memory work in different ways and develop at different times. Stress hormones, for example, tend to inhibit the hippocampus, possibly preventing the formation of a conscious memory of the event. The amygdala, however, which develops earlier and has no trouble forming unconscious emotional memories, will form even stronger memories because of stress hormones. Children who are abused at an early age, for example, may form strong emotional memories to which they will never have conscious access (LeDoux, 1999).

Thus, neuroscientists have found that emotions have a memory of their own and can generate attitudes and behavior without our conscious awareness, despite conscious desires to the contrary (Damasio, 1994, 1999; Gilbert, 1991; LeDoux, 1986, 1994, 1996, 1999; Libet, 1996; Rorty, 1979, 1980). Although conscious thought and action are always influenced by emotional states and attitudes, it does not work the other way around. There are many more systemic connections and pathways leading from the limbic system to the cortex than cortical pathways leading to the limbic system. As LeDoux (1999) stated,

Once the amygdala is turned on, it can influence information processing in the cortex from the earliest stages onward, but only the later stages of cortical processing affect the amygdala. In other words, even though communication goes two ways, it's not equally effective in both directions. In general, the projections from the amygdala to the cortex are much stronger than vice versa. (LeDoux, 1999, p. 145)

MEMORY FALLIBILITY

Experiments by Loftus (1979a, 1979b, 1993a, 1993b, 1994, 1997) and others (Restak, 2000) have shown how easily fictitious childhood events (e.g., getting lost in a shopping mall, staying overnight in the hospital with an ear infection) may be convincingly remembered and even elaborated on by adults who become convinced of their actual occurrence. In one experiment, preschool-age children were merely told that they had undergone a traumatic event: They caught a finger in a mousetrap and were taken to a local hospital. Eventually, the children elaborated such highly detailed stories that even psychologists who specialized in interviewing children became convinced that the event had actually happened.

Key elements that allow for false memories seem to be the: (a) essential plasticity of memory in general, (b) susceptibility of dual-memory systems to absorbing misinformation, and (c) presence of three learning factors—use of imagination, mental rehearsal, and self-involvement. Because, unlike the cognitive system, the brain's emotional system makes no distinction between actual experience and media experience, media memories can and do mix readily with memories of actual experience, providing the basis for future decision and action. "Just as there is no firm dividing line between illusions of perceiving and remembering," researcher Roediger (1996) observed, "there is no firm line between illusions of remembering and those of judging and deciding" (p. 95).

Steven Pinker (1997) explained: "When we watch TV, we stare at a shimmering piece of glass, but our surface–perception module tells the rest of the brain that we are seeing real people and places . . . we cannot erase the assumption. . . . Even in a life-long couch potato, the visual system never 'learns' that television is a pane of glowing phosphor dots, and the person never loses the illusion that there is a world behind the pane" (p. 29). This is why the limbic system reacts to both horror films and actual horrific experience in the same way with typical fight-or-flight response. Regardless of what we already consciously know to be true, the basic emotional system of the brain reacts immediately to the senses in both actual and mediated experience, triggering a whole array of physical reactions: the heart beat quickens, breathing accelerates, pupils dilate, temperature drops, and blood is redirected to the muscles to prime them for action.

As some critics have suggested, for example, film audiences may use movies to place themselves virtually but safely within critical circumstances to rehearse how to act if the situation were to actually occur. This works *only* because visual experience is always real to the emotional system. Only the cognitive system, which enters perceptual processing at a later point, really knows the difference between film and reality. The essence of what Coleridge called "the willing suspension of disbelief" is that we have to suspend rational judgment only a little (and after the fact at that) to fully enter into a mediated experience.

Albert Bandura (1968) found that film and TV reduce children's inhibitions against violence, increase aggressive behavior, and teach children how to attack others. Bandura theorized that children learn aggression through media exposure when it is distinctive, simple, and prevalent; when they observe it as being evaluated positively; and when it is apparently useful. When any emotion is experienced, the body relies on the brain's amygdala to remember the emotional shape of the situation, and it keeps this shape in memory to act as a preselective kind of framing that biases interpretation and action in a survival-favorable way. This primary framing stage is essential if we are to get a sense of how to act in a threatening situation, and so it has become an essential and overriding response through evolution. With vicarious experience through media as well as with actual experience, the emotional system lays down an emotional memory as if the event really is happening, but both emotional and hippocampal memories change with time and circumstance.

Therefore, memory is not a videotape of past events, but a fluid construction that selects out key details and condenses information. Patients with frontal-lobe damage seem to be more susceptible to false recollections, however, because remembering is a constructive process that initially depends on perception. It is subsequently susceptible to a variety of distortions and illusions, so that memory in general is more likely to contain falsehoods than not (Hilts, 1996; Johnson, Hashtroudi, & Lindsay, 1993; Roediger, 1996; Schacter, 1995, 1996). Each time we recall a memory, it is altered by the current context of emotion and cognition. Preconceptions, prejudices, and unexamined assumptions all influence memory. The misinformation effect paradigm introduced by Loftus and Palmer (1974), for example, illustrates how information introduced after an event can alter the memory of that event, both in terms of forgetting the original event and in remembering a merely suggested event as actually having occurred (Lindsay & Johnson, 1989; Loftus, 1979a, 1979b, 1993a, 1993b; Ross, Read, & Toglia, 1994; Weingardt, Toland, & Loftus, 1994).

Source amnesia, in which we remember the fact or occurrence but not the source of the knowledge, is linked with the frontal lobes, the last of the cortex to mature and the most vulnerable to the aging process (Restak, 2000). A closely related phenomenon called the *sleeper effect* allows the impact of information from a low-credibility source to increase over time (Hannah & Sternthal, 1984; Hovland, Lumsdaine, & Sheffield, 1949; Mazursky & Schul, 1987). As the source becomes less strongly associated with the message over time, false information is more likely to be accepted as true. Underwood and Pezdek (1998) suggested that the cognitive processes underlying the sleeper effect are similar to those underlying memory suggestibility. Failures in source monitoring constantly color our memory for events and continue to influence both the development and expression of our knowledge and beliefs (Johnson et al., 1993).

In ordinary long-term memories, the hippocampus, responsible for processing contextual or episodic memory, works closely with the amygdala, the center of the emotional system, to generate and remember the emotion accompanying the event. Although a number of circumstances can interfere with the process of laying down long-term memories, one of the most common nonpathogenic causes for memory loss and confusion is stress. Eventually, too, memory also fades by a process of what is called *graceful degradation*, losing sharpness and detail over time (Restak, 2000). We forget slowly and almost imperceptibly because long-term memories are distributed throughout the brain, rather than stored together in specific localized areas as short-term or working memory is. Additionally, each time we recall a particular memory, we place it into a current context that in turn influences it and changes it yet again. Each time we recall an event from memory, the memory changes according to current circumstances and emotions.

REPETITION AND TYPES OF MEMORY

One of the most significant influences on memory formation and recall is repetition, particularly a repetition rich in association, self-involvement, and elaboration. This aspect of memory is particularly relevant to videogame play, which relies on repetition in shifting scenarios to train players to respond in particularly effective ways to traumatic encounters. Neurologist Restak (2000) explained how this repetition sets up a neuron network that results in preferred action: "Memory storage within the brain depends upon patterns of electrical and chemical activity among neurons. . . . Coordinated and repetitive activity between any two neurons strengthen(s) their connections. . . . Neurons that are active together retain stronger synaptic connections; when one neuron is activated, it tends to rouse the others, which collectively re–create the original pattern" (p. 116). Neurologists in general condense this basic principle into a simple axiom: Neurons that fire together wire together. Neurons that are wired together create an automatic response on a level below conscious awareness.

Although the hippocampus is the brain's entry point for the encoding of information into declarative memory, procedural memories (which function like a kind of auto pilot) do not require the hippocampus. Procedural memories depend heavily on repetition and on the ability of the limbic system to learn without conscious thought or effort. Repetition also plays a key role in solidifying memory and routinizing the abnormal. The anterior cingulate, located in the frontal brain, acts like an alarm bell detecting false patterns in the thinking process, but relaxes when things become routine.

At the unconscious level, each repetition of a simultaneous neural firing pattern makes it more likely that it will become the natural way to respond, given an appropriate stimulus or associative cue. For athletes, for example, this is good news. The body can be trained to the point where the perfect swan dive or double axel can be initiated automatically and carried through without thought. Systems activated in this way utilize more and more complex circuits in the brain. Areas of the motor cortex that control hand and finger movements are much bigger in professional keyboard and string players than in nonmusicians, and the increase in size correlates with the age at which the musician began training. The earlier the training, the larger the relevant areas of the motor cortex.

For those with negative or destructive habits of thought or action, the news is bad: If you are a former smoker who is used to responding to the anxiety of talking on the phone by lighting up a cigarette, for example, every time the phone rings, the desire for a cigarette will well up into the conscious mind. Habit modification necessarily requires a *lessening* in the strength of the synaptic connections at the cellular level in that circuitry for that habit to diminish (Restak, 2000).

The repetition of patterns of violence as a preferred response or repeated patterns of sexual behavior in media can be dangerous to the psyche, particularly to the developing brain of the child, which reasons through the amygdala. When we are continually exposed in real-life experience or through media to limited patterns of violent response, those scenarios not only come to be seen as normal over time (Huesmann & Miller, 1994), but can also become activated as a thoughtless way of responding to the natural stresses of life.

Once the scenario is established as reinforced neural patterning, conscious thought is not required to decide on an action, particularly when one is under stress or in the throes of an emotionally overpowering situation. Lessening the synaptic connections at the level of circuitry, which is the only way to alter habitual response patterns, is not a matter of conscious thought. Conscious thought can act *only* as a braking system to counteract or prevent us from acting on impulse. Thus, weakening synaptic connections can only be a matter of disuse over time, so that the emotional system can essentially deprogram itself by weakening destructive patterns of response and strengthening positive ones. In the case of traumatic memories, the emotional stress may be so great that the memory and its associations may never be dispelled.

FALSE VERSUS TRUE MEMORIES

The difference in the functioning between the cognitive and emotional systems is also significant in determining false memories from true ones. As experiments by neurologist Schacter and others have shown, a true memory calls up both the conscious experience and some sensory detail from the moment when the learning took place, and the result may be detectable through positron emission tomography (PET) scans of the brain, which measure glucose uptake as the memory is recalled. Although false memories only light up the area adjacent to the left of the hippocampus, which is the center of conscious recall, true memories light up *both* the hippocampal area *and* the sensory area where the experience was initially processed (Hilts, 1996; Schacter, 1995, 1996).

This is an important distinction in determining actual memories from false memories. Suggested by association within the brain's own system, false memories and details may be recalled because they fit the pattern in memory, and therefore seemingly *could have been* part of the original experience. False memories verbally suggested or inadvertently implanted have also been implicated in what has been called *repressed memory syndrome,* in which a patient may come to believe that he or she has been the actual victim of abuse that has merely been suggested by an inept counselor or interviewer.

VIDEOGAMES AND MENTAL LIFE

The process by which videogames inculcate habitual response patterns in game players follows a pattern of specific emotional learning and implicit procedural skill development. In the videogame player, the kind of emotional learning associated with both simple repetition and traumatic experience is initiated and conditioned by repeated patterns of interaction with programmed characters, settings, and actions. Videogames, in effect, train a player how to interact with the game by developing and rewarding certain automatic reactions through point systems; they also condition the emotional system to initiate a preferred violent response to all ranges and degrees of provocation. By utilizing the built-in fear response of the emotional system, videogames also engender physical changes in the brain. Although every new communication medium engenders different effects in both individuals and the society that embraces it, there is little doubt in communication research that there is a positive correlation between antisocial behavior and violence and viewing media violence.

In 1994, for example, Paik and Comstock statistically combined more than 200 correlational and experimental studies involving over 1,000 comparisons between violent media and control groups and found that media violence is a significant contributor to violent and hostile behavior. In a 10-year review of research on the impact of media on children and adolescents, in keeping with the research prior to 1990 documenting that children learn behaviors and have their value systems shaped by media, Villani (2000) concluded that the primary effects of media exposure are increased violent and aggressive behavior, increased high-risk behaviors, including alcohol and drug use, and accelerated onset of sexual activity. Calvert and Tan (1996) clearly showed that the impact of this violence is intensified by the immersive environments that characterize virtual reality and interactive videogames.

Because they are interactive in nature, videogames cause players to initiate violence, not merely to watch it. As a result, their potential for altering brain structures and function is significant. As videogames become even more realistic than TV and more like film in their capacity to involve people and absorb them into the screen reality, there is an even more pressing need for neurological research on media effects.

According to a 1997 survey conducted by the National Institute on Media and the Family and the University of Oklahoma, 84% of all teens play video/electronic games, and 92% of boys play games. Of these, 90% say their parents never check ratings before allowing them to rent or buy video games, and 89% of teens and 91% of boys say their parents never put time limits on their videogame play. This is especially alarming in view of the growing popularity of videogames like "Kingpin" ("mature" rating, Xatrix, Los Angeles) where the player, according to a review by *PC Gamer*, "turns the player into a street thug traipsing through a life-like ghetto with a lead pipe, bludgeoning thick-necked bar bouncers and heroin-addled hookers" (Lawrence, 1999, p. 4). In the game, players can trade up for a crowbar once they pummel the next street person to death and then lift $10 from his pockets to buy it. As the action heats up, a Cypress Hill hip-hop soundtrack keeps time to the beatings. Retailers may sell any game to customers of any age.

As the public becomes more aware of the connection between media experience and real-life violence suggested by thousands of media studies, the issue of responsibility has inevitably found its way into the legal system, where manufacturers of violent images usually claim first amendment freedom of speech rights, and plaintiffs argue that media violence provides a fertile training ground for impressionable kids. In April 1999, for example, the parents of children killed in the West Paducah, Kentucky school shooting by shooter Michael Carneal, filed suit against makers of violent videogames for honing his killing skills by playing point-and-shoot games. In December 1997, the 14-year-old killed three students and wounded five others; he hit eight children with eight shots, each one in the head or upper torso. According to the FBI, the average marksman succeeds with less than one bullet in five. According to Lt. Col. Dave Grossman, West Point teacher who specialized in psychologically preparing cadets to kill, Carneal was able to hit each human target with uncanny accuracy because the point-and-shoot videogames he played are so much like the simulators used to teach soldiers and police officers (Grossman & DeGaetano, 1999). When he walked into the prayer meeting at the high school, allegedly trained as a marksman by videogames and inspired by the film *Basketball Diaries*, Michael Carneal had already logged hundreds of hours of practice killing realistic human figures and earning bonus points for head shots (Fields, 1999).

Today, over 2,000 studies link media violence with violent behavior. Although most researchers agree that violence is a complex behavior with multiple causes, media plays a special role in legitimizing violence, promoting attitudes that result in violence, and glamorizing violence as a pleasurable activity. Bandura (1977) suggested that people must learn aggressive behavior, and that they do learn it through imitation, especially as children, if it seems useful in getting what they want. From 1996 to 1997, during which Michael Carneal went on his shooting binge, the U.S. Dept of Education recorded 11,000 incidents of school violence involving weapons. In the April 20, 1999, incident in Littleton, Colorado, Eric Harris, 17, and Dylan Klebold, 18, may have showed just how influential media could be in the lives of adolescents. Fans of goth music and Marilyn Manson, the two were also obsessed with the violent videogame "Doom" and, according to media interviews with friends, played it every afternoon. Introduced first in 1993, "Doom" and its successor, "Quake," introduced in 1996, were within the first wave of videogames to develop the point-and-shoot strategy, which transformed the player into the shooter and used the percentage of kills at the end as the means of scoring. The games use realistic graphics, including eviscerated prisoners in rooms filled with bloody skulls and body parts. On June 25, 2003, 14- and 16-year-old stepbrothers, William and Joshua Buckner, opened fire on automobiles on Interstate 40 in Tennessee, emulating "Grand Theft Auto," killing one motorist and wounding many others. A gang of youths calling themselves the "Nut Cases," in Oakland, California, were charged in 2003 with dozens of robberies and five killings inspired by "Grand Theft Auto" as well. As technology has allowed the videogames to become faster and more detailed, the variety of ways to kill have multiplied, including brass knuckles, nail guns, pump–action shotguns, and even grenade launchers that literally blow apart whatever moves within the view of the player.

The significance of this in terms of perceptual process lies in repetitive play and the fact that the visual experience of the videogame is always real to the emotional system. If, while we are watching a film or TV, the experience gets too uncomfortable, we can suspend our emotional belief by calling on our intellect to restore emotional balance. But this kind of rational action can only counteract the experience to a certain extent, and it has limitations, as everyone who has experienced nightmares after watching a scary movie knows. The brain's amygdala remembers the emotional shape of the viewed experience and stores it for future survival. Emotions are an integral and holistic preparatory part of reasoning; logical reasoning influences behavior only by serving as a delayed rational check on intuitive perceptions.

MAPS FOR THE FUTURE

Because of the evolutionary development of our perceptual system, we continue to learn from mediated and actual experience alike and use them to construct the maps by which we can understand future experience. The more often a particular pattern of experience (e.g., a film scenario or videogame violence) is repeated, the more automatic and deeply engrained the neuronal circuitry becomes in the brain. In the same way that athletes train long hours to educate the unconscious mind to move the body automatically when certain circumstances are initiated, the more conditioned our responses and thinking become when we are continually exposed to patterns of experience, whether in actual life or in media exposure.

Because evolution is a relatively slow process of development, the perceptual system does not have a built-in module for separately processing images that come from media and those that do not. The mammalian brain sees media images as reality and responds emotionally as if they were reality, learning emotionally from both media and actual experience in the same way. As computer memories become greater and processors speedier through such developments as nanotectic logic chips and virtual reality without helmets and data gloves, videogames will inevitably become so much like real-life experience that they may in fact become indistinguishable from real life in cognitive and emotional terms.

Damasio (1999) explained that, "images [i.e., mental patterns created through the senses] allow us to choose among repertoires of previously available patterns of action and [to] optimize the delivery of the chosen action" (p. 24). When the neurological maps that we use to navigate reality are drawn from the repetition of patterns of action provided by the entertainment industry, we not only essentially place the parameters of our behavioral choices within the agency of commercial interests, we also distort or displace the process of social and intellectual growth that the process of natural play promotes.

Once taken for granted as a "carefree and exuberant way to pass the time before the hard work of adulthood," play is now being taken seriously by neuroscientists as a primary means of evolving intelligence within the human species. For example, recent research has shown a strong positive link between playtime and the size of mammalian brains, showing a clear correlation between the amount a brain grows between birth and maturity and the amount of play in which the species is involved (Iwaniuk, Nelson, & Pellis, 2001). Because spontaneous, self-directed play involves the complex assessment of playmates, social signals, and reciprocity necessary for social development, some researchers believe that free play creates a brain with greater behavioral flexibility and learning potential as well as creativity, whereas organized sports and otherwise structured play do not (Bekoff, 2001; Furlow, 2001). When videogames take the place of spontaneous play or are allowed to direct the imagination in unnatural ways, overall emotional and cognitive development may suffer irreparable stultification or worse.

Media critic Taylor Stoehr (2001) believes that the formula stories of media "pull fantasy into line and keep us from dancing off on private paths" and likens TV watching to meditation, in which the audience slips off into a trance, becoming one "with whatever 'universe' the medium represents," forcefully replacing the function of daydreaming and fantasy with a "restless limbo of consciousness, where everything seems to be on hold." Such media training, he argues, establishes patterns of awareness that are regarded as "normal." This tuning out of consciousness, which parallels the effect of alcohol or drugs, directs attention somewhere other than the present. Virtual reality, he believes, "represents a move of the media towards such a condition of physical transformation, without the drugs or alcohol."

TRAUMA, STRESS, MEMORY, AND THE ULTIMATE COST

Severe emotional trauma not only scars the psyche; it physically damages the brain. Because the body is not built to handle psychologically induced stress, if stress mechanisms do not turn off, the body, especially the brain, can suffer irreversible damage. In terms of memory, a major point of concern of neurologists is that stress hormones eventually damage the hippocampus, which is vital to both learning and memory. The hippocampus is, in fact, one of the first parts of the body to reveal the structural changes caused by stressful conditions. Combat veterans suffering from posttraumatic stress disorder (PTSD) show significant reduction in the volume of the hippocampus, and research shows that both combat veterans and survivors of child abuse have performed at levels averaging 40% lower on tests of verbal memory than people of comparable age and education (Goleman, 1995).

Because the hippocampus plays a key role in moderating the hormone cascade to the body, continuous stress over time causes it to shrink, and eventually stress and anxiety can become chronic. When stress responses are chronically kept in overdrive, the effect is also to exacerbate diseases such as hypertension, diabetes, gastric ulcers, colitis, and asthma, as well as damage to the immune system. Although minor stress causes the amygdala to signal cortical areas to strengthen memory, too much agitation disrupts concentration and interferes with memory by heightening levels of cortisol, which is ultimately toxic to the hippocampus. Although the stress response is a survival mechanism preparing us to meet physical dangers in the short run, the prolonged secretion of cortisol and adrenaline associated with the stress response ultimately cause "allostatic load," which leads to illnesses such as stroke and atherosclerosis and the increased risk of heart attack (see Figure 2.3). If stress is considerably prolonged, the damage can be permanent, destroying the hippocampal neurons (McEwen, 1999).

Because the fight-or-flight fear response can be initiated by actual conditions of life such as combat or abuse, or by artificially induced media events such as movies or videogames, the effect of prolonged stress on the brain is similar in both. Symptoms of stress and anxiety cannot be willed or

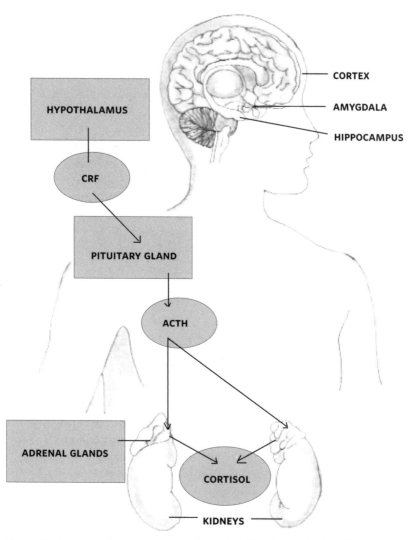

Figure 2.3. Prolonged stress causes "allostatic load" which ultimately leads to illnesses such as stroke and increased risk of heart attack. If stress is considerably prolonged, cortisol damage can be permanent, even destroying hippocampal neurons themselves.

wished away, and the allostatic load of real and mediated experience has real physical and psychological consequences. One of the most significant consequences of trauma and prolonged stress is that it biases the brain in such a way that the thalamic pathways to the amygdala predominate over the cortical ones, allowing these low–level emotionally based processing networks to take the lead in the learning and storage of information (Restak, 2000).

The ultimate effect of this cannot be overestimated because this privileges the amygdala pathway at the expense of the cortical pathway, and therefore sets up a thinking and behavior pattern dominated by emotional processing and quick response, as well as a dulled sensitivity to the lower level natural pleasures of everyday life, such as birds singing, sunsets, and quiet moments of sharing. The emotional learning associated with stressful activity not only rewires the synaptic connections in the brain, but also privileges negativity and depression as the lenses through which we perceive reality. In people who are anxious, attention is drawn toward threatening stimuli in the environment, resulting in the tendency to both overestimate the likelihood of bad things happening and interpret ambiguous stimuli as negative. Such neurological understanding explains not only why fears associated with a specific experience can evolve into phobias that are difficult or impossible to reverse through reasoning, but also the phenomenon of what George Gerbner et al. (1978, 1980) called *mean world syndrome,* where the repeated exposure to negative messages causes people to become convinced that the world they live in is an inherently dangerous and primarily mean one.

Repeated negative media messages show up on PET scans the same as injury to the left hemisphere. Experiments by Richard Davidson at the University of Wisconsin–Madison have shown that repeated display of negative images induce marked changes in the mood of the participants, and as the mood worsens, it is accompanied by changes in the brain's glucose metabolism registered on a PET scan. These scans appeared similar to those in people who had suffered damage to the left hemisphere. With the left hemisphere less active, the right takes control (Restak, 2000). This is particularly significant because the left side of the brain is concerned with positive emotions and the right side with negative ones. Because the left hemisphere controls emotions in the right side of the brain, damage to the left side, which dampens our response to negative events by inhibiting the amygdala, results in negativity and depression.

A 2002 study using functional Magnetic Resonance Imaging (fMRI) brain scans by researchers at Indiana University Medical School (Matthews et al., 2002) showed that hours of playing violent videogames affect the brain on a cellular level, causing misfiring of signals between nerve cells or slowing brain activity in the frontal lobes, which controls impulses and attention span. Adverse effects were most apparent among teens diagnosed with a "disruptive behavior disorder" (DBD), who are the ones most likely to "act out by harming animals or property or fighting with other kids." Videogames, it appears, sharpens reflexes and visual skills for violence while dampening the powers of logical reasoning.

As it becomes clearer that the primary effects of media exposure include increased violent and aggressive behavior, increased high–risk behaviors, including alcohol and drug use, and accelerated onset of sexual activity, the correlations between emotional memory and media experience become more and more crucial to understand. As media researcher Murray (1997) has noted, the next frontier of media effects studies in the 21st century must be biologically based studies on the effects of mass media and interactive media, both immediately and in the long term.

Emotional stress induced by the repetitive patterns of vicarious media experience not only reduces memory; it also reduces rationality and a positive outlook on life. Hippocampal damage decreases our ability to form and consolidate declarative memories; when this happens, we not only make up reasonable explanations to fill in the memory gaps, but we also believe them. Ultimately, we do not remember falsely so much as we remember selectively those aspects that are meaningful to us at the time in terms of our attitude, and our unconscious provides fictitious details that fit the pattern we expect to see. With a prevalent negative attitude induced by stress and exposure to real or media violence, and with the damage caused to the memory and homeostatic balance of emotions by overstimulation through prolonged exposure, media can not only alter our perception, our ability to process information accurately, and our memories, it can also profoundly and irrevocably alter the substance of our thinking and the quality of our lives.

REFERENCES

Anderson, C. A., & Dill, K. E. (2000). Video games and aggressive thoughts, feelings and behavior in the laboratory and in life. *Journal of Personality and Social Psychology, 78*(4), 772–790.

Anderson, C. A., & Ford, C. M. (1986). Affect of the game player: Short terms effects of highly and mildly aggressive video games. *Personality and Social Psychology Bulletin, 12,* 390–402.

Ballard, M. E., & Weist, J. R. (1996). Mortal Kombat: The effects of violent\video game play on males' hostility and cardiovascular responding. *Journal of Applied Social Psychology, 26,* 717–730.

Bandura, A. (1968). What TV violence can do to your child. In O. Larsen (Ed.), *Violence and the mass media* (pp. 123–139). New York: Harper & Row.

Bandura A. (1977). *Social learning theory.* Englewood Cliffs, NJ:Prentice Hall.

Bekoff, M. (2001). Social play behaviour: Cooperation, fairness, trust and the evolution of morality. *Consciousness Studies, 8,* 81.

Calvert, S. L., & Tan, S. L. (1996). Impact of virtual reality on young adults' physiological arousal and aggressive thoughts: Interaction versus observation. In R. Carter (Ed.), *Mapping the mind*. Berkeley: University of California Press.

Damasio, A. (1994). *Descartes' error: Emotion, reason and the human brain*. New York: Avon.

Damasio, A. (1999). *The feeling of what happens*. New York: Harcourt Brace.

Dill, K. E., & Dill, J. C. (1998). Video game violence: A review of empirical literature. *Aggression and Violent Behavior: A Review Journal, 3*, 407–428.

Emes, C. E. (1997). Is Mr. Pac man eating our children? A review of the effect of videogames on children. *Canadian Journal of Psychiatry, 42*, 409–414.

Fields, S. (1999, October 25). Seeking clues why teens slaughter teens. *Boston Herald, 2*, 23.

Furlow, B. (2001, June 9). Play's the thing. *New Scientist, 170*, 28–31.

Gerbner, G., Gross, L., Jackson–Beeck, M., Jeffries–Fox, S., & Signorelli, N. (1978). Cultural indicators: Violence profile no. 9. *Journal of Communication, 28*, 176–206.

Gerbner, G., Gross, L., Morgan, M., & Signorelli, N. et al. (1980). The mainstreaming of America: Violence profile no. 11. *Journal of Communication, 30*, 100–127.

Gilbert, D. T. (1991). How mental systems believe. *American Psychologist, 46*, 107–117.

Goleman, D. (1995). Severe trauma may damage the brain as well as the psyche. In N. Wade (Ed.), *The Science Times book of the brain*. New York: Lyons Press.

Grossman, D., & DeGaetano, G. (1999). *Stop teaching our kids to kill: A call to action against TV, movie and video game violence*. New York: Crown.

Hannah, D. B., & Sternthal, B. (1984). Detecting and explaining the sleeper effect. *Journal of Communication Research, 11*, 632–642.

Hilts, P. (1996). In research scans, telltale signs sort false memories from true. In N. Wade (Ed.), *The Science Times book of the brain* (pp. 95–98). New York: Lyons Press.

Hovland, C. I., Lumsdaine, A. A., & Sheffield, F. D. (1949). *Experiments in mass communication*. Princeton, NJ: Princeton University Press.

Huesmann, L. R. (1986). Psychological processes promoting the relation between exposure to media violence and aggressive behavior by the viewer. *Journal of Social Issues, 42*, 125–139.

Huesmann, L. R. & Miller, L. (1994). Long-term effects of repeated exposure to media violence in childhood. In L. Huesmann (Ed.), *Aggressive behavior: Current perspectives* (pp. 153–188). New York: Plenum Press.

Irwin, A. R., & Gross, A. M. (1995). Cognitive tempo, violent video games, and aggressive behavior in young boys. *Journal of Family Violence, 10*, 337–350.

Iwaniuk, A., Nelson, J., & Pellis, S. (2001). Do big brained animals play more? *Journal of Comparative Psychology, 115*, 29.

Johnson, M., Hashtroudi, S., & Lindsay, D. (1993). Source monitoring. *Psychological Bulletin, 114*, 3–28.

Kandel, E . (1999). Of learning, memory, and genetic switches. In R. Conlan (Ed.), *States of mind* (pp. 151–178). New York: Wiley.

Lawrence, J. M. (1999, May 3). "Violent, depraved," videogame has some questioning content. *Boston Herald*, p. 4.

LeDoux, J. (1986). Sensory systems and emotion. *Integrative Psychiatry, 4*, 237–248.

LeDoux, J. (1994). Emotion, memory and the brain. *Scientific American, 27*, 50–57.

LeDoux, J. (1996). *The emotional brain: The mysterious underpinnings of emotional life.* New York: Simon & Schuster Touchstone.

LeDoux, J. (1999). The power of emotions. In R. Conlan (Ed.), *States of mind* (pp. 123–149). New York: Wiley.

Libet, B. (1996). Neural time factors in conscious and unconscious mental functions. In S. R. Hameroff et al. (Eds.), *Toward a science of consciousness* (pp. 337–347) Cambridge: MIT Press.

Lindsay, D. S., & Johnson, M. K. (1989). The eyewitness suggestibility effect and memory for source. *Memory and Cognition, 17*, 349–358.

Loftus, E. (1979a). *Eyewitness testimony.* Cambridge, MA: Harvard University Press.

Loftus, E. (1979b). The malleability of memory. *American Scientist, 67*, 312–320.

Loftus, E. (1993a). The reality of repressed memories. *American Psychologist, 48*, 518–537.

Loftus, E. (1993b). Made in memory: Distortions in recollection after misleading information. In D. L. Medin (Ed.), *The psychology of learning and motivation: Advances in theory and research* (pp. 187–215). New York: Academic Press.

Loftus, E. (1994). *Myth of repressed memory.* New York: St. Martin's Press.

Loftus, E. (1997, September). Creating false memories. *Scientific American*, 51–55.

Loftus, E., & Palmer, J. C. (1974). Reconstruction of automobile destruction: An example of the interaction between language and memory. *Journal of Verbal Learning and Verbal Behavior, 13*, 585–589.

Lynch, P. (1994). Type A behavior, hostility, and cardiovascular function at rest and after playing video games in teenagers. *Psychosomatic Medicine, 56*, 152.

Lynch, P. (1999). Hostility, type A behavior, and stress hormones at rest and after playing video games in teenagers. *Psychosomatic Medicine, 61*, 113.

Matthews, V. et al. (2002). Aggressive youths, violent video games trigger unusual brain activity. 88th Scientific Assembly and Annual Meeting of the Radiological Society of North America in Chicago. December 2, 2002. See also: Indiana University Medical School news release <http://medicine.indiana.edu/news_releases/archive_02/violent_games02.html.>

Mazursky, D., & Schul, Y. (1987). The effects of advertising encoding on the failure to discount information: Implications for the sleeper effect. *Journal of Consumer Research, 15*, 24–35.

McEwen, B. (1999). Stress and the brain. In R. Conlan (Ed.), *States of mind* (pp. 81-101). New York: Wiley.

Murray, J. P. (1997). Studying television violence: A research agenda for the 21st century. In J. K. Asamen & G. L. Berry (Eds.), *Research paradigms, television and social behavior* (pp. 369–410). Thousand Oaks, CA: Sage.

Paik, H., & Comstock, G. (1994). The effects of television violence on antisocial behavior: A meta–analysis. *Communication Research, 2*, 516–46.

Pinker, S. (1997). *How the mind works.* New York: W. W. Norton.

Poole, S. (2000). *Trigger happy: Videogames and the entertainment revolution.* New York: Arcade Publishing.

Restak, R. (2000). *Mysteries of the mind.* Washington, DC: National Geographic.

Roberts, D. (2000). Media and youth: Access, exposure and privatization. *Journal of Adolescent Health, 27*, 8–14.

Roediger, H. L. (1996). Memory illusions, *Journal of Memory and Language, 35*, 76–100.

Rorty, A. O. (1979). *Philosophy and the mirror of nature.* Princeton: Princeton University Press.

Rorty, A. O. (1980). *Explaining emotions.* Berkeley: University of California Press.

Ross, D. F., Read, J. D., & Toglia, M. P. (1994). *Adult eyewitness testimony: Current trends and developments.* Cambridge: Cambridge University Press.

Schacter, D. L. (1995). Memory distortion: History and current status. In D. L. Schachter, J. T. Coyle, G. D. Fishbach, M.–M. Mesulam, & L. E. Sullivan (Eds.), *Memory distortion: How minds, brains and societies reconstruct the past* (pp. 1–43). Cambridge, MA: Harvard University Press.

Schacter, D. L. (1996). Recognition memory for recently spoken words. *Neuron, 17*(2), 267–74.

Stoehr, T. (2001). http://www.adbusters.org/campaigns/tvturnoff/toolbox/trance.html.

Underwood, J., & Pezdek, K. (1998). Memory suggestibility as an example of the sleeper effect. *Psychonomic Bulletin & Review, 5*, 449–453.

Van Schie, E. G. M., & Weigman, O. (1997). Children and video games: Leisure, aggression, social integration, and school performance. *Journal of Applied Social Psychology, 27*, 1175–1194.

Villani, S. (2000). Impact of media on children and adolescents: A 10-year review of the research. *Journal of American Academy of Adolescent Psychiatry, 40*, 392–401.

Weingardt, K. R., Toland, H. K., & Loftus, E. F. (1994). Reports of suggested memories: Do people truly believe them? In D. F. Ross, J. D. Read, & M. P. Foglia (Eds.), *Adult eyewitness testimony: Current trends and developments* (pp. 3-26). New York: Springer Verlag.

Winkel, M., Novak, D. M., & Hopson, M. (1987). Personality factors, subject gender and the effects of aggressive video games on aggression in adolescents. *Journal of Research in Personality, 21*, 211–223.

SECTION II
COLLECTIVE IDENTITIES,
VISUAL RHETORIC, AND
PUBLIC SPACE

CHAPTER THREE

The Speed of Immanent Images[1]
The Dangers of Reading Photographs

KEVIN MICHAEL DELUCA
UNIVERSITY OF GEORGIA

> Writing about music is like dancing about architecture.
>
> —Unknown

S IMILARLY, WRITING ABOUT PHOTOGRAPHY is also like writing about music. Such skepticism is warranted on many grounds and certainly highlights the question of translation. That said, we academic critics write and talk, so it is not surprising that when we finally set our sights on photography, we write and talk about it. More than that, however, we encounter photographs as loyal scribes from the Gutenberg Galaxy, all too quickly turning photographs into texts. So this chapter may, I fear, add to the pile of words obscuring photographs.

I use the word *obscure* advisedly, noting how words conceal photographs, keep them from being seen; further, noting how photography emerges from the camera obscura and suggesting that photographs remain a dark chamber to us. As Deleuze and Guattari (1977) claimed, "The eye no longer sees, it reads" (p. 206). Despite pointing to the impossibility of seeing photographs through words, I still believe in trying. As the Queen in *Alice's Adventures in Wonderland* explains, "Why, sometimes I've believed as many as six impossible things before breakfast." So, sharing the Queen's optimism (or insanity), I embrace our turn to the visual. It is certainly apropos now, as atrocity images flood our public screen, from newspapers to televisions. Today I want to briefly interrogate our encounter with images, especially photographs. Many disciplines have yet to engage images/photographs. Our studious gazes at images are always askew, filtered through the terministic screens of old habits, old practices, old concepts.

---

1. When talking about images, I am mostly referring to photographs. Though focusing on rhetoric, my comments apply to many disciplines in the humanities, including history, political science, cultural studies, and so on.

The stark choice we face was most eloquently described by Roland Barthes over two decades ago, when he suggested that the exorbitant thingness of photos arrests interpretation, that a photo's intractable immanence, utter singularity, interrupts the quest for transcendent knowledge. That is, we study the studium, the cultural field that allows us to place the photograph and ignore the punctum that pierces the studium and interrupts interpretation. Given that Roland Barthes is the patron saint of visual cultural studies, I hesitate to be critical; however, I want to suggest a friendly amendment. The punctum is an unshared and unsharable personal experience. Yet in Part Two of *Camera Lucida* the punctum drops out and in the concluding five pages Barthes seems to want to discuss a socially shared intractable immanence—the madness of photographs. To quote Barthes (1981), "Society is concerned to tame the Photograph, to temper the madness which keeps threatening to explode in the face of whoever looks at it" (p. 117). This madness, which is recognized communally and threatens *anyone* who looks, this "*shared* hallucination" (p. 115) is the photograph's excess, the exorbitant, what Barthes termed "the photographic *ecstasy*" (p. 119). What I fear is that as critics we are participating in this taming of the photograph, the taming of its ecstasy, its excess, its exorbitant.

NEGLECTING IMAGES

We can see this taming in four dominant responses to images in the discipline of rhetorical studies. I briefly mention three responses before focusing on the fourth. The traditionally dominant response is one of disciplinary blindness. Too often rhetoricians live in a universe devoid of images. A paradigmatic example is the analysis of the U.S. civil rights movement. In rhetoric, the civil rights movement is reduced to its linguistic manifestations—primarily the speeches of Martin Luther King Jr. and, as lesser luminaries, Malcolm X, John Lewis, and Stokely Carmichael. Yet any reckoning must account for the rhetorical force of images of Emmett Till and of black bodies at risk from Birmingham police dogs and fire hoses. These images still await rhetorical analysis.[2]

An obvious defense of this disciplinary blindness would be that rhetoric is about words, speeches. Such an assumption does not survive scrutiny. Let us look at Aristotle's (1991) definition: "Let rhetoric be an ability, in each case, to see the available means of persuasion . . . rhetoric seems to be able

---

2. Christine Harold and I are trying to do some of this work in "Behold the Corpse: Violent Images and the Case of Emmett Till," *Rhetoric and Public Affairs*, 2005.

to observe the persuasive about 'the given'" (pp. 36–37). It is worth noting that Aristotle did not limit the "available means" to speech. That Aristotle's elaboration on the three forms most important in his context later solidified into a formulaic neo-Aristotelianism is not solely his fault. His definition has a wonderful openness about it that suggests rhetoric is always a seeing anew of a social field in constant flux. For instance, there is no reason to expect speeches to be eternally and universally an available means. Although public address conventionally defined as speeches has been the heart of the discipline of rhetoric, in the case of late 20th-century United States, it is hard to see speeches as the predominant current available means (Gronbeck, 1995; Jamieson, 1988; McGee, 1990). It is much easier to see the corporate discourses of public relations and advertising, both heavily dependent on images, as potent available means.

Fundamentally, then, rhetoric is characterized by contingency, *arrangiasti*, the art of making do in civic space. In technical terms, rhetoric is dependent on emergent forms. *Emergent* is an old literary term adopted by evolutionary biology and being reclaimed for the humanities by literary theorist Wlad Godzich (1994). Emergent suggests something unprecedented, unpredictable, unexpected. In biology, an *emerging* characteristic would be limbs, which emerged in a linear way from fins. An *emergent* characteristic would be consciousness, which occurred outside of a teleological frame. It was unpredictable, contingent. Godzich argues that an example from literature is the novel, whose emergence could not have been predicted from earlier forms of literature. I want to suggest that the most interesting aspect of rhetoric is its emergent character, its contingent quality. Rhetoric is the art of discerning and deploying the available contingent means of constructing, maintaining, and transforming social reality in a particular context.

A second response is to look at texts dominated by images without noticing or acknowledging the images. This trend is most evident in the rhetorical treatment of television. In study after study—of the "Mary Tyler Moore Show," of television news, of Budweiser commercials, and so on—we study television without the vision thing, as if television were radio. We study the transcripts, the words, and the ideological content suggested by the words, and we leave the images virgin territory. To study television as if it were radio, as if it were a speech, is more than silly. It is a reduction and mutation of one form, say television or film, into another form, speeches or writing. To ignore the form of visual media prevents us from getting at the force of a medium in society. The effects of radio and television have been different, and images play no small part in that difference.

A third response acknowledges the rhetorical force of images, but then quickly retreats to words and traditional rhetorical methods. Michael Hogan's (1996) book termed the U.S. nuclear freeze movement a *televisual movement*, but then proceeded to study it through television transcripts. Olson and Goodnight's (1994) study of the protest practices of PETA acknowledged the existence of images, but focused on slogans and captions as if the images were merely decorative. This approach is more dangerous than the first two because, while they blissfully neglect images, this third approach purports to be studying images, but does so in a manner that domesticates images for the house of logos. Neglect may be benign. Domestication never is.

READING IMAGES

The fourth approach is achieving a certain currency in our discipline and warrants a more sustained treatment. This approach takes images seriously. The scholars analyze images with care and diligence. These are not bad qualities! And yet . . .

And yet in the study of images, perhaps care and diligence are a problem. I will explain presently. Before getting to my curmudgeon carping, however, let me praise the current renaissance of visual rhetoric as epitomized by this last approach. Scholars such as John Lucaites, Robert Hariman, Cara Finnegan, Lester Olson, Tom Benson, and others make it impossible for me to simply complain that the discipline of rhetoric studies images by focusing on words, that we think images are captured by captions, that we think images are a sideshow. Now, clearly with respect to images, we can declare, quoting the famous jazz musician, "This ain't no sideshow." The scholars I proceed to criticize are careful and judicious. Keep that in mind as I proceed to my criticisms. They are all doing much of what is right in the study of visual rhetoric. They all attempt close study of images. This is a crucial, yet often neglected, practice. Second, they read both fine art and prosaic images as rhetoric, not art. This distinction is vital. Third, they read images as political—both instrumentally political in a particular situation and generally political on a cultural level. Some work has the additional merit of extending the historical range of the importance of visual rhetoric. If Mitchell is right in announcing the displacement of the linguistic turn by the pictorial turn, such work pointedly discourages our solipsism and reminds us of earlier instances of image politics.

So, what is my problem? To reiterate, I am worried about how we as a field use context, morality, and transcendent theory to reduce the rhetorical force of images to meaning, domesticating them for our studies.

The scholars I praise are all careful in their work to provide historical context. Yet historical context too quickly can slip into facile understanding—a comfort that dulls awareness of the rhetorical force of images. Context is always a fiction of our own making—an illusion that fosters delusions. A good example of this is a picture from the Iraq invasion that appeared on the front page of *The New York Times* and other newspapers around the United States. The photo, by Damir Sagolj, shows a sitting U.S. marine holding a small Iraqi girl in his lap moments after a firefight killed her parents. The little girl is dressed in pink, with the sweater sleeve of her right arm stained by blood. She is touching the marine's camouflage jacket. She is barefoot. The marine, dressed all in camouflage and with a helmet and visor, looks grim as he gazes down on the little girl in his lap. In the background, the legs and guns of camouflage-attired soldiers are walking away. This photograph engendered diametrically opposite reactions, some people reading it as U.S. military propaganda, others reading it as evidence of the wrongness of the invasion. Neither reading is wrong, but rather, they suggest that context cannot determine the meaning of a text. Historical texts, with their possible contexts being multiplied across time as well as space, further amplify this point. As Derrida (1982) explains: "Every sign, linguistic or nonlinguistic . . . can break with every given context, and engender infinitely new contexts in an absolutely nonsaturable fashion. This does not suppose that the mark is valid outside its context, but on the contrary that there are only contexts without any center of absolute anchoring" (p. 320).

My second fear revolves around moral responses to images, the iconophobia or fear of images that infects the concept of the public sphere. Indeed, the fear and moral condemnation of images in the public sphere is so endemic as to warrant junking the concept of the public sphere in favor of the public screen (DeLuca & Peeples, 2002). This moralism is rampant, and prominent examples include the work of Kathleen Hall Jamieson and Neil Postman, two authors who have provided insightful analysis of images, but then regress into moralistic condemnations of images and nostalgia for an imaginary Golden Age. Good or bad, thumbs up or down, gets us nowhere. This sort of moralism creeps into the work of many scholars. In an interesting essay on the Elian spectacle, Anne Demo (2003) suggests that she is wary of moral condemnations of the spectacle, but then does not disavow the claim that "the seductive power of images dulls critical sensibilities." Later the author complains that the spectacle as infotainment "effaces content," and that her critique is concerned with both "the normalization of infotainment" and "the inversion of reality and illusion." In sum, the essay concludes that the Elian spectacle "exemplified many of the characteristic ills associated with media spectacles," ills termed "civic poisons."

Of course, in our moral condemnations of images, we rhetorical critics are in good company. In her seminal *On Photography*, not only did Sontag (1977) open the book by chastising us for lingering unregenerately in Plato's cave, reveling in mere images of the Truth, in the first chapter alone she described photography as "ghostly traces that give us an imaginary possession of an unreal past and make us complicit with an oppressive status quo, the slaughter-bench of history. Photographs corrupt, anesthetize, and deaden conscience. To take a photograph is to commit a sublimated murder. Photos can only give a semblance of knowledge, a semblance of wisdom" (pp. 3–24). Sontag concluded that photography's reductive approach to reality is a form of "mental pollution" that turns us into "image junkies." Moral judgments and terminology such as civic poisons and image junkies short-circuit thinking about what work images do. The question is not whether photographs are good or bad, real or illusory, authentic or twisted, but rather, "What sort of public and what forms of knowing does a photocentric media matrix produce?" Sontag got it exactly wrong. We scholars have not reveled enough. We need to practice a certain debauchery.

Finally, scholars such as Cara Finnegan, Robert Hariman, and John Lucaites offer concepts for making sense of images. With reservations, I applaud this move. Instead of trying to domesticate photographs with rhetorical terms irreducibly tied to words—metaphor, enthymeme, and so on— assuredly an involuntary and yet unfortunate reflex for rhetorical scholars, Finnegan, Hariman, and Lucaites are actually thinking, for the task of thinking is to create concepts. As Deleuze and Guattari (1994) put it, thinking is "the art of forming, inventing, and fabricating concepts" (p. 2). The question then becomes, what is their thinking producing, what is it getting us with respect to the rhetorical force of photographs? Here it is important to distinguish between transcendent and immanent concepts; if photography is anything, it is immanent, radically contingent—Barthes' "that has been." Finnegan offers circulation as a concept for making sense of photographs, and Hariman and Lucaites offer icon. Circulation and icon are interesting forays, though I worry that they are the sort of transcendent concepts that produce a donut theory of photography that allows us to circle around photos without engaging them.

Finnegan (2003b) makes explicit my fear when she explains that to understand the Farm Security Administration (FSA) photos as inventional resources, "then what I needed to do was not so much study the photographs, but study circulation." Finnegan (2003a) elaborates on her notion of circulation in her important book on the FSA photographs, *Picturing Poverty: Print Culture and the FSA Photographs*: "I contend that the power of the FSA photographs' visual rhetoric may best be understood by situating the images in the contexts of print culture within which they appeared and by paying close attention to the uses to which they were put" (p. xii). In focusing on contexts instead of the intractable immanence of individual images, Finnegan enacts her "belief that the study of images must remain grounded in the materiality of their rhetorical circulation" (p. 224). With this move, Finnegan opts to retreat to reading contexts rather than seeing photographs. There are two problems with Finnegan's turn to contexts and circulation. First, such a "grounding" is the sort of "taming" that Barthes warned us about—a taming that enables us to avert our eyes away from the madness, excess, and ecstasy of the singular photograph. Second, as the plural in Finnegan's contexts suggests, because of the absolute heterogeneity of audiences, context is always utterly undecidable—a fiction of the critic's imagination. As critics we can still look at the multiple partial and contingent contexts of any photograph, but we cannot turn to contexts as the repository of rhetorical power/force. We must resist the tendency to let concepts distance us from the intractable immanence of images.

Icon displays the same flaws. Since Hariman and Lucaites have fleshed out their concept of icon in several articles, I want to explore in a bit of detail what is at stake with deploying it. Hariman and Lucaites (2002) study what they term *iconic photographs,* such as "Migrant Mother," "Flag Raising on Iwo Jima," and "Accidental Napalm." In their definition, most explicitly elaborated in the essay "Performing Civic Identity: The Iconic Photograph of the Flag Raising on Iwo Jima," iconic photographs have four traits: they are widely recognized, they are representations of historically significant events, they activate strong emotional response, and they are reproduced across a range of media, genre, or topics.

Note that the definition of an iconic photograph has nothing to do with the singularity of the photograph itself, the contingency of its material manifestation. Indeed there is no way under this definition to look at a photograph in its initial present and discern it to be iconic. Iconic is a retrospective historical designation. Indeed this definition has a circular feel—a photo is iconic because it is iconic. Iconic functions as a transcendent concept, denying the particularity of any singular photograph. It becomes a genre designation. Further, arguably the definition of an iconic photograph is not even particular to photography as a medium. Quite clearly, a speech—let us say Winston Churchill's "Their Finest Hour" or "Blood, Toil, Tears, and Sweat"—can be widely recognized, represent a historical event, activate an emotional response, and be reprinted.

According to Hariman and Lucaites (2002), the icon performs two major functions: It "organizes a field of interpretations" and it "manage[s] a basic contradiction or recurrent crisis within the political community" (p. 367). As in the definition, the description of the functions of iconic photos suggests nothing particular to a singular photograph or even to photography itself. The concept of icon can just as easily be applied to a speech.

In erasing the singularity of any particular photograph, at best Hariman and Lucaites limit their analysis to studium—the cultural conventions that allow us to read a photograph. Their definition and list of functions suggest there is no need at all to view the photograph in its singularity. Studying the surrounding context, contradictions in the political community, is sufficient. This position erases that which distinguishes the photograph from the linguistic, what Barthes (1981) described as the photograph's Intractable "that-has-been," its irrefutable presence given without mediation, the emanation, not representation, of a referent.[3]

So, what do I want? Just two things. Attention to studium gives us a context for making sense of photos, for taming them with meanings. Such an approach rarely captures rhetorical force. As Guattari (as quoted in Deleuze, 1995) exhorts us, "The only question is how anything works, with its intensities, flows, processes, partial objects—none of which *mean* anything" (p. 22). To account for rhetorical force, analysis must at least acknowledge both what Barthes terms the *punctum* and the *ecstasy* of the photograph that exceed linguistic domestication. This does not mean we must completely abandon the methods that yield studium, but it does suggest we need to transform our orientation. We still read images from the traditional ground of rhetoric through the screen of words. First, then, we need to acknowledge how images transform rhetoric, politics, and history. Finnegan, Hariman, and Lucaites, among others, are beginning to do that in rhetorical studies. More than that, though, we need to do criticism in an image world. We need to perform rhetorical criticism from the orientation of images. As academics, we still reside in Gutenberg's Galaxy. Approaching images with the

---

3. In an essay on the "accidental napalm" photo Hariman and Lucaites (2003) briefly gesture to the singularity of the photograph when they admit that the photo "automatically represents both the event and the gap between the event and any pattern of interpretation" (p. 55).

mindset and methods of print ensures we will misread them. Adopting an image orientation is a necessary first step.

DOING IMAGES: SPEED AND ECSTASY

To quote the theorist du jour, in "Publics and Counterpublics," Michael Warner (2002) suggests that public discourse is poetic—it brings a world into being, it makes a public "have this character, speak this way, see the world in this way." Echoing numerous media theorists, Warner further asserts that different media produce different worlds—McLuhan's now cliche "The medium is the message" or Kittler's updating in his preface to *Gramophone, Film, Typewriter,* "Media determine our situation, which—in spite or because of it—deserves a description." A linguistic-centered media matrix enacts a language ideology that privileges rational-critical dialogue by independently existing persons with agency. If we take photographs seriously as public discourse, then what sort of public, what sort of world, does an image-centric media matrix call into being?

Our image world is made possible by and privileges speed. In the ceaseless circulation of images in our media matrix, speed annihilates contemplation, surface flattens depth, flow drowns moments, distraction disrupts attention, affect eclipses meaning, the glance replaces the gaze, reiteration erases originals, and the public screen displaces the public sphere. As habits of reception and modes of perception are transformed, our habits of analysis are challenged. In a world moving at the speed of images, criticism premised on the gaze, sustained attention, focus, rationality, and depth of research is rendered archaic. Criticism seeking the rhetorical force of photographs oscillates between two tasks—first, to face the intractable immanence of this photograph in its absolute particularity, and, second, to describe the world called into being by this photograph as part of the public discourse of an image-centric media matrix. This leaves us with the question: How do we perform such a criticism of images from the ground of images—a criticism premised on speed, on distraction, on glances?

I am suggesting speed, distraction and glances as immanent concepts, not transcendent categories that corral photographs, interpret photographs, give us their meaning. Speed, distraction, and glances as modes of orientation, practices for engaging photographs, modes of intensities. Perhaps the most pressing problem with concepts like "circulation" and "icon" is that they are dependent on habits of analysis indebted to print, calling for the studious gaze of the academic and reinstantiating the print perspective. Academic criticism can be understood as akin to the general habits of reading—an intensification, but not different in kind. To read photographs is to skew them into objects palatable for the print gaze. To reconceptualize practice through speed, distraction, and glances, however, calls for critics to encounter images in a manner akin to the general habits of seeing, such as the habit of seeing described by Barthes (1981), "I cannot penetrate, cannot reach into the Photograph. I can only sweep it with my glance" (p. 106). My goal here is not to put forth a method for better capturing the meaning or essence of photographs. Speed, distraction, and glances suggest not a subject dominating an object, but a relationship of simultaneous becoming. Photographs engaged not as objects of study, corpuses, corpses, but Deleuzian bodies—modes that introduce relations of speed and slowness into the social and produce affects. To briefly elaborate on photographs as compositions of speeds and slownesses, Hariman and Lucaites (2003), following others, note that "the iconic photo can delay or stop time. The traumatic structure of the napalm photo freezes an action" (p. 61). Yes, and the photo also accelerates time, enabling the action to appear everywhere virtually immediately, so that the present of the napalm accident, the present of the Vietnam War, the present of the attack on Iraq also occur in middle America on that very same day.

The work of Walter Benjamin offers directions for performing a criticism of images from the ground of images by arguing for a necessary revalorization of distraction and glances through the model of the flaneur/flaneuse. Eschewing judgment, Benjamin sought to understand distraction as the mode of perception most appropriate to the technologically transformed conditions of the 20th century. In his famous "Art in the Age of Mechanical Reproduction," Benjamin (1973) writes of the audience as "a collectivity in a state of distraction" and asserts that "the tasks which face the human apparatus of perception at the turning points of history cannot be solved by optical means, that is, by contemplation, alone. They are mastered gradually by habit, under the guidance of tactile appropriation" (pp. 232–233). Benjamin is suggesting here and across his scattered, eclectic work, the form and objects of which mimic his critique, a model for the rhetorical critic—to displace the focused gaze with the distracted look of the optical unconscious, the glance of habit, which is tactile in the sense that one is not an observer gazing from a critical distance, but an actor immersed in a sea of imagery, a body pressed upon by the play of images and driven to distraction to survive, a self-utilizing, "a way of looking and experiencing the world in which the eye does not act to hold external objects in a firm contemplative gaze, but only notices them in passing and while also keeping a series of other objects in view" (Latham, 1999, p. 463; for others who see Benjamin as a theorist of distraction, see Taussig, 1992; Abbas, 1996).

Benjamin (1999) both conceptualizes and performs this distracted actor, the flaneur, in *The Arcades Project* (Passagen-Werk). The practice of distractedly wandering the streets produces the flaneur, the poet Baudelaire, the thinker Benjamin, for "An intoxication comes over the man who walks long and aimlessly through the streets," an "anamnestic intoxication" that produces knowledge "as something experienced and lived through" (p. 417), "for the fruits of idleness are more precious than the fruits of labor" (p. 452). In wandering among the ruins of the Paris Arcades in a state of distraction, in glancing at the detritus of the capital of the 19th century, Benjamin produces a criticism of the progress of the West, of industrial capitalism, and offers a model for contemporary critics wandering the image arcades of our public screen.

The key point, of course, is that Benjamin understood distraction not as a lack of attention, but as a necessary form of perception when immersed in the technologically induced torrent of images and information that constitutes public discourse in the 20th century. Speed and images, singly and in concert, annihilate contemplation. In our present moment of the public screen, glances of distraction emerge as a way of making do in this new civic space. In response, to see images, critics need to become intoxicated and distracted wanderers reveling in debauchery. There are worse fates.

REFERENCES

Abbas, A. (1996). Cultural studies in a postculture. In C. Nelson & D. Gaonkar (Eds.), *Disciplinarity and dissent in cultural studies* (pp. 289-312). New York: Routledge.

Aristotle. (1991). *On rhetoric: A theory of civic discourse.* New York: Oxford University Press.

Barthes, R. (1981). *Camera lucida.* New York: Hill and Wang.

Benjamin, W. (1999). *The Arcades Project,* Cambridge: Harvard University Press.

Deleuze, G. (1995). Gilles Deleuze and Felix Guattari on Anti-Oedipus. *Negotiations.* New York: Columbia University Press.

Deleuze, G. & Guattari, F. (1977). *Anti-Oedipus.* New York: Viking.

Deleuze, G. & Guattari, F. (1994). *What is philosophy?* New York: Columbia University Press.

DeLuca, K., & Peeples, J. (2002). From public sphere to public screen: Democracy, activism, and the violence of Seattle. *Critical Studies in Media Communication* 19(2), 125-151.

Demo, A. (2003). Policy and spectacle culture. Unpublished paper presented at the 2nd Annual Kern Conference: Visual Communication: Rhetoric, Technology and Social Change, Rochester Institute of Technology, Rochester, NY.

Derrida, J. (1982). *Margins of philosophy*. Chicago: University of Chicago Press.

Finnegan, C. (2003a). *Picturing poverty*. Washington: Smithsonian.

Finnegan, C. (2003b). Rhetorical circulation and visual politics. Unpublished paper presented at the 2nd Annual Kern Conference: Visual Communication: Rhetoric, Technology and Social Change, Rochester Institute of Technology, Rochester, NY.

Godzich, W. (1994). *The culture of literacy*. Boston: Harvard University Press.

Gronbeck, B. E. (1995). Rhetoric, ethics, and telespectacles in the post-everything age. In R. H. Brown (Ed.), *Postmodern representations* (pp. 217–238). Urbana: University of Illinois Press.

Hariman, R., & Lucaites, J. (2002). Performing civic identity: The iconic photograph of the flag raising on Iwo Jima. *Quarterly Journal of Speech, 88*(4), 363–392.

Hariman, R., & Lucaites, J. L. (2003). Public identity and collective memory in U.S. iconic photography: The image of "Accidental Napalm." *Critical Studies in Media Communication, 20*, 35–66.

Hogan, J. M. (1996). *The nuclear freeze campaign, rhetoric, and foreign policy in the telepolitical age*. East Lansing: Michigan State University Press.

Jamieson, K. (1988). *Eloquence in an electronic age*. New York: Oxford University Press.

Kittler, F. (1999). *Gramophone, film, typewriter*. Stanford: Stanford University Press.

Latham, A. (1999). The power of distraction: Distraction, tactility, and habit in the work of Walter Benjamin. *Environment and Planning D: Society and Space, 17*, 451-473.

McGee, M. C. (1990). Text, context, and the fragmentation of contemporary culture. *Western Journal of Speech Communication, 54*, 274-289.

Olson, K. M., & Goodnight, G. T. (1994). Entanglements of consumption, cruelty, privacy, and fashion: The social controversy of fur. *Quarterly Journal of Speech, 80*, 249–276.

Sontag, S. (1977). *On photography* New York: Farrar, Straus, & Giroux.

Taussig, M. (1992). *The nervous system*. New York: Routledge.

Warner, M. (2002). Publics and counterpublics. *Quarterly Journal of Speech, 88*(4), 413–425.

CHAPTER FOUR

Memorializing Affluence in the Postwar Family

Kodak's Colorama in Grand Central Terminal (1950–1990)

DIANE S. HOPE

ROCHESTER INSTITUTE OF TECHNOLOGY

B EGINNING IN 1950 AND LASTING UNTIL 1990, Eastman Kodak Company promoted itself and color photography through a changing display of 565 giant images installed in Grand Central Terminal in the center of New York City. The imposing exhibit, measuring 18 feet by 60 feet, was the largest advertisement ever seen. Promoted as "the world's largest photographs," the images exemplified the wonders of color photography made available by Eastman Kodak (Kerr, 1998a; Nordstrom & Roalf, 2004). In intense color pictures, the Colorama combined the most common expressions of image consumption existent in the popular culture: advertising and snapshots.

Color images were appearing in movies, advertising, and magazines by the 1940s, yet color print film was undependable, and equipment and reproduction processes were expensive. In 1949, only 2% of Kodak's market was in color film (Roalf, 2004). Although Kodachrome processing, introduced 10 years earlier, produced brilliant, long-lasting transparencies (Rijper, 2002), color print photography was not ready for the mass consumer market (Czech, 1996; Roalf, 2004). Family snapshots, newsprint images, and everyday uses of photography were produced and circulated primarily in monochromatic shades of black, white, and gray. Although color images were made to record and document World War II, images that circulated in newspapers, magazines, newsreel film, and personal snapshots memorialized the war in black and white (Coleman, 2002). But the shades of everyday photographic memory were about to change.

Postwar affluence and the abundant mass production of consumer goods solidified Kodak's determination to become the leader of color film photography in the mass market. The seizure and worldwide distribution of the trade secrets of Germany's Agfa Company[1] intensified competition for the mass marketing of color film and bolstered Kodak's own ongoing research for the "Ektacolor family of products" (Roalf, 2004, p. 77). In 1950, when Kodak displayed the first Colorama image, the advertising campaign launched color into the market for snapshot photography and became one of the most successful campaigns in corporate history (Kerr, 1998a).

This chapter focuses on the advertising rhetoric of the Colorama as a major expression of postwar memorializing. With the technologies of color film processing ready for mass consumption, Kodak intensified the established strategy of memorializing the family in snapshots by promoting the value of color photography as a celebration of postwar affluence. The Kodak images pictured the nuclear family as a consumer unit; Kodak marketed the affluent nuclear family as a collective consumer enterprise, engaged in the production and consumption of color images as commodities. Consumer goods were a perfect showcase for the bright hues of Ektacolor, and each image featured commodities as signs of ritualized family life.

In color-saturated pictures, Kodak advertised a fantasy world in which the ritual of making color photographs coincidentally highlighted material consumption as a domestic value. The Colorama punctuated the national ethic with images that valorized and conjoined affluence and the nuclear family as twin standards for a new U.S. culture. From 1950 through the middle years of 1970, the visual narratives in Kodak's images were remarkably consistent. No indication of the sociocultural changes occurring through those decades found reflection in Kodak portrayals. Targeting the young family as the most important market for postwar consumption of film and cameras, the Kodak Colorama froze the happy family and its possessions in an array of staged color photographs displayed in the "busiest intersection in the world."

Each day half a million people, mostly New York commuters, moved past the Colorama display, and every 3 weeks the picture changed (Roalf, 2004) (Plate 4.1, p. 277, Grand Central with Colorama). Located in the vaulted space of what had been designed in 1913 as the "gateway to the continent," the stationary Colorama became an icon of commercial sentimentality. Although the images did not circulate, New York was the center of advertising, publishing, and, in the early days, TV. The cultural production at work in New York

---

1. The American military seized the Agfa plant in Wolfen and "claimed the company's trade secrets for Agfacolor negative film as 'war indemnity'" and distributed the information (Roalf, 2004, p. 77).

set the standard for the nation's popular cultural agenda. Located in the rapidly deteriorating terminal building, the snapshot advertisements presented New Yorkers with a mythical vision of life in suburban small towns and rural settings. A full account of the parallel story of Grand Central Station's fall and rebirth is not possible here, but the intertwined history of Grand Central and the Colorama informs the chapter. Framed by the grand architectural space of the east balcony, the space occupied by the Colorama had figured prominently in the history of the landmark building during World War II.

During the war, the terminal was especially important as a hub of the rail system. In 1941, the Farm Security Administration (FSA) used the east balcony space to exhibit 22 photographs (enlarged by Kodak) in a montage 118 feet wide and almost 100 feet high as part of the war bond drive, that served to black out the east windows of the terminal for the duration of the war (Kerr, 1998a). In 1943, the east wall of the balcony housed a 75-foot high, 30-feet wide patriotic mural depicting flags, bombs, and soldiers to raise money for a second U.S. Defense Bonds campaign. Below the balcony, soldiers waiting for trains gathered in the Service Men's Lounge (Belle & Leighton, 2000). From 1944 to 1947, an average of 520 trains were accommodated every weekday. The peak of terminal use occurred in 1947; 65 million passengers, or over 40% of the U.S. population, were served by the station (Nevins, 1982).

Yet by 1949, New York Central Railroad, the operator of the terminal, was losing money; air travel, bus travel, and private automobiles had diminished the use of rail as the primary transportation system of the country. Government subsidies for airports and highways, corrupt and inefficient rail management, and the popular love of automobiles combined to drain railroad finances (Belle & Leighton, 2000). The rail company was eager to find revenue, and Kodak was eager to advertise color photography. Paying over $300,000 per year to rent the space in Grand Central Terminal, Kodak installed the Colorama in 1950 (Kerr, 1998a).

With few exceptions,[2] two types of color images were displayed in the 40-year period of the Colorama display. The first type, snapshot advertising,

---

2. Notable exceptions include the 1967 image of Earthrise from the moon, photographed by NASA's Lunar Orbiter I on Kodak film, and in 1969, the Apollo 11 moon landing, a Colorama displayed a day before the images were seen in weekly news magazines (Roalf, 2004). "During each of the final four years of the Colorama's lease, Grand Central's owner, the Metropolitan Transportation Authority, required that one subject be of their choosing" (Kodak e-Magazine). For example, the choice for 1986 was a photograph of the Metro-North commuter train traveling along the Hudson River, made by Kodak photographer Bob Clemens.

the primary focus of this chapter, depicted middle-class families in the act of making snapshots together. Attractive models depicted picture-takers and their families staged in moments from affluent lives, at play, on holidays, on vacation, or as tourists. In nearly every image displayed from 1950 to the mid-1970s, the family—making pictures—was the subject. The second type of Coloramas were color spectacles that professionally reflected the travel slide shows amateurs produced as family entertainment. Exhibited from the mid-1970s until the final image of 1990,[3] the spectacle images celebrated Kodak color photography in panoramas of national rituals, nature, exotic locales, theme parks, sentimental subjects, sports scenes, and Kodak-sponsored events.[4] The picture-making family was no longer in the frame. By the mid-1970s, it was no longer necessary to sell color photography to families; the nearly total success of Kodak's campaign was complete. American families remembered themselves in color and identified themselves as a collective of consumers.

Image-based advertising exhibits a particular form of visual rhetoric. The critic, seeking to answer the basic question "What's going on here?", can consider the rhetoric of advertising from a variety of standpoints, including target audience, circulation, visual arguments and claims, aesthetics, semiotics, themes, effectiveness, and technology of production and reproduction. Scholars from communication, sociology, and marketing contribute to our understanding of advertising as a ubiquitous form of visual communication. Yet advertising's explicit persuasive goal—to market and sell goods, services, or brands—determines that the central set of questions must involve the rhetorical critic in direct consideration of a commercial enterprise intended to create profit through the circulation of representations (Goldman & Papson, 1996). Thus, the rhetoric of

---

3. Roalf (2004) wrote, "The very last Colorama, which was displayed from November 1989 to February 1990, is now steeped in a nostalgia that has altered the photograph's original meaning since the events of September 11, 2001. In this picture, a glittering nighttime view of the New York City skyline features the Twin Towers of the World Trade Center, with the only digital enhancement ever created for the Colorama program—an oversize red apple nestled among the buildings to the towers' left. The copy that ran with the photograph reads: 'Kodak thanks the Big Apple for 40 years of friendship in Grand Central'" (p. 77).

4. In addition to TV shows (e.g., *The Adventures of Ozzie and Harriet* and *The Ed Sullivan Show*), Kodak-sponsored events included America's Junior Miss Pageant, various world Olympic meetings, world's fairs, and theme park exhibits.

pictorial images in advertising cannot be separated realistically from their ideological roots. This approach to advertising's rhetoric follows the tradition of the early Marshall McLuhan (1951), Stewart Ewen (1976), Erving Goffman (1976), Roland Marchand (1985), and most important, Nancy Martha West (2000), for her detailed examination of Kodak's early advertising history.

Marchand borrowed the phrase "Capitalist Realism"[5] to describe some of the "serious distortions in advertising's mirror" as "inherent in the nature of advertising" (p. xviii). Like Socialist Realism, emergent in the cultures of socialism, the images of Capitalist Realism at work in advertising depict "the ideals and aspirations" of capitalism more "accurately" than does the reality of U.S. culture (p. xvii). Goffman (1976) used a similar term, *commercial realism*, to describe "the standard transformation employed in contemporary ads, in which the scene is conceivable in all detail as one that could *in theory* have occurred as pictured" (p. 15; italics added). It is this theoretical picturing that dominates the snapshot advertising of the Colorama. Further complicating our analysis of the rhetoric is that the advertised product in the Colorama was color photography. In the case of the Colorama, photography advertised itself by promoting the making of color snapshots as a postwar ritual of family cohesion. As Norman Kerr (1998a), Kodak's Colorama historian, wrote, "One dramatic photograph could capture attention and communicate values to even the most diverse of audiences" (p. 1). Cultural values in use of snapshots becomes part of the frame for understanding Colorama advertising. Technology is another aspect of the Colorama advertising considered in this analysis. The size and place of the installation, and the mechanics of changing the image every 3 weeks for 40 years, influenced the content and presentation of the representations.

The practice of translating experience into instant memories was enhanced by snapshot photography as an amateur pastime. As West (2000) documented in her detailed examination of Eastman Kodak's advertising history from 1888 to 1932, Kodak was especially influential in promoting snapshots as nostalgia. Yet Kodak's advertising strategies reflected a crucial shift in focus during the early 40-year span: "Snapshot photography was transformed from a leisure activity—which like all forms of play, celebrates freedom, spontaneity, and the pleasures of the present—to an obligatory act of preserving memories as defense against the future and as assurance

---

5. The term was coined by Michael Schudson (1984) in his book, *Advertising, the Uneasy Persuasion: Its Dubious Impact on American Society* (pp. 214–218).

of the past" (p. 13). The turning point in Kodak's advertising, West argued, was World War I, "when Americans . . . desperately needed photographs to perform as confirmations of family unity" (p. 13). Like snapshots, advertising images were effective at "assuaging the anxieties of consumers about losses of community and individual control" brought on by modernity (Marchand, 1985, p. xxi). Some 40 years later, after the end of World War II, Kodak revitalized its early advertising strategy in the promotion of color photography as the means to preserve family memory as a defense for future unknowns—in the "age of affluence," the vehicle for making reassuring memories was color. For Kodak, the Colorama "depicted the rebirth of human spirit after World War II, with the emphasis on expanding lifestyles, enticing destinations for jet age travel, triumphs in space exploration and momentous special events" (Kerr, 1998a, p. 1).

Kodak had always sought a mass market for its cameras and films, and the triumph of Kodak's earliest advertising campaigns is legendary. "Eastman's genius lay less in invention than in marketing" (Nickel, 1998, p. 9). Kodak's advertising campaigns rarely faltered from the strategy developed by George Eastman at the turn of the century—an appeal that combined the technical ease of producing a photograph with nostalgic portrayals of middle-class life, "for the easy availability of snapshots allowed people for the first time in history to arrange their lives in such a way that painful or unpleasant aspects were systematically erased" (West, 2000, p. 1). When Eastman patented his simple box camera in 1888, he immediately began to market photography as a pleasurable activity, a hobby available to all. Largely credited with making photography available to "ordinary people . . . to make pictures of themselves as they pleased" (Nickel, 1998, pp. 9–11), Kodak's focus on the amateur in its early mass advertising campaigns featured children making photographs as play or, in the case of the long-running *Kodak Girl* campaign, on the new independent and adventurous woman.[6] Kodak's advertising strategy emphasized photography as a leisure activity—a way

---

6. The fashionable *Kodak Girl* was interested more in the camera as an accessory to her ensemble, rather than in its technical properties, and was used to market Vanity Kodak cameras (available in five colors), as well as other products. For an extended discussion of Kodak's use of women in their ads, see West (2000), chapter 4, "Proudly Displayed by Wearers of Chic Ensembles: Vanity Cameras, Kodak Girls, and the Culture of Female Fashion." Marchand (1985) discussed Kodak ads for the Vanity Kodak as part of the "Mystique of the Ensemble" and as "the crowning achievement of advertising's emphasis on color, beauty, and style" in the 1920s (pp. 132–140).

for amateurs to play with the camera, "the sheer pleasure and adventure of taking photographs are the main subject" (West, 2000, p. 13).

Kodak's early marketing goals were in sharp contrast to the practices of established photographers who sought to define photography as a profession. The success of Kodak's famous slogan, "You press the button, we do the rest," dismayed Alfred Stieglitz, who wrote in 1899, "It is due to this fatal facility that photography as a picture-making medium has fallen into disrepute" (cited in Nickel, 1998, p. 11). Nickel argued that Stieglitz and others were able to establish photography as an art form, in part by redefining the snapshot as something other. "Art photography defined itself against the example of the snapshot by asserting a new, symbolic, essentially public function for the medium" (Nickel, 1998, p. 11). As an artistic medium circulated in galleries, museums, and specialized publications, photography focused on the artist and on the aesthetics of the image for anonymous viewers. With the marketing of the Brownie cameras, Kodak's definition of photography as a leisure time performance defined the makers, subjects, and viewers of images as private consumers with individual, spontaneous desires.

West argued convincingly that Kodak's advertising themes shifted from play to memory, to emerge during World War I as a ritualized performance of domestic nostalgia residing in the family. Kodak advertisements were moral lessons about creating authentic memories for the family's future cohesiveness. The successful slogan, "Let Kodak Keep the Story," lasted over 20 years and reinforced ad copy and images that seem to suggest to consumers that, "the horrors of war could be balanced and neutralized, even forgotten, through reassuring narratives implicit in photographs of home and family" (West, 2000, p. 167). Decades later, after the end of World War II, Kodak was to carry its marketing strategy of family nostalgia to new intensity in the Colorama program. In addition to family unity, themes in the Colorama display emphasized consumer goods as necessary props for middle-class family narratives. The maker, subject, and viewers of snapshots were pictured as the same people, telling stories of themselves as families and consumers.

STRATEGY AND TECHNOLOGY OF COLOR MARKETING

Kodak correctly identified a ready mass market for color photography after World War II in the growing affluence of the middle class. The *Cavalcade of Color*, a Kodachrome slide exhibit by Kodak at the World's Fair in 1939, had been a popular attraction, and Kodak was eager to repeat the success of the monumental installation to promote color film for the consuming public (Kerr, 1998a; Nordstrom, 2004). Although Walker Evans and other professionals initially disdained color photography as corrupt and vulgar[7](Eauclaire, 1984; Eklund, 2000), Kodak reasoned that the amateur photographer—the taker of snapshots—was ready to embrace color photography as the perfect means to document the experience of postwar security and to subjugate the gray memories of the decade with visions of domestic affluence. To this end, Kodak seized the opportunity to install the Colorama in Grand Central Station.

Kodak applied the marketing conventions of mass advertising to the selling of color photography primarily and to its film and cameras secondarily. Adolph Stuber, vice president of sales and advertising, sharply instructed the staff of the Colorama information booth, "I want it made clear that you are here to promote photography—talk photography first—Kodak next" (Kerr, 1998b, p. 6). Rarely including any text but a title caption, the Colorama's snapshot advertising was an ostensive demonstration of what the amateur could do with a camera and color film. The images "were not billboard advertisements in the ordinary sense . . . seldom imposing a blatant sales pitch"; instead "photographic vision was the message" (Kerr, 1998a, p. 1). Kodak's vision of its target market was racially and sexually biased. Families were white[8] and young, headed by men, depicted as groups of attractive heterosexual couples, babies, children, teenagers, and grandparents, and staged in scenes where "nothing but blue skies" provided locations for "dreaming in color" (Nordstrom & Roalf, 2004, p. 5). For approximately 25 years of the 40-year span, the Colorama vision of the postwar family embodied an ordered hierarchy in which "men photograph women, women photograph children, children photograph other children, and everybody photographs a scenic view" while other family members "eagerly look on" as an appreciative audience for the picture-taking session (Nordstrom, 2004, p. 7).

---

7. Evans might have been describing the Colorama when he wrote that they "blow you down with screeching hues alone . . . a bebop of electric blues, furious reds, and poison greens" (cited in Eauclaire, 1984, p. 40). Evans eventually produced some color images, but preferred muted colors: "If you tone it all down it's just about bearable, and that's the only thing to do with it, make it as monotonous as possible" (cited in Eklund, 2000, p. 124).

8. Coleman (2002) reported the technical relationship of imaging whiteness to color processing: "The entire tonal palette of Kodachrome was premised on the necessity of rendering in a pleasing manner the skin tones of those who would be its principal consumers: Caucasians" (p. 10, f2).

At the heart of the Colorama project was Eastman Kodak's central marketing ploy voiced by Stuber: "Everyone who sees the Colorama should be able to visualize themselves as being able to make the same wonderful photo" (cited in Nordstrom, 2004, p. 5). The visual strategy was simple: Each image pictured someone in the frame taking a picture with a camera that was large enough to be identified as a Kodak. The picture-taker, looking through the lens at family members or a spectacular scene, was the focal point of every image, a management decision that irked many photographers, including Ansel Adams.[9] In an information center, Kodak staff offered help and instructions to consumers for making the best pictures, reinforcing the pretense that anyone armed with a simple Kodak camera and color film could produce images similar to those displayed in the Colorama. This despite the fact that all 565 Coloramas were taken by professional photographers, including Adams, Ernst Haas, Eliot Porter, Gordon Parks, Jon Abbot, Valentino Serra, and Ozzie Sweet (Handy, 2004; Kerr, 1998a; Nordstrom, 2004). Kodak professionals, including photographers and technical staff, produced most of the images, inventing technique as they went along.

The technology of producing and assembling the colorful images was a professional challenge. The original plan of duplicating the projection techniques used for the 1939 World's Fair *Cavalcade of Color* was abandoned because of the ambient light in Grand Central. Kodak's installation blocked natural light from reaching the Grand Concourse, negating one of the most remarkable features of the building's Beaux Arts design (Nevins, 1982), a fact that would later figure prominently in the effort to restore the terminal.[10]

---

9. Adams made six pictures for the Colorama. The first in May/June 1951, *Yosemite Valley in Snapshots,* featured two families taking pictures of the scenery and each other. Adams' objections to the selection of the photo with "the most prominent placement of the camera-user in the scene" were overruled. "Management's response was that the Colorama should not be ambiguous in promoting the excitement of color photography." A year later in July/August 1952, Adams made *Grand Canyon, Arizona,* the first Colorama "where strong emphasis was placed on the view itself, not the obligatory Kodak camera being used," in defiance of company policy. "However, Adams' contradictory and more pictorial choice was accepted—probably after some internal management debate" (Kodak e-magazine).

10. Removal of the Colorama was an event designed to impact public opinion: "The morning after the dismantling was finished and the protective curtain was taken down, the architects stood quietly watching the first commuters stream

To overcome the lighting problem, the images were backlit, producing the effect of giant transparencies. The panoramic layout of most of the images was impossible to achieve with available snapshot technologies, and the size of the negatives mandated special equipment, including a custom-designed enlarger that had to be set up in Kodak's recreational building in Rochester. Kodak technicians wallpapered the images together, splicing negatives in rolls 20 feet long, weighing hundreds of pounds. The images were trucked from Rochester to Manhattan about every 3 weeks (Kerr, 1998a).

The disparity between Stuber's insistence on the illusion of the amateur snapshot and the actual production of the image was frequently ludicrous. Producing uniform color mandated lighting techniques that were a reoccurring challenge, even for Kodak professionals (Plate 4.2, p. 277, Christmas Carolers, 1961). The technique used to light this image of Christmas Carolers, made by Kodak photographer Neil Montanus, is described and commented on by Norman Kerr (1999):

> Two-thirds of this Colorama's display area was devoted to a complex set erected in Kodak's photo illustration studio (the side panel showed the newest snapshot camera). The set was lit "outside" with blue-filtered electronic flash to simulate moonlight. This illusion was reinforced by Neil's clever application of urea and alcohol to create frosted windows, and by artificial snow on potted nursery plants. Neil's meticulous attention to lighting his exuberant cast, including his young son, conveys a convincing sense of reality. Management's insistence on including a snapshot camera seen being used from inside wasn't challenged, though it's doubtful that taking a flash picture through a window would have worked. (p. 31)

It is clear from the many references to *management decisions* in Kerr's history of the Colorama that the illusion implicit in the advertising campaign took precedence over fidelity to amateur possibilities.

Considerations of "how the ideology of the family and the technology of photography support and reinforce each other" permeate theoretical explorations of the snapshot (M. Hirsch, 1997, p. 48). More significant than amateur cameras in determining the subject and framing of images were the size, shape, and color saturation of the negatives demanded for the Colorama installation. The shape of the Colorama frame encouraged horizontal lines in landscapes, and rows of things as subjects: babies, surfboards,

---

into the Main Concourse from the train platforms" (Belle & Leighton, 2000, p. 133). As the natural light came in, commuters were treated to a sight that had been blocked for 40 years, and public support for the project was enthusiastic.

kittens, and hot-air balloons were popular Colorama images.[11] Before the development of techniques to make one long negative, the horizontal rectangle made proportions a problem that was solved by dividing the screen into a central frame with two sidebar images. This device allowed Kodak to picture the same family and the same event in different shots. Sidebars showed pictures that might have been taken by the picture-taker in the center (Plate 4.3, p. 278, Farm Scene and Family Snapshots).

Collective memory of the 1950s family is largely a mediated creation in which the photo technologies of advertising performed an important role. The Colorama not only displayed images of what the proper family should look like, but the images instructed families in how to produce their own mediated memories *in color*. As Coleman (2002) pointed out, "Whenever the technology and economics of color photography have come abreast of monochrome closely enough to be competitive with it, color is automatically preferred. . . . Especially via the applied and vernacular usages and forms of color photography, the primacy of color in photography has been established by democratic vote" (p. 10). The circulation of color images in movies, fashion ads, and celebrity shots, popular in the 1940s and 1950s, stimulated the consumer demand for color in their own snapshots.

Sontag (1973) remarked on another dimension of photography's relationship to family especially pertinent to reading the interwoven demands of technology and ideology presented in *Farm Scene*: "As that claustrophobic unit, the nuclear family, was being carved out of a much larger family aggregate, photography came along to memorialize, to restate symbolically, the imperiled continuity and vanishing extendedness of family life" (p. 9). After the war, the extended family was fractured further, and Kodak was ready to market color photography in sentimental appeals to traditional family mythologies. Although popular culture was rife with performances counter to the claustrophobic family, no trace of rebelliousness appeared in the Colorama images.[12] The farm scene in this image reflects the divided screen technique in a typically nostalgic image: a family farm in rural New York State. The red barn, dirt road, wooden fence, and horse and buggy reference a backward

---

11. *15 Babies* was one of the most popular of Kodak's images and was duplicated twice as the babies became toddlers and school children. When the Colorama came down, a number of New Yorkers isolated the Kodak Babies as something they would miss (Grundberg, 1989; Handy, 2004).

12. *Rebel Without A Cause*, the James Dean cult film of 1955, is a classic example. Filmed in color, the movie depicted a smothering family and adolescent rebellion.

glance to a mythical past. Three generations of a family—cute kids, animals, a hint of some ritual in the corsage pinned on the mother's blouse, and especially, the picture-taking man—mark the photo as a Kodak ad.

As a collective unit, the family was producer, subject, and audience for memorials to itself and to the affluence of its domesticity. The collectiveness of the endeavor establishes the photographic act as an event whose significance equals or surpasses the subject of the snapshot. "Through photographs, each family constructs a portrait-chronicle of itself—a portable kit of images that bears witness to its connectedness. . . . It hardly matters what activities are photographed so long as photographs get taken and are cherished" (Sontag, 1973, p. 8).

Postwar advertising for family snapshots added another layer to the production and consumption of family images. The staging of family rituals, celebrations, and holidays in the advertisements tortured family memories into standardized commercial visions. The Colorama illuminated the postwar nuclear family as an intimate collective of consumers. No matter who was taking the photograph, family occasions were portrayed as celebrations of consumption.[13] Some images were subtle in the promotion of consumption, whereas others were not. In Colorama #155, made in 1959, *Camping at Lake Placid, New York*, photographed by Herb Archer (Plate 4.4, p. 278), the mother is photographing the children who sit in a fishing boat, framed by the Adirondack Mountains in the background. Framing the family in the foreground is a wealth of camping equipment. Tents, bikes, stoves, a cooler, sleeping bags, and assorted utensils compete with the family as the object of our gaze.

Norman Rockwell directed another Colorama, *Closing up a Summer Cottage*, photographed by Ralph Amdursky and Charles Baker, in which a

---

13. By the end of World War II, the ensuing affluence of the middle class and the enactment of the G.I. Bill enabled thousands of veteran-headed families the means of home ownership. "Eighty-five percent of the new homes were built in the suburbs, where the nuclear family found new possibilities for privacy and togetherness" (Coontz, 1992, p. 24). The push by industry and government to encourage women to leave jobs created by the absence of men during the war was framed as a desire for a traditional family life that had rarely existed outside the network of extended families and communities. In fact the family of the 1950s reflected a reversal of trends: "For the first time in more than 100 years, the age for marriage and motherhood fell, fertility increased, divorce rates declined, and women's degree of educational parity with men dropped sharply" (Coontz, 1992, p. 25).

family attempts to load a station wagon with a surplus of possessions that includes garden equipment, toys, boats, suitcases, and golf clubs (Nordstrom, 2004). In a nostalgic image, a young boy photographs the neighborhood children.[14] This focus on affluence merged family sentimentality with commodities and paved the way for advertising's accepted presence in American life. Technically, the ideal snapshot promoted in the Colorama mimicked advertising images in production value and pictorial quality; each image had to be "perfectly" framed, lit, and staged (Kerr, 1999, p. 1)—a model that reinforced the dominance of consumerism as a primary frame for domestic meaning. Colorama images stressed the features that distinguished the family of the 1950s from previous generations: a calcification of gender roles, a focus on the child, and an emphasis on material goods (Coontz, 1992).

IN MEMORY OF THE FAMILY

Family snapshots have engendered theoretical speculation as authentic artifacts of record. Yet as J. Hirsch (1981) concluded, conventional family photographs reference myths about families: "Pleasure has replaced stability as the most important family goal. And yet we still treasure paintings and create photographs which relate, no matter how tenuously, to ancient metaphors of family unity and cohesion: we still seem to acknowledge the values we have shed" (p. 32). The mythology of families may explain the interest in family snapshots as found objects. A scattering of museum exhibits, catalogues, and essays attends to anonymous snapshots as discoveries with "a license to circulate . . . at a flea market, photographic fair, or historical society" (Nickel, 1998, p. 13). Yet the separation of the family photo from the specific family of its making shifts the contextual relationship away from a focus on the collectivity of image makers, subjects, and viewers, the defining characteristic of family snapshots. Snapshots as found objects highlight the relationship between the image and a curious viewer uninvolved with the subject as a known person. For example, Graves and Payne (1977) collected and published anonymous photographs, " . . . which were complete visual statements, needing neither explanation nor rationalization" (p. 9), effectively making the family photo a work of art—however unintended by the maker.

---

14. Although predating them by nearly 40 years, these images look like and connect the anticonsumer visual arguments made by Peter Menzel (1994) in his collection of global families and their possessions, *Material World: A Global Family Portrait.*

Roland Barthes' (1981) famous remarks emanating from his consideration of a single photograph of his mother as a child offer a stark contrast to the conventions of found snapshots and the staged images of the Colorama. In his *Camera Lucida,* Barthes discussed his mother's childhood image, made in 1898. The photograph touched the grown man after his mother's death. He wrote, "And no more than I would reduce my family to the Family, would I reduce my mother to the Mother" (p. 74). For Barthes, "what founds the nature of Photography is the knowledge that a living being for an instant was caught motionless in front of the lens" (p. 78). This sense of singularity is in exact opposition to the use of photography in advertising, and especially to the family scenes promoted by the Colorama. Goffman (1976) focused on the "pictured scenes" of advertising images as stand-ins for real situations and concluded: "Presumably what the advertisement is concerned to depict is not particular individuals. . . . Pictured scenes show examples of categories of persons, not particular persons" (p. 19). Just so, the rhetoric of the Colorama invites the production of interchangeable family images, using the specific conventions of consumerism: a display of goods and the identification of self with commodities.

In advertising images, American families are identified and reduced to the same events, the same poses. The whole family is implicated in the manufacturing of the myth. Commenting on the inadequacy of Barthes' musings as a way to understand snapshots, Nickel (1998) protested: "Barthes sought the essence of photography, its unique and inimitable feature (its *noeme,* as he calls it) in its capacity to ratify the existence of a particular moment in the past, something the snapshot often does well. But simple logic rules here—while all snapshots may be photographs, not all photographs are snapshots" (p. 9). Colorama advertisements for the color snapshot presented yet another kind of family photograph, the staged dramatization of a happy family inexorably embedded in consumer ideologies, a performance picture-takers were invited to mimic.

In Colorama images, real lives often merged with mediated fictions. Perhaps nothing demonstrates more the eerie quality of the Colorama images than those featuring the family of Ozzie, Harriet, David, and Ricky Nelson. Kodak sponsored *The Adventures of Ozzie and Harriet* TV show, and the Nelson family appeared in four Colorama images. As the Nelsons did on TV (in black and white), they did in full color for Kodak. The Nelsons merged their real family life with that staged by media promoters. By presenting themselves as staged representations of themselves, the fictional Nelsons became emblematic commercials for real families. The last Colorama Nelson family image, made in 1960, captures Harriet doing a hula dance on Waikiki beach while Ricky plays the guitar, David gazes fondly, and Ozzie films them all for a home movie (with a Kodak camera; Nordstrom, 2004). The melding of reality with representation is of course the seduction of photography in general and advertising in particular. Bruce Handy (2004), writing from a contemporary look backward, compared the Colorama with Roman inscriptions and medieval churches: "The Colorama was arguably the closest midcentruy [sic] America came to narrating its own stories and celebrating its own secular myths in a similar epic, inspiring, and sometimes bludgeoning fashion" (p. 331) (Plate 4.5, p. 278).

At just about the same time the Colorama went up in Grand Central Terminal, Marshall McLuhan (1951) published *The Mechanical Bride*, his early examination of popular media at work in the culture of postwar America. McLuhan's probes into the "folklore of industrial man" identified the consistent links among technology, consumerism, and sex in the visual artifacts of advertising as "some sort of collective dream" (p. v). He described his method of inquiry as "providing typical visual imagery of our environment and dislocating it into meaning by inspection" (p. vi):

> Where visual symbols have been employed in an effort to paralyze the mind, they are here used as a means of energizing it. It is observable that the more illusion and falsehood needed to maintain any given state of affairs, the more tyranny is needed to maintain the illusion and falsehood. Today the tyrant rules not by club or fist, but, disguised as a market researcher, he shepherds his flocks in the ways of utility and comfort. (McLuhan, 1951, p. vi)

From the vantage point of the 21st century, some of McLuhan's observations seem both naive and obvious, yet it may be that the marriage of photography to advertising, so ubiquitous a stream of our collective consciousness, forecast the victory of consumerism as the tyranny McLuhan feared.

The perfected family snapshot exemplified in the Colorama underscores the production of the image as a collective project necessary to the commercialization of family life. Family members, mimicking advertising images, do more than agree to be photographed: They participate by arranging themselves, posing and smiling, dressing in appropriate costume, and displaying the props of consumer life. The collective effort provides further evidence of domestic cooperation in the creation of memory. In the final decades of the Colorama, the families disappeared from the display, replaced by lush panoramas of exotic locals or beautiful scenes of nature, absent the mandatory picture-taker. Although slide shows declined as a family activity,[15] the family photograph had become, by then, a firmly ritualized performance of memorializing.

When the New York community learned that the Colorama would be removed, commentary reflected a love–hate relationship with the advertising monument. "Love it (as a spectacular display) or spurn it (as an esthetic intrusion), there is one thing you cannot do in the presence of the Kodak Colorama in Grand Central Terminal: miss it. That may change in coming months" (Anderson & Dunlap, 1985, p. 5). Sadness, relief, anger, and approval were linked to the tragic condition of Grand Central Terminal in the 1970s and 1980s. The bitter letter of Joel Sachs, writing to the *New York Times* in 1989, is worth quoting for its passion:

> For almost 40 years, jaded New Yorkers, harried commuters and gawking tourists walking through the terminal have paused to observe the ever vibrant, ever colorful, ever changing Colorama. Oftentimes, it brightened up the gloomy stroll through an otherwise cold and impersonal space.
>
> Now with the demise of the Colorama those passing through Grand Central will have to be content with watching the somewhat less colorful and less exciting visual display of winos, panhandlers, and the homeless who have taken over the terminal, not to mention its ever-expending array of gritty, fast-food establishments and downscale shops.
>
> Hats off to Metro-North. You've done it again.
>
> Joel H. Sachs

Other writers and commentators were sad, but resigned: "It's the first thing I look for when I come here . . . it's a changing picture postcard of the world." The missed "pictures of China at sunrise, the Taj Mahal at dawn, and pandas at the Bronx Zoo" (cited in Kendel, 1990, p. 8A) reference the last 15 years of spectacle images that dominated the Colorama. Less frequently missed were the family snapshots, perhaps because they were least remembered, having ended 15 years earlier. Yet the family images were ambivalent constructs in the public mind. Grundberg's (1989) remarks on the images may reflect a common sentiment: "My least favorites were idealized pseudo-snapshots of happy families doing happy-family things. Scenes like these might be perfectly natural in Rochester, Kodak's home, but they were out of place in the context of Grand Central Terminal with its sorry popu-

---

15. The last slide projectors came off Kodak's assembly lines on October 22, 2004. The company made 35 million slide projectors in seven decades—the single most successful piece of equipment in Kodak's 125-year history (Rand, 2004).

lation of homeless men and women and its wonderful diversity of races, creeds, and lifestyles" (p. 94).

Acknowledging the ambivalence of public sentiment, Grand Central's restoration committee removed the Colorama as a rhetorical act designed to influence public opinion of the project:

> We concluded that with one preemptive strike, it would be relatively simple and inexpensive to show the public something of the real Grand Central by dismantling the Kodak sign. . . . As the sunshine burst through three windows that had not been seen since 1950, it was as if life were being breathed back into the building. Many commuters stopped in their tracks, speechless and amazed at the change that had so instantly bought back the majesty of the space. (Belle & Leighton, 2000, p. 133)

Public support of the restoration project solidified.

Narratives of wars, racial unrest, poverty, violence, and the continual challenge of modern and postmodern urban existence have no life in advertising or family photographs. Amateur family photographers have been taught to use photography as a talisman—a magical tool that denies family disruption and ultimately denies death itself. "Recently, photography has become almost as widely practiced an amusement as sex and dancing—which means that, like every mass art form, photography is not practiced by most people as an art. It is mainly a social rite, a defense against anxiety, and a tool of power" (Sontag, 1973, p. 8). The Colorama was a historic milestone in presenting Americans a vision of themselves as Kodak thought they wanted to be in the postwar years of affluence. Although snapshot photography and especially digital technology may once again encourage amateurs to play with images, the ritual family photo persists to document and mythologize ritualized consumerism. The Colorama images, with their colorful narratives of happiness, affluence, and material comfort, produced the pictures that pointed the way to the commodity future of families.

REFERENCES

Anderson, S. H., & Dunlap, D. (1985, November 26). New York day by day: At Grand Central, Kodak could lose its beam. *New York Times*, p. B5.

Barthes, R. (1981). *Camera lucida* (R. Howard, Trans.). New York: Hill & Wang.

Belle, J., & Leighton, M. R. (2000). *Grand Central.* New York: Norton.

Coleman, A. D. (2002). Mama, don't take our Kodachrome away. In E. Rijper (Ed.), *Kodachrome: The American invention of our world* (pp. 1939–1959). New York: Delano Greenidge Editions.

Coontz, S. (1992). *The way we never were: American families and the nostalgia trap.* New York: Basic Books, HarperCollins.

Czech, K. P. (1996). *Snapshot: America discovers the camera.* Minneapolis: Lerner.

Eauclaire, S. (1994). *New color/new work: Eighteen photographic essays.* New York: Abbeville.

Eklund, D. (2000). The harassed man's haven of detachment: Walker Evans and the Fortune portfolio. In M. M. Morris Hambourg, J. L. Rosenheim, D. Eklund, & M. Fineman (Eds.), *Walker Evans* (pp. 121–129). New York: The Metropolitan Museum of Art, in Association with Princeton University Press.

Ewen, S. (1976). *Captians of consciousness.* New York: McGraw-Hill.

Goffman, E. (1976). Picture frames. In *Gender advertisements* (pp. 10–23). New York: Harper & Row.

Goldman, R., & Papson, S. (1996). *Sign wars: The cultured landscrape of advertising.* New York: Guilford.

Graves, K., & Payne M. (1977). *American snapshots.* Oakland, CA: Scrimshaw.

Grundberg, A. (1989, December 3). Camera; One of the city's most spectacular traditions will cease to exist at the end of the month. *New York Times,* Section I, p. 94

Handy, B. (2004, September). Call of the wide. *Vanity Fair,* pp. 321–325.

Hirch, J. (1981). *Family photographs: Content, meaning and effect.* New York: Oxford University Press.

Hirsch, M. (1997). *Family frames: Photography, narrative and postmemory.* Cambridge, MA: Harvard University Press.

Kendel, B. (1990, Febuary 22). Grand Central's facelift takes it back to the future. *USA Today,* p. 8A.

Kerr, N. (1998a). A capsule history. In *A history of Kodak's Colorama.* Rochester, NY: George Eastman House Archive.

Kerr, N. (1998b). The Kodak Colorama display and information center site. In *A history of Kodak's Colorama.* Rochester, NY: George Eastman House Archive.

Kerr, N. (1999, May/June). The Kodak Colorama: Lighting on a grand scale. *Photo Techniques Magazine, 20*(3), 31–35.

Kodak, e-magazine: The Kodak Colorama http://www.kodak.com/US/en/corp/features/coloramas/colorama.html

Marchand, R. (1985). *Advertising the American dream.* Berkeley: University of California Press.

McLuhan, M. (1951). *The mechanical bride.* New York: Vanguard.

Menzel, P. (1994). *Material world: A global family portrait.* San Francisco, CA: Sierra Club Books.

Nevins, D. (Ed.). (1992). *Grand Central terminal: City within the city.* New York: The Municipal Art Society of New York.

Nickel, D. R. (1998). *Snapshots: The photography of everyday life.* San Francisco: San Francisco Museum of Modern Art.

Nordstrom, A. (2004). Dreaming in color. In A. Nordsrom & P. Roalf (Eds.), *Colorama: The world's largest photographs* (pp. 5–11). New York: Aperture Foundation.

Nordstrom, A., & Roalf, P. (2004). *Colorama: The world's largest photographs*. New York: Aperture Foundation.

Rand, B. (2004, November 19). Kodak projector, 67, slides into history. *Rochester Democratic & Chronicle*, pp. 1A–2A.

Rijper, E. (Ed.). (2002). *Kodachrome: The American invention of our world: 1939-1959.* New York: Delano Greenidge Editions.

Roalf, P. (2004). Picture perfect. In A. Nordstrom & P. Roalf (Eds.), *Colorama: The world's largest photographs* (pp. 77–79). New York: Aperture Foundation.

Sachs, J. H. (1989, August 13). Colorama [Letter to the editor]. *New York Times*, Section 10, p. 10.

Schudson, M. (1984). *Advertising, the uneasy persuasion: Its dubious impact on American society*. New York: Basic Books.

Sontag, S. (1973). *On photography*. New York: Picador, Farrar, Straus & Giroux.

West, N. M. (2000). *Kodak and the lens of nostalgia*. Charlotteville: University Press of Virginia.

CHAPTER FIVE

Looking for Matthew Shepard
A Study in Visual Argument Field

SUSAN J. BALTER-REITZ AND KAREN A. STEWART
MONTANA STATE UNIVERSITY-BILLINGS

O N THE EVENING OF OCTOBER 6, 1998, Aaron McKinney and Russell Henderson met Matthew Shepard at the Fireside Lounge, a college bar in Laramie, Wyoming. Although there has been some dispute over exactly what transpired after the three left the bar,[1] McKinney and Henderson most definitely beat Shepard with a .357 handgun, took his wallet, and left him tied to a deer fence about a mile outside the town limits. Eighteen hours later, on the evening of October 7, Shepard was found by Aaron Kreifels, who had been riding his bicycle when he came across Shepard tied to the fence. Initially, Kreifels mistook Shepard for a scarecrow, his body was lying limply on the ground, and his hands had been tied behind him to a fencepost. Shepard had been beaten so severely that his face was unrecognizable, and his assailants had left him without shoes or a coat on a typically frigid Wyoming evening.

The media coverage of the event was extraordinary. Within days, Laramie had become a media circus (Loffreda, 2000). High-profile political figures quickly condemned the attack on Shepard; President Clinton called for the passage of the Hate Crimes Prevention Act (Crowder, 1998). Candlelight vigils were held across the country; initially in Shepard's honor and, after he died from his injuries, in his memory. Shepard's murder drew national attention to the Hate Crimes Prevention Act, legislation that had previously

---

1. The dispute about the events of October 6 revolved around the nature of the relationship among McKinney, Henderson, and Shepard. McKinney claimed during his trial that Shepard made a pass at him, and this is what caused him to brutally beat Shepard (Janofsky, 1999). Henderson's story was not aired in open court; he plea bargained at the last minute to avoid the death penalty (Hughes, 1999).

stalled in Congress. Many gay-rights advocates were hopeful that the tragedy in Laramie would lead to tougher penalties for hate crimes against gays and lesbians (Dunn, 2000).

Although the media certainly gave presence to this story (Ott & Aoki, 2002), a substantial amount of the coverage did not focus on the alleged perpetrators of the crime or the victim, but instead on the town and people of Laramie. News coverage of the legal hearings and trials of McKinney and Henderson often began with the phrase, "In Laramie, Wyoming today. . . . " Both the *Advocate* (Curtis, 1999) and the *New York Times* ran stories on the first anniversary of Shepard's murder, which prominently featured Laramie.[2] The questions about Matthew Shepard's death seemed to focus on "How could this have happened here?", rather than on "How could this have happened?"

The debate over the death of Matthew Shepard has not centered on the traditional issues of crime—the victim, the perpetrator, or the circumstances—but instead on the place where the murder occurred. In subsequent months, as the stories of the legal proceedings were reported in the national media, the attention of the press remained on the town of Laramie. Moises Kaufmann (2001) and the Tetonic Theater Company's play, *The Laramie Project,* further focused Shepard's story on the *place,* rather than the actors or actions. From an argumentation standpoint, the direction of the media and public discourse about this event seemed irrational. A closer examination of the visual rhetoric surrounding Shepard's death explains why the discourse was directed from the issues of how and why to the issue of where.

We argue that the photographs which accompanied the news stories about Matthew Shepard's murder limited the range of discourse about this event because it directed the narrative to the Western landscape. Photographs of the fence where Shepard was found tied and unconscious dominated the print media coverage of the case; photographs of Matthew Shepard, Aaron McKinney, and Russell Henderson are noticeably absent from much of the coverage. The most prominent of these photographs was the cover image that appeared on *Time* magazine's October 26, 1998 issue.

Ott and Aoki (2002) sought to understand why the media attention given to Shepard's death did not translate into stronger anti-hate legislation. They were disturbed that the public had "already forgotten, or worse, reconciled these events" (p. 484). Following a thorough analysis of the media framing of Shepard's murder, Ott and Aoki concluded that the roles

---

2. Other news sources also ran articles that concentrated on Laramie and the West. See Corry (1998), Kass (1999), and Lopez (1998) for examples of this coverage.

created for Shepard, McKinney, and Henderson by the media led the public to distance themselves from this crime. We would add that the visual representation of the story created another dimension to the public's framing of Shepard's murder.

The photographs of the fence played against a backdrop of American's attraction to the Western myth. Media representations of the West, both fictional and nonfictional, struggle with the incongruity between the romantic West and the realities of the contemporary West (Limerick, 2000). The West has historically symbolized hope and prosperity; it is now the site of bitter disputes between private and public, between the wealthy and the working class, and between the individual and the community. Matthew Shepard's murder has been read in the midst of these conflicts, and the story of his death has been blurred with the public's understandings of the mythical West.

THE WESTERN MYTH

The West is both physical and metaphysical; it exists as a geographical entity and a state of mind. For Industrial America, the dualistic nature of the western mystique permitted a sense of promise to a population confined to eastern and midwestern cities. For many Americans, the West represented a fantastic promise that might one day be fulfilled. Working-class city dwellers viewed the West as a way to escape the drudgery of their lives; the concept of the West created a feeling of potential that served to mollify the population, even if this potential would never be actualized (Murdoch, 2001). Those who undertook the journey into America's frontier discovered that the guarantee of freedom and wealth had been overstated; they had embarked on a dangerous journey only to find a more difficult life in the West than the one they left behind (Limerick, 1987). Despite the empirical evidence that life in the West was no easier than life in the East, Americans continued to give credence to the western myth.

Limerick (2000) argued that the western myth perseveres because it is a creation story "the place where the virtues and values of the nation were formed" (p. 314). Lewis and Clark's expedition, the building of the transcontinental railroad, and the countless people who traversed the Oregon Trail all contributed essential elements to the western mythic story. Although each of these are verifiable events, they are also part of the morality tales of the American public—stories that entail the hardships of the land, the perseverance of the people, and the possibility of American freedom.

As a place, the American West may seem easy to locate, but in academic circles the boundaries of the West are often difficult to pinpoint (Hausladen, 2003). The West has been identified in a number of different geographical dimensions: west of the Mississippi, the area of the Rocky Mountains, Texas, the Southwest, and the Pacific Northwest. Each of these geographic descriptions is problemtized as descriptive of the West; each area has a distinct culture, landscape, and population. Although historians of the American West may never settle their disputes over the true definitions of the territory, the debate is telling about the importance of place in the cultural history of the United States. Neel (1996) argued the interconnection between the landscape and the culture:

> Nature and culture together have made this place called the West. By attending as much to the workings of the natural world as to the human one, western history can serve to remind us that in being part of nature we are bound by it and that humans alone are not the measure of all things. (p. 106)

The West has been one focus of the American mythic story for close to 200 years. Although the adventures of Lewis and Clark may be identified as one of the first manifestations of this country's obsession with the West, historians trace human beings' infatuation with the West as beginning much earlier. Ideals of freedom, individuality, and destiny have been intertwined with geographic place for centuries. It is no wonder that in this country, which for years had an actual place of unexplored wilderness, that the West takes on such mythic proportions.

The Horatio Alger sensibility that pervades American culture roots itself in the possibility of great success—a possibility that is fed by the myth of an untamed wilderness full of resources waiting to be exploited by an individual with enough talent and work ethic to make a go of it. Aquilla (1996) wrote, "Although the West offered the potential for immeasurable success, it also held the possibility of abysmal failure through dashed hopes, broken dreams, financial ruin, or even tragic death at the hands of brutal bad guys or unrelenting forces of nature" (pp. 2–3). The brutality of the lands and the people who lived there is not a simple parable. Although the Western mystique has clearly identifiable heroes and villains, often those who suffered at the hands of the villains possessed a tragic flaw. Their death in the West created a nuanced morality tale: Those who fail in the West do so because of a defect in their own character. Death in the West was both predictable and natural, and the tales that emerged from the western genre of stories reinforced the moral that only the strong could survive such brutality. Janet Hocker Rushing's (1983) analysis of western films illustrates the archetypal roles that humans play in the western landscape. Male heroes must demonstrate rugged individualism to survive on the frontier. Other male characters generally exhibit a fatal flaw that usually results in their death; they succumb to violence because they do not belong in the West.

Both the state of Wyoming and the town of Laramie are unique sites within the Western myth. Wyoming is the least populous state in the United States (Wyoming Department of A & I, 2001); photographs of its landscape are often bereft of signs of civilization. Much of Wyoming's economy is still driven by extraction of natural resources and ranching. Although there is a great deal of wealth in Wyoming, the income gap is large, and the discrepancy between rich and poor continues to increase ("Pay Gap High in Teton Country," 2003). Minkowitz (1999) found Laramie to be a place of inexpensive luxury for those few who could afford it, but whose amenities were out of reach for many of the town's population. The battle between the mythic West and the new West rages in Laramie and in most of Wyoming, even as the tourist brochures and popular media invite America to experience the Real West that still exists there. Fictional representations of Wyoming further reinforce its role as keeper of the mythic West. Films and TV series perpetuate the West as an empty landscape where those who have the ability to succeed find wealth, redemption, and freedom.

The myths of the western landscape are confronted by the realities of a nation that no longer possesses open territory. Starrs (2003), commenting on the postmodern mythic West, found "The visceral disputes over land and life in each Western state come as a complete shock to newcomers" (p. 87). Inherent in the mythic West is the vision of open space and escape from civilization. Places that were, as little as 10 years ago, wide open land are now crowded with large houses on small lots. In 2003, it was almost impossible to find a place where no vestiges of civilization are visible. In the photographs of the fence, the landscape appears to be remote, but in fact the fence where Shepard died is behind a Super Wal-Mart and only a half mile to one of the more expensive subdivisions in Laramie (Loffreda, 2000). *Time*'s photograph captures the essence of the Western myth and reifies its dominance over the story of Shepard's death.

VISUAL ARGUMENTATION

In recent years, visual rhetorical theory and criticism has generated a vibrant and compelling body of literature. Taylor's (2003) essay found "expanding engagement by communication critics with particular visual genres" (p. 3). No archetype theory or method for the analysis of visual argument has yet emerged from these writings, but it is clear that the visual turn in rhetoric has emerged as one of the dominant themes of contemporary theorizing.

Visual theory and criticism in argumentation is still in a formative stage. The classical argumentation model of claim, evidence, and inference does not seem to provide much insight into the working of visual artifacts. Yet scholars sense that visuals do function as argument, and much of the research that has emerged from argumentation has been an attempt to define the function of visuals in argument.

Visual argument analysis has two dominant foci: one interested with the substance of the argument, the other with the interaction that the audience has with a visual argument. Shelly (1996) and Blair (1996) are both concerned with understanding the substance of visual argument. Shelly's work creates a schema for identifying the different functions of visual argument; she distinguished two types of visual appeals: the demonstrative and the rhetorical. Although Shelly cautioned that her categories are not mutually exclusive and should not be viewed as a closed system of categorizing, her primary concern is with understanding the purpose of the visual in an argument system. Blair's task is much more fundamental; he asked what should count as visual argument. To this end, he constructed criteria that are useful in determining what constitutes visual argument.

Birdsell and Goarke (1996) and Finnegan (2001) investigated the intersection of the visual form with audience assent. Birdsell and Goarke argued that, to understand how a visual argument works on an audience, a critic must examine three types of context: "immediate visual context, immediate verbal context, and visual culture" (p. 6). The first two contexts are read in relation to the visual; the third requires a critic to understand how the public reads the visual in relation to its interaction with other visuals. Birdsell and Goarke (1996) claimed "The meaning of a visual claim or argument obviously depends on a complex set of relationships between a particular image/text and a given set of interpreters" (p. 5). Mitchell (1994) and Finnegan (2002) both made similar arguments: Visuals cannot be separated from the surrounding symbol systems. News photography in particular offers viewers a specific way to interpret its images.

The preceding theories of argument substance and argument assent imply an understanding of how audiences are primed to respond to visuals. Their focus is primarily on how visuals function as either claim or evidence.

We are in accordance with theories. We would add, however, that a consideration of field is also important to understanding how visuals work as argument. Toulmin's (1958) classic treatise instructed argument critics that argument analysis must always consider the field in which the argument is taking place:

> The arguments which we put forward, and the steps which occur in them, will be correspondingly various: depending on the logical types of the facts adduced and of the conclusions drawn from them, the steps we take—the transitions of logical type—will be different. (p. 13)

Argument fields serve to direct audiences to the appropriate realm in which to analyze the strength of a particular argument. Each field has a different set of criteria for the worth of an argument based on the expectations of members of that field. For example, arguments about the quality of art are different when directed to art critics than to the general public. Fields control the quality of evidence, the type of reasoning statements being used, and even the claims that may be advanced. We argue visuals direct audience response because they establish the field on which an argument should be judged. In the case of Matthew Shepard, the visual changed the field from legal realism to the western myth.

PHOTOJOURNALISM

Much attention has been paid to photojournalism and documentary photography in visual scholarship. Hariman and Lucaites' (2003) investigations of iconic photography, Zelizer's (2003) analysis of how news photographs intervene in discourse about traumatic events, and Finnegan's (2002) work on FSA photographs exemplify contributions to the field. It is no surprise that photojournalism has seized the attention of so many of our colleagues; it is a powerful rhetorical form. Newton (2001) explained the attraction of photojournalism to researchers:

> Images of reportage are both agents and artifacts. They are agents in the sense that they are part of the cultural dialectic of formation, change, response, and so forth. They are artifacts in the sense that they tell us something about individuals, moments in time, and places for which we may no longer have other evidence. (pp. 101–102)

Scholars are not the only parties interested in photojournalism; public interest in news photography is also great. Photography allows the public to witness events. Despite their knowledge that the photograph is mediated, the public is able to imagine they are close to the event they are seeing. The technology of photography creates a clear, crisp, vividly representational image; the photograph looks like the familiar world. In this way, photojournalism allows audiences to feel more connected to a news story than if they only experienced the written text. By experiencing the event photographically, audiences believe in the veracity of the event.

The ability of audiences to attribute truth to photographic depictions of events is one of the most powerful elements of photojournalism. Finnegan (2001) argued that audiences are likely to respond to pictorial representations based on the naturalistic enthymeme. In other words, the audience will give credibility to a photograph because they participate in the enthymeme by granting that the visual is real. Despite awareness by contemporary audiences that technology may be used to manipulate photographs, audiences seem willing to believe what they see. Barbatsis (1996) found "The power of pictorial realism in collaboration with a compelling camera metaphor blurs the distinction between an act of constructing images in a fictional world and an act of constructing images in a real world" (p. 78).

Audiences presume that photojournalism presents an absolute truth. The truth, however, is subject to the choices made by the photographer attempting to capture the essence of the news story. The image taken by the photographer is inherently constrained by the parameters of the viewfinder and the need to consolidate a complex story into a photograph. Additionally, the photographer is working to produce an image that succeeds editorially; the image must work in concert with both the journalistic presentation of that image and the textual content. Because this photograph is in a news source and because it accompanies a news text, it directs the audience as to how to read the story.

Photojournalism allows audiences to feel as if they are experiencing events first hand. A familiar depiction generates an acceptance of truth to that depiction. This is despite the audience's understanding that the photograph is mediated and subject to the processes of photojournalism. These processes of photojournalism create the frame that enables the audience to experience the event. It is through the selection of the subject of the photograph, as well as the artistic choices made by the photographer to enhance the subject, that audiences are cued to the meaning of the event. The implication of this is that a frame is created in which the audience interprets the event which the photograph represents.

Although photographs of the fence dominate pictorial representations of Shepard's murder, for purposes of our analysis we have chosen to concentrate on *Time*'s October 26, 1998 cover. *Time*'s cover image was one of the first to use the fence to represent Shepard's death. Additionally, *Time* has strong credibility as a news source. It claims 44% of news magazine readership ("About Time," 2003). *Time* is also renowned for its photojournalism; each year it receives numerous awards.

The choice of the fence as the cover image negates other possible visual icons to represent this story. The editors could have chosen to use photographs of candlelight vigils, Shepard's parents, McKinney and Henderson's arraignment, or even a large portrait of Shepard, all of which appear on subsequent pages within the issue. The fence most likely emerged as the dominant image because it was already imbued with iconic meaning. Fences are inherently associated with the West. Deer fences, in particular, have a specific western association because of their design to regulate wild life without restricting access to public land. The design of deer fences also evokes a secondary iconic meaning. Deer fences are constructed by crossing logs; visually they remind viewers of crosses. Shepard, who was found tied to the fence, was not literally crucified, but the proximity of his body to the fence implied crucifixion.[3] The decision by *Time* to capitalize on the iconic nature of the fence directed viewers to the western landscape as embodied by the fence, the grass, and the sky.

Time's cover photograph was employed as a full-page image, placed behind the *Time* masthead and contained within the characteristic red cover border identified with *Time* magazine. The focal point of the photograph was a basket of flowers, interpreted as a memorial, hanging from the top of the fencepost. The Laramie, Wyoming, landscape, divided into two-thirds sky and one-third land, contextualized the fence and the flowers.

Although the memorial basket was the focal point of the photograph, the rustic deer fence was the photograph's dominant image. The dominance of the fence was expressed not only through its predominance as the foreground image, but also through the compositional employment of the angular nature of its construction. The angled posts led the viewer through the cover design, first highlighting the basket of flowers, then leading the

---

3. In early media reports, the position of Shepard's body on the fence was misrepresented. Some reported that he had literally been strung up on the fence in the image of a crucifixion (Loffreda, 2000).

Time Magazine, October 26, 1998. Photograph courtesy of Steve Liss and Getty Images.

eyes down into the landscape, and finally drawing the eyes to an inset photograph of Shepard. Dominance of the fence was also reiterated by the decision to minimize interruption of the fence by any additional design elements incorporated into the cover. The fence was allowed to penetrate the masthead, covering the lower portion of the uncharacteristically subtle letters, to remain intact.

The western characteristics of the fence were emphasized through the use of natural light and landscape. Sunlight fell on the rough-hewn fence posts, contrasting the irregular surfaces of the fence. The typified portrayal of the western landscape, with sweeping prairie grass, a domineering sky filled with indications of inclement weather, and the complete absence of signs of urban development encased the fence. The fence was located less than a half mile from a subdivision, yet all signs of urban development were absent from the photograph. Houses, power lines, cell phone towers, and retail outlets were selectively eliminated from the photograph.

The headline accompanying the cover photograph read, "The War Over Gays." A relatively small inset photograph of Shepard was placed under the headline, imposed over the turbulent sky of the photograph of the fence. It is apparent that the photograph was not taken professionally. It was a snapshot of Shepard taken in a casual setting. In the snapshot, Shepard was posed in profile, turned to his right, with his gaze fixed downward. In the cover layout, the inset photograph was placed to the left of the fence. In doing so, Shepard's gaze faced the spine of the magazine, not the fence. The placement of the Shepard photograph broke the standard design practice of orienting portraits to face other design elements to imply a relationship between the images. The awkward placement of the Shepard photograph was further exaggerated by the thick black border surrounding the image, and by the inability of Shepard's photographic gaze to direct the viewer from its placement on the left to the dominant image of the fence located to the right.

Matthew Shepard's name does not appear in the headline or secondary headlines on the cover. Underneath Shepard's photograph, "Murder in Laramie" was typeset. Additional lines identically typeset and placed in succession, followed: "Changing Gay Politics," "Do Hate-Crime Laws Work?," and "Showdown Over Gay Marriage." The style of typesetting indicated themes addressed within the pages of the magazine. In the lower left-hand corner of the cover, a photo caption identifies the inset photograph as Matthew Shepard and the main photograph of the fence as the location Shepard was left to die.

THE FENCE AS VISUAL ARGUMENT CUE

Visuals are not read by audiences in isolation; they are cued by the text and context that surrounds their display. In the case of *Time*, viewers are told how to interpret the cover image by reading the headlines that accompany that image. Two headlines from this issue are most relevant: the largest headline, "The War Over Gays," and the first subheadline under Shepard's picture, "Murder in Laramie." Each of these headlines focuses the viewer on the landscape as instrumental to the story.

The dominant headline, "The War Over Gays," read in conjunction with the audience's historical knowledge that westward expansion was filled with land battles, equates Shepard's murder with epic acts of purification. Wars in the West were fought to make way for civilization; battles were waged against American Indians, Spanish, and Mexicans to secure land for farms and railroads. The erasure of these peoples from the landscape was the goal of the war; the battle was won when the land was emptied or purified. Shepard's elimination from the landscape signifies the importance of the land over his life. The prominence of the land over Shepard's life is reinforced by the subheadline, "Murder in Laramie." Instead of naming Shepard, *Time*'s verbal and visual cues erase Shepard from the story. Laramie is named and, in doing so, is given the featured role in the story. The text prepares the audience for the focus of the narrative and solidifies the landscape as the leading character in the story.

Absent the text, the photograph does not represent an act of violence. The scene is idyllic. The sky is big, the land is pristine, and nature is not contained. The fence is constructed of rustic poles, designed to complement the landscape. Even the basket of flowers attached to the fence does not signify a place of mourning; the flowers retain the same charm as the fence. The photograph provides an easily accepted characterization of the Laramie landscape, familiar to audiences predisposed to western imagery. Even without textual cues, viewers would understand that this photograph is the West.

The only visual signifier of Shepard on the cover is the small, inset photograph located between the headlines on the far left side of the page. Shepard is marginalized by the layout. Not only is his photograph notably diminutive in size, it is further reduced by a thick, black restraining border. Shepard's photograph is not contextualized by the rest of the cover. It requires a caption to clarify Shepard's relationship to the fence and to explain his inclusion in the story. Matthew Shepard is not the center of his own story; he is overpowered by the character of the landscape.

Time's cover photograph framed Shepard's murder so that the public was directed to consider the crime as part of the western myth. The visual cues offered by the cover superimposed a mythic story over a contemporary narrative, which changed the discourse from who was responsible for killing Matthew Shepard to a discussion about western values. The murder was reframed, and public argument shifted from subject to place.

Our reading of this shift indicates that one way visuals function in argument is to establish a frame that directs audiences to the field they should use to judge an argument. The field shift shortcuts the discursive process in the public sphere. It is much more complex to argue the culpability of McKinney and Henderson than the power of the western landscape to eliminate impurities. Western lore imbues the land with extraordinary presence; the presence of the land overshadows the presence of McKinney and Henderson. The land is the frame, and McKinney and Henderson are not even in the picture. The argument frame places the story of the crime squarely in the culture's mythology, which in turn prepares the audience to evaluate the murder in terms of the place where it occurred. Olson (1987) argued, "Both visual and verbal rhetoric entail a commitment to use a community's representational systems in endeavors to enlist the will of the audience" (p. 18). *Time*'s cover played against the representational system of the mythic West. In doing so, it incorporated the mythic West into Shepard's story.

The shift in field from law to landscape disavows human agency. Henderson and McKinney are cast not as villains, but as agents of the land. Instead of murderers, they become stewards of the West. In historic times, they would have been hailed as heroes; they purified the landscape by eliminating the disruptive influence personified by Shepard. Throughout the narrative of his death, Shepard is described as a gay University of Wyoming student. His sexuality is his first characteristic, his position as a student second. He is never described as a native of Wyoming, never placed in the scene as a natural part of the landscape. Students in Laramie are seen as outsiders—necessary interlopers in an otherwise settled community. Despite the fact that Wyoming students are responsible for the relative prosperity of Laramie, they do not belong. Although Henderson and McKinney have certainly been punished for their crimes, there is no doubt that their role in this drama was mitigated by the focus on scene. Burke (1969) is instructive here. When scene dominates the drama, the actors are engaged in the realm of motion. They are not responsible or accountable for the act; McKinney, Henderson, and Shepard are pawns of the scene.

EXPLORING VISUAL ARGUMENT FIELD

The ability of a photograph to control the field of argument is premised on the audience's presumption that the photograph is truthful. Photojournalism is an extension of journalism and, as such, retains the inclination of the audience to perceive the practice as unbiased, accurate descriptions of news worthy events. Photojournalism is granted permission by the audience to frame the narrative. In the Shepard story, the dominance of the scene is accepted as important to the narrative because of the overwhelming presence of the landscape. The prioritizing of the character of the land over Shepard in the discourse that followed the distribution of the *Time* cover serves as evidence that the visual frame given to the story is taken to be the truth.

The frame of the photograph instructs audiences what field they should use for evaluating the quality of a visual argument. In the case of the Matthew Shepard cover, the link is evident because the photograph is easily located within the corpus of the western landscape genre. The photograph of the deer fence recalls western artistic themes: dramatic landscapes, atmospheric forces, and the sublime (Goetzmann & Goetzmann, 1986). Western images exert a powerful influence in American culture and a dramatic pull on the imagination of American audiences.

Continued explorations into the interactions between argument fields and visuals would augment our knowledge of visual communication. Analysis of additional visual arguments that employ the genre of the American West would seem a natural starting point. DeLuca and Demo's (2000) work on Yosemite provides a foundation for this inquiry. As a genre, the American West is easily identifiable; obviously it is not the only visual genre with distinction. We would encourage visual scholars to investigate other possible genres that may lend themselves to framing audience response to visual argument. Finally, we would hope that research in visual argumentation goes beyond the study of photojournalism and documentary photography to explore other visual media such as fine art and illustration. Expanding inquiry into multiple visual forms can only increase our knowledge of the processes of visual communication.

REFERENCES

About *Time*. (2003, September 8). Retrieved November 29, 2003 from http://www.time-planner.com/planner/about_time/index.html.

Aquilla, R. (1996). Introduction. In R. Aquilla (Ed.), *Wanted dead or alive: The American west in popular culture* (pp. 1–16). Urbana: University of Illinois Press.

Barbatsis, G. S. (1996). Look and I will show you something you will want to see: Pictorial engagements in negative political campaign commercials. *Argumentation and Advocacy, 33,* 69-78.

Birdsell, D. S., & Goarke, L. (1996). Toward a theory of visual argument. *Argumentation and Advocacy, 33,* 1-10.

Blair, J. A. (1996). The possibility and actuality of visual arguments. *Argumentation and Advocacy, 33,* 23-39.

Burke, K. (1969). *A grammar of motives.* Berkeley: University of California Press.

Corry, J. (1998, December). Murder in Wyoming. *American Spectator,* pp. 72–73.

Crowder, C. (1998, October 11). Clinton saddened by Wyoming hate assault. *Rocky Mountain News.* p. 5A. Retrieved November 6, 2003, Lexis Database.

Curtis, P. (1999, October 12). A town reflects on itself. *Advocate,* pp. 44–48.

DeLuca, K. M., & Demo A. T. (2000). Imaging nature: Watkins, Yosemite, and the birth of environmentalism. *Critical Studies in Media Communication, 17,* 241-260.

Dunn, A. R. (2000, May 1). Fighting for equal rights on all fronts. *National Law Journal,* p. B1. Retrieved October 31, 2003, Lexis Database.

Finnegan, C. A. (2001). The naturalistic enthymeme and visual argument: Photographic representation in the "skull controversy." *Argumentation and Advocacy* 37, 133-149.

Finnegan, C. A. (2002). *Picturing poverty: Print culture and the FSA photographs.* Washington, DC: Smithsonian Books.

Goetzmann, W. H., & Goetzmann, W. N. (1986). *The West of the imagination.* New York: W.W. Norton.

Hariman, R., & Lucaites, J. L. (2003). Public identity and collective memory in U.S. iconic photography: The image of "accidental napalm." *Critical Studies in Media Communication, 20,* 35-66.

Hausladen, G. (2003). Introduction. In G. J. Hauslauden (Ed.), *Western places, American myths: How we think about the West* (pp. 1–20). Reno: University of Nevada Press.

Hughes, J. (1999, April 6). Shepard assailant pleads guilty. *Denver Post,* p. A1. Retrieved October 31, 2003, Lexis Database.

Janofsky, M. (1999, November 2). Judge rejects "gay panic" as defense in murder case. *New York Times,* p. A14. Retrieved October 31, 2003, Lexis Database.

Kass, J. (1999, March 23). A collision of values in rural west. *Christian Science Monitor,* p. 1.

Kaufman, M. (2001). *The Laramie project.* New York: Vintage Books.

Limerick, P. N. (1987). *The legacy of conquest.* New York: Norton.

Limerick, P. N. (2000). *Something in the soil.* New York: Norton.

Loffreda, B. (2000). *Losing Matt Shepard.* New York: Columbia.

Lopez, S. (1998, October 26). "To be young and gay in Wyoming." *Time,* pp. 38–40.

Minkowitz, D. (1999, July 12). Love and hate in Laramie. *Nation,* pp. 18-22.

Mitchell, W. J. T. (1994). *Picture theory.* Chicago: University of Chicago Press.

Murdoch, D. H. (2001). *The American West: The invention of a myth.* Reno: University of Nevada Press

Neel, S. R. (1996). A place of extremes: Nature, history and the American West. In C. A. Milner II (Ed.), *A new significance: Re-envisioning the history of the American West* (pp. 105–224). New York: Oxford.

Newton, J. H. (2001). *The burden of visual truth: The role of photojournalism in mediating reality.* Mahwah, NJ: Erlbaum.

Olson, L. C. (1987). Benjamin Franklin's pictorial representations of the British colonies in America: A study of rhetorical iconology. *Quarterly Journal of Speech, 53,* 18-42.

Ott, B. L., & Aoki, E. (2002). The politics of negotiating public tragedy: Media framing of the Matthew Shepard murder. *Rhetoric and Public Affairs, 5,* 483-505.

Pay gap high in Teton County. (2003, November 28). *Billings Gazette,* p. 10C.

Rushing, J. H. (1983). The rhetoric of the American Western myth. *Communication Monographs, 50,* 14–32.

Shelly, C. (1996). Rhetorical and demonstrative modes of visual argument: Looking at images of human evolution. *Argumentation and Advocacy, 33,* 53-68.

Starrs, P. F. (2003). Land tenure: The spatial musculature of the American West. In G. J. Hauslauden (Ed.), *Western places, American myths* (pp. 57–84). Reno: University of Nevada Press.

Taylor, B. C. (2003). "Our bruised arms hung up as monuments": Nuclear iconography in post-cold war culture. *Critical Studies in Media Communication, 20,* 1-34.

Toulmin, S. (1958). *The uses of argument.* Cambridge: Cambridge University Press.

Wyoming Department of A & I. (2001). Resident population for U.S. and all states 1990 and 2000. Retrieved November 27, 2003, from http://eadiv.state.wy.us/demog_data/pop2000/states00.htm.

Zelizer, B. (2003, November). *Visual communication in a time of crisis.* Paper presented at the meeting of the National Communication Association, Miami, FL.

CHAPTER SIX

Amber Alert
The Subject Citizen and Technologies in Transformation

JULIE BORKIN
WAYNE STATE UNIVERSITY

I N EARLY AUGUST 2002, two teenage California girls were found alive just 12 hours after an abductor forced them away from their broken-down vehicle to a location over 100 miles away. The suspect, who according to the sheriff was "just minutes away from killing them," was shot and killed in a shootout with police, and the girls returned home unharmed ("Kidnapped Teens Are Rescued," 2002). The story spread quickly across the nation, yet another tale in the summer of 2002's heavy media attention on child abduction cases. Police credited the rapid and successful outcome to the newly implemented Amber Alert System—an emergency communication program designed to intervene quickly in child abduction situations by enlisting public involvement as "the eyes and ears of local law enforcement" ("Missing Kids Amber Alert Project," n.d.). Motorists receive suspect information via a variety of traditional media, including radio and TV messages, as well as new hypermedia sources, including even the electronic highway traffic signs usually used to alert motorists of construction projects, traffic backups, or estimated travel times. Strategically positioned along busy interstates and connecting highways nationwide, in an Amber Alert, these changeable sign messages are quickly switched to report pertinent details that may help motorists identify a suspect's vehicle. Typically, abbreviated details form two or three lines of text alternating between two message screens (see figure 6.1, p. 128), including "Amber Alert," and then some available information including the vehicle description, license plate, and phone number to call if the vehicle is spotted. These flashing messages convey a sense of urgency and proximity that commands attention and relevance. Perhaps too much so because in some cases already, not only have enthusiastic motorists jammed phone lines to report only partially

Figure 6.1. Changeable message signs, rapid response, and community involvement are integral to Amber Alerts. Photograph courtesy of Ken Borkin.

matching information, others have chosen to intervene, even chasing similar vehicles for miles rather than alerting authorities (Lee, 2002).

The Amber Alert program is a particularly interesting opportunity to consider the subject citizen's participation in a community concern—as rousing a community into action is a complex goal in a culture largely consumed with a myriad of personal concerns instead. Advertisers spend millions trying to gain, hold, and refresh market segments; educators anguish over how to position features and benefits of higher education; and religious groups work to repackage spiritual conventions to appeal to a preoccupied public. Yet shifting contemporary practices remain embedded in particular affective attachments, in conformity with the pathetic component named at least as long ago as Aristotle. The constitutive powers of rhetoric move beyond a classical understanding of persuasion and focus instead on how audiences are always already positioned to act in a particular way. Put another way, through constitutive rhetoric, a subject is embodied or created and marshaled toward particular practices, normalizing a range of legible or appropriate positions or responses as an effect. In this chapter, I trace the development of community participation and law enforcement norms, and then trace the shifting context of post-9/11 law enforcement conditions through examination of the Amber Alert system, a context that challenges the subject citizen's role and responsibility to the community in important ways.

Community participation might be anticipated in times of emergencies of various kinds. Public health concerns such as epidemic diseases, threat of war, and crime management are often issues that gather community attention and action through informal and institutional means. In the matter of crime management specifically, citizen response to the institution of law enforcement in a participatory capacity can be traced back to at least the times of Alfred the Great, who mandated a "mutual pledge" program obliging subjects to report criminal activity or face fines (Burns, 2001). In the United States, early colonists rotated responsibility for standing night watch in the village, normalizing a participatory capacity with institutional law enforcement, but this tradition proved inadequate for managing local populations in emerging urban communities by the time of the Industrial Revolution. According to Fleissner and Heinzelmann (1996), much of the 20th century relied on a "professional era" in policing, leaving crime management almost exclusively to law enforcement agents.

Activating the community's involvement with law enforcement returned as a police priority in the 1970s and 1980s as part of an effort to break down the perceived "wall" of divide between the police and the public. Following the release of the "broken windows" work (Wilson & Kelling, 1982), which suggested that disorder in the neighborhood is a source of public fear, indicated by such markers as broken windows, additional governmental attention and resources were directed toward community policing. This effort was fueled by hopes of managing costs, freeing police officers to identify underlying causes of crime, and invigorating a more active relationship between the community and the police. In practice, public participation in such efforts, dubbed *community policing,* is familiar to most only through education programs such as drug or rape prevention seminars. The Neighborhood Watch program, an "extra eyes and ears" approach primarily for keeping home burglars away, normalized a commitment to citizen participation, yet criminal justice scholars agree that most community members have maintained a 911 mentality in law enforcement matters, merely reporting crime. Over the last century, other public concerns for health and safety surrounding fears of disease, nuclear threat, war, or terrorism have also been managed almost exclusively through a variety of institutional or directly governmental civil defense programs that, for reasons of cost and scope, serve primarily as information distribution centers (Amacher, 2003).

In the matter of crime management, however, the normalized division between citizen and law enforcement does not mean that Americans are uninterested or unaware of criminal activity. Public attention is directed across a host of media from "Most Wanted" fliers still tacked on post office walls, local and national media news programming, or the ubiquitous milk carton displays of missing children. Law enforcement encourages leads from citizens about possible criminal information through "tip" hotlines and reality TV, including shows such as *America's Most Wanted* and *Unsolved Mysteries*, which extend the awareness and potential public involvement to some degree. Such opportunities open new possibilities for citizen responsibility, but have served mostly to satisfy the viewers' curiosity, maintaining their role as spectator and serving as an opportunity to observe law enforcement successfully manage various social order situations. Even in national criminal matters such as the Oklahoma City bombing, illegal immigration, and drug trafficking, citizens have left crime management to law enforcement representatives. Hence, although community policing strategy seeks to partner citizens in law enforcement efforts that reduce the fear of crime and increase a community's sense of control (Fleissner & Heinzelmann, 1996), it appears the public has preferred to watch and listen, but not much more.

Although public concerns and expectations about domestic safety are certainly nothing new, the American public's preoccupation with personal and national security appears significantly transformed subsequent to the bombings of the World Trade Center and the Pentagon, and the plane crash in Pennsylvania. Those and other events, along with incidents including the anthrax scare and the Washington, DC, sniper killings, call into question the traditional role of government and law enforcement agencies as reliable structures to protect, anticipate, or guarantee citizens safety in any environment. The sense of panic widely evoked after 9/11 slowed travel and consumer spending, and reoriented national security priorities. Although people may no longer attribute heightened public safety concerns directly to the events of 9/11, during the recent sniper scare, Washington officials closed schools for several days in the name of child safety, raising concern that officials could no longer provide safety in even the most essential places.

These events have substantially changed the dynamics of citizenship, perhaps forever transforming the expectations and rules of citizens and their relation to government agencies. Indeed a new climate seems to have taken hold of the national sensibility, one in which citizens are actively called to participate in public safety regulation. We are seeing the signs of this transformation repeated again and again: potential terrorist suspicions reported by wary observers, corporate whistle blowers, and even a trucker willing to risk life and rig in the apprehension of the Washington, DC, snipers ("Alert Trucker," 2002).

A host of new practices and proposals partnering citizen responsibility and law enforcement efforts have been proposed in recent months. Government and corporations are negotiating for the conditions allowing the appropriation of new communication technologies, or hypermedia, including cell phone, pager, Internet service messaging, and even lottery terminals for particular emergency situations ("What Is AOL's Role?" 2002). In one example, the National Communications System (NCS), a federal agency, is proposing that government officials take over the wireless networks used by cellular telephones in the event of an emergency for the safety and protection of national security (Blair, 2002). Legislative measures on local, state, and national levels seek such partnerings as well. One recently implemented program, a major component of the newly created Department of Homeland Security, names its goal as the "cooperation of the public and the private sector" (U.S. Office of the President, 2002, p. 7). Toward this end, the governmental organization priorities work in tandem with a unified military, the FBI, local law enforcement, and the community with a goal to fight terrorism, protect the economy, defend liberty and justice, and allow "children to be educated and to live free from poverty and violence" (p. 4). These objectives allow a protocol that approves information sharing in matters both foreign and domestic through phone tapping, tracking e-mails, and more. Such moves point toward interesting material partnerings and environments changed by this shift of relations between the community and law enforcement.

To understand the rhetorical and political force of some of these developments without presuming that it is merely a series of government initiatives put over on a duped populace, it is useful to examine the range of possible responses and rewards subjects get from such investments through a particular textual formation. The radical and quickly shifting transformation described here has far-reaching implications. Thus, although this chapter examines the possibilities of this transformation through the lens of just one program, Amber Alert, it is paradigmatic of a particular historical context in which the role of citizen is being articulated into a deputized citizen beyond the confines of a single text. Amber is a particularly useful text of examination toward this end precisely because of its localized urgency and specified focus of suspicion as determined by the law enforcement community. Here, too, Amber offers a particular set of operating logics symbolized in innocence and reliance on institutional structures including legislative and law enforcement agencies. I argue that Amber works to interpellate individuals into a collective identity of *good citizen,* deputized to act with an illusion of agency and forging a transhistorical identity, including future responsibility directed to law enforcement's goals and shaping material conditions that may normalize further interpellations. This chapter, then, provides a critical look at the ways in which the identity of the public citizen is articulated into one of public deputy by drawing on the theoretical frameworks of Maurice Charland's constitutive rhetoric and Ronald Greene's work on materiality.

This theoretical assemblage is essential if we want to understand both how identities may be reconstructed as well as conjecture about the implications of such maneuvers. Greene's (1998a, 1998b) emphasis on materiality helps move constitutive rhetoric beyond the requisite, but incomplete, effort to understand the way in which identifications have been forged, and it allows us to project outward and anticipate some of the material, cultural, political, and ethical entailments of those identifications—or as Greene (1998b) stated, to "draw a portrait" of the future. Here I follow Greene on the importance of tracking these material effects when he suggested rhetorical responsibility and clarity comes in "understanding that in acting decisively one participates in fixing forces that will continue after the purposes for which they have been immediately instrumental and will, to some extent, bind others who will inherit the modified traditions" (p. 22).

This ground offers an opportunity to examine the role, including expectation and responsibility, of both individual and collective. Here a political rationality is at work, in which the individual, or citizen subject, responds and reaffirms the authority of the collective, or national sovereignty, circulating power. Toby Miller (1993), for instance, argued that Americans consistently privilege the role of citizen over being a "mere" individual, following Foucault's pastoral model of the institution of the Christian church in four aspects—enacting the fulfillment of heavenly salvation, laying down the self for others, promising care for both the community and the self, and maintaining a need to know those that it is to care for. The subject citizen identifies with the greater whole and participates in the production of categories of censure that normalize particular subjects while excluding other subjects as deviant subject positions. In this way, individuals can be made productive to social concerns through means other than force. This pastoral model speaks to the American national sentimentality that values national identity concomitantly with individual subjectivity.

AMBER ALERT

The public attention, visibility, and concern for the matter of child abduction has brought the Amber Alert system a mushrooming amount of publicity and support. Many of the recent child abduction narratives have featured a potent affective entailment centering largely on tropes of innocence and vulnerability, and the public discourse about Amber works in tandem with these messages. Amber discussions avoid focusing attention on potential weakness in existing community or law enforcement practices, instead animating the themes of innocence and vulnerability and directing attention and resources toward criminal apprehension and legislative intervention.

By example, the recent high-profile coverage of the Elizabeth Smart abduction became connected with the Amber Alert program, emphasizing both the vulnerability and innocence of the girl and the national legislation that would facilitate and fund the Amber Alert program. When Smart disappeared in June 2002, the nation shared in detailed accounts of the middle-of-the-night abduction. We heard about the slit window screen and the terrorized little sister, watched images of the young fair-haired Elizabeth playing her harp, and shared the tears of grieving family members pleading for her return.

The vulnerability and innocence of the children and their families as suffering victims becomes a critical part of the how individuals are drawn into participation, acting and supporting the process of various kinds of intervention and normalizing the victims' right to vindication through media access and public policy. Just one day after his daughter's safe return, Ed Smart held a news conference demanding politicians' immediate attention and approval of Amber Alert, despite that Amber had no known role in Elizabeth's return. Within that same day, both the House and Senate conducted a news conference blaming one another for inaction, and the Amber measure bypassed its order on the schedule, becoming law within the month (Huse, 2003). The public sentiment stirred by the news conference and Smart's comments functioned in a particular way precisely because of the force of the perception of innocence.

Other aspects of Amber Alert also draw on affective attachments. The program, designated Amber Alert, hails the memory of Amber Hagerman, the namesake, recounting another high-profile child abduction case that ended with the 9-year-old's murder 7 years ago. This narrative, inextricably attached to the Amber Alert program, has appeared in virtually all of the surrounding media coverage. The lingering unspoken threat that "this" is what "usually" happens to abducted victims continues to animate the intensity and urgency of the perceptions and responses. A *New York Times* article noted that such "legislation by anecdote" works powerfully because "in the battle over legislation, there is no weapon as powerful as a victim" (Stolberg, 2003). Similar connections have recently linked legislation and high-visibility victim narratives, including the recent Laci Petersen murder and the "James Brady" gun bill. The victim's publicity so successfully rouses public sentiment that legislative opponents are often unwilling to appear publicly for fear of appearing insensitive, effectively silencing other perspectives. Such practices extend the role of Amber well beyond a telephone tip reporting suspicious activity.

Just as the attention and support of Amber legislation cannot be detached from the perception of innocent victims in the contextual attachment including Ed Smart's news conference discourse, other political influences seem particularly attentive to public sentiment in the matter of child safety as well, citing a joint responsibility between community and institutional efforts. For example, Bush convened a special day-long conference in October 2002 as part of a response to the heightened concern during the summer-long media focus on abductions. In his speech that day, Bush said, "Our first duty as adults is to create an environment in which children can grow and thrive without fearing for their security" ("Bush Promises $10 million," 2002). He "listened with tears in his eyes . . . to wrenching stories from the parents of missing or murdered children, then announced that the federal government would spend $10 million to improve the Amber Alert systems" (Bumiller, 2002), saying, "our society has a duty, has a solemn duty, to shield children from exploitation and danger" ("Bush Backs Amber," 2002).

Here the emphasis on the Amber program implementation suggests that policy and financial support are the elements that will appropriately shield children from such crime. The discourse of "our" society and "our" duty constitutes the unstated, but implied and expected, public participation in the program, accepting the community's responsibility to prevent such dangers through criminal apprehension and legislative intervention. In this way, "our" very concern about public safety, so long left in the hands of law enforcement, is folded into a joint agreement to reinvest confidence in governmental structures, even while participating to reinforce and extend its surveillance, accepting the "eyes and ears" role spelled out in Amber.

Addressing one successful Amber apprehension, a police officer's comments gesture more specifically toward this responsibility to partner with police. Crediting the Amber Alert system in returning a young California victim, he said, "Contra Costa (officials) did an outstanding job of moving quickly and getting the information out there. . . . It's an example of the system working, of the public and law enforcement working together" (Hendricks, 2003, p. A28).

This public responsiveness signals a shift in citizen involvement with law enforcement goals. According to a spokesperson for the National Center for Missing and Exploited Children, the dwindling number of child abductions by strangers each year may be due, in part, to this community policing function. Reflecting on Smart's return, Scofield said this "reflects the change that has occurred in how our nation handles child abductions. We are a more educated nation . . . with a public more ready to participate in search and recovery" ("Experts: Most Abducted Children," 2003, n.p.).

Although taking extraordinary measures for children's safety may be laudable, the efforts may not be representative of children's safety at all. First, child abductions are rare regardless of the media coverage of summer 2002. "Every year many more children die from bicycle accidents than are abducted and murdered" (Fox, 2002). Of the over 2,000 child abductions reported each day, most involve parents or caregivers, and only about 100 child abductions by strangers are reported nationwide in an entire year. The summer-long media spectacle, a special presidential child abduction conference, the $10 million funding boost for Amber, and a nationwide legislative implementation proceeded virtually without opposition despite such statistics.

Despite its minimal contribution to public safety, Amber works to give the citizen "something to do"—not unlike the "go boil some water" advice once proffered to the pacing father waiting for the birth of a child. In the act of believing we are "doing" something, we have accepted a role of doing what someone else has determined useful and necessary to the public's interests, believing that we have, as Foucault's pastoral model suggests, both risked ourselves and cared for the community. On the one hand, we may be concerned that Amber puts an untrained commuting citizen subject at risk in a heightened context of urgency and emotion; on the other hand, we may need to attend to how a suspect subject is positioned as a deviant requiring citizen activism in a hastily deputized capacity.

For the investment into Amber's purported protection, the citizen in return may gain a sense of satisfaction for supporting or even participating in the reanimation of a longed-for past in which the community seemed better. Contemporary despair over unexplainable tragedy, including the shock and panic surrounding the events of 9/11 and subsequent concerns, may animate a sense of longing and nostalgia for the "good old days" when community members seemed to truly know and care for one another. Following the work of Salecl (1998), I believe that today's global and technological advances bring a sense of disarray and loss that limits the range of intelligible responses to particular crises. Sanctioning a reporting system like Amber or supporting legislative protection of innocent victims seems appropriate in a culture anxious for solutions that minimize personal responsibility and grant a sense of pseudocommunity that symbolizes fulfillment of that longing. In some sense, the gesture can be no other because the logics of innocence and vulnerability resonate with the vulnerability, particularly recently, that we know in our world and ourselves. This temporary identification with a group gathered against some suspect stands in for a lack of personal or collective identity, granting a temporary perception of wholeness to carry back to more daily matters.

Normalizing this process of communication opens the door for the messaging systems and the citizen to be marshaled for other purposes as well. Just as the protocol that was designed to warn of nuclear attack has been repackaged first for weather alerts, and now for the sake of the children, I argue that it also opens a space for other rhetorical and material elements to be partnered to manage other socially constructed deviants, including those labeled *criminals* or *terrorists*. Further, the messaging system requires an immediate response, placing a precarious urgency for the citizen to act on fragments of information that can quickly coalesce suspicion and judgment. In other words, a heightened sense of urgency pushes a citizen to act, perhaps without the luxury of reflection or clarification, toward a fellow citizen who, although still classified legally as a suspect, incurs a range of potential judgments in the process of justice practiced by these hastily hailed law enforcement assistants. "Innocent until proven guilty" may be difficult to negotiate if a speeding trucker is attempting to enact roadside intervention with a suspect's automobile. Third, such a move creates a dependence on media and law enforcement to define emergencies and establishes their position of authenticating various identities.

The genealogical work urged by Foucault, Nietzsche, and others allows us to turn the matter away from the specifics of this particular project and toward a larger frame of consideration. Specifically, rather than question the value of safety and security, one must ask whether the technology of Amber as a protocol of protection indeed accomplishes what it purports, or perhaps instead works to serve a different purpose altogether. In offering benefit to a specific and localized audience, I believe it is possible that other interests are served. Valorizing the innocent may cover over a larger realm of less manageable national concerns, including the economy, white-collar crime, and political interest groups, creating a substitute conquest for the nation to applaud.

The Amber response serves a constitutive function, paradoxically inventing criteria that reinscribes loyalty and participation with a law enforcement system just as public confidence in the social order's capacity to manage world events seems most lacking. Although this particular technology seems to have been made possible by the patriotic fervor and child abduction media hype in recent days, it is perhaps useful to remember that official announcements throughout the World Trade Center buildings assured workers that all was well and instructed them to return to their offices. Like Charland's (1987) Quebecois, the citizen is driven to act in the illusion of agency, here reinscribing loyalty to keepers of the social order. Finally, the production of a deviant in need of policing by the deputized subject citizen in the name of the children occupies the subject citizen with a specific and normalized construction of relevant criminal behavior—putting public attention toward what Liazos called "crime in the streets," instead of the large-scale institutional "crime in the suites" (Henderschott, 2002).

Further considerations beyond Amber might probe what defines a *child abduction* or how a particular suspect or criminal becomes the most wanted. The support for Amber, regardless of its future legislative direction or policing successes, raises important questions about how the need for safety and the current climate of fear have been affiliated together. This transformation is possible at whatever level the citizen acts, whether merely to observe, report, or participate directly with a suspect. Such a shift changes long-standing norms of citizen dependence on governmental bodies and law enforcement to maintain social order. Additionally, to follow through on exploring the portrait of the future as noted in Greene's materiality, other traces outside the Amber scene must be tracked to demonstrate how relationships enabled by the Amber discourse may also work to forge a new sensibility among citizens that goes far beyond child protection issues.

REFERENCES

Alert trucker: I'm no hero. (2002, October 24). From CNN.com. Retrieved from http://www.cnn.com/2002/US/South/10/24/sniper.truck.driver/

Amacher, P. (2003). Civil defense: You're on your own again. *Bulletin of the Atomic Scientists*, 59, 34-37, 40–43. Retrieved from http://www.thebulletin.org/issues/2003/mj03/mj03amacher.html

Blair, J. (2002, December 12). A nation challenged: Telecommunications; U.S. considers restricting cellphone use in disasters. *New York Times*. Retrieved September 16, 2002 from *http://www.nytimes.com*.

Bumiller, E. (2003, October 3). Bush unveils upgrade of Amber Alert system. *New York Times*. Retrieved from nytimes.com.

Burns, R. (2001, September). "Amber plan: Hue and cry." *Partnerships*, a publication of Community Policing. Retrieved from http://www.communitypolicing.org/publications/comlinks/cl16/cl16_burns.htm.

Bush backs Amber Alert expansion: Adds coordinator at Justice Department. (2002). Retrieved October 22, 2002 from http://c1.zedo.com/ads2/i/3853/172/167000003/0/i.html?e=i;s=11;m=101;w=49;b=;z=0.9768179788902742

Bush promises $10 million for Amber system. (2002, October 3). *Free Press News*

Service. Retrieved October 21, 2002, from http://www.freep.com/news/nw/amber3_20021003.htm.

Charland, M. (1987). Constitutive rhetoric: The case of the peuple Quebecois. *Quarterly Journal of Speech, 73*, 133–150.

Experts: Most abducted children are returned safely. (2003, March 12). Retrieved from http://www.cnn.com/2003/US/West/03/12/smart.missing.children.ap/index.

Fleissner, D., & Heinzelmann, F. (1996, August). *Crime prevention through environmental design and community policing*. National Institute of Justice Research in Action newsletter. U.S. Department of Justice.

Fox, J. A. (2002, August 17). Amber Alert's dangers. *New York Times*. Retrieved September 16, 2002, from http://www.nytimes.com.

Greene, R. W. (1998a). The aesthetic turn and the rhetorical perspective on argumentation. *Argumentation and Advocacy, 35*, 19–29.

Greene, R. W. (1998b). Another materialist rhetoric. *Critical Studies in Mass Communication, 15*, 21–31.

Henderschott, A. (2002). *The politics of deviance*. San Francisco: Encounter Books.

Hendricks, T. (2003, March 16). Richmond girl found safe by tow truck driver in L.A.: Amber Alert leads to capture of suspect, rescue of 12-year old, p. A28. *San Francisco Chronicle*. Retrieved November 25, 2003, from http://www.sfgate.com/cgi-bin/article.cgi?file=/chronicle/archive/2003/03/16/BA126709.DTL

Huse, C. (2003, March 14). Lawmakers rush to back a national alert system. *New York Times*. Retrieved May 25, 2003 from http://nytimes.com.

Kidnapped teens are rescued just in time: Man was close to killing California girls; alert system is credited. (2002, August 2). Retrieved from http://www.freep.com/news/nw/kidnap2_20020802.htm.

Lee, H. (2002, August 31). Amber Alert runs into snags in Bay Area. *San Francisco Chronicle*. Retrieved October 22, 2002 from http://www.itsa.org/itsnews.nsf/$All/84693A184E9869A185256C28007C01D7.

Miller, T. (1993). *The well-tempered self: Citizenship, culture, and the postmodern*. Baltimore: Johns Hopkins University Press.

Salecl, R. (1998). For the love of the nation: Ceausescu's Disneyland. In *(Per)versions of love and hate* (pp. 79-103). London: Verso.

Stolberg, S. G. (2003, May 8). From CNN to Congress, legislation by anecdote. *New York Times*. Retrieved from nytimes.com.

U.S. Office of the President. (2002). *The National Security Strategy of the United States*. Retrieved September 21, 2002, from http://www.nytimes.com and http://www.whitehouse.gov/homeland/book/nat_strat_hls.pdf.

What is AOL's role in AMBER alerts? (n.d.). Retrieved October 21, 2002, from www.aol.com keyword AMBER.

Wilson, J. Q., & Kelling G. (1982, March). Broken windows. *Atlantic Monthly*. Cited in D. Fleissner & F. Heinzelmann (1996, August), Crime prevention through environmental design and community policing. National Institute of Justice Research in Action newsletter. U.S. Department of Justice.

CHAPTER SEVEN

A Content Analysis of Sex Bias in International News Magazines

YANA VAN DER MEULEN RODGERS
RUTGERS UNIVERSITY

JING YING ZHANG
COLLEGE OF WILLIAM AND MARY

THIS CHAPTER USES A CONTENT ANALYSIS to explore the degree to which pictures in the leading international news magazines contain sex bias. In a dual interpretation of sex bias, the methodology focuses on how frequently the magazines portray females in their pictures relative to males, and the extent to which pictures of females and males contain sexual images. Sexual images include nudity, provocative clothing, or a suggestive pose. This dual approach to examining sex bias conforms with a well-established technique in content analyses, based on quantity and quality criteria, used to study gender and race in the media. The sample, taken from five widely read news magazines with international coverage, includes all photographs and cartoon pictures accompanying feature news articles. To maintain focus on images in the featured news, pictures accompanying advertisements and short news briefs are excluded.

The analysis contributes to the broader research agenda on how women are depicted in the international mass media. This rich body of literature covers numerous countries, a long time span, and a range of media types, including TV and films, newspapers and magazines, radio, and advertising (see Dines & Humez, 1995; Rhode, 1999; Sapiro, 1999). The cumulative body of research on media impacts has demonstrated the power of the media in shaping public perceptions of women and in influencing public discourse. Findings specific to news magazines indicate that the typical reader of news magazines looks at most, if not all, of the pictures, but reads far fewer of the stories (see Gilens, 1999). Furthermore, readers of news stories are more likely to remember the pictures, than the words. News magazines have a wide audience: About 20% of American adults claim to be regular readers of news magazines, and the leading news magazines are the most frequently cited news sources for other journalists. Finally, pictures can enhance the visibility and persuasiveness of a text message. Despite the apparently strong influence of news magazines in shaping perceptions, except for advertising images little previous work has examined sex bias in their published feature-related pictures. Hence, this study's documentation of sex bias in news-magazine pictures will improve our understanding of the channels through which news magazines—as integral parts of the mass media and as sources of information in the classroom—shape perceptions of women.

THE BROADER RESEARCH AGENDA

Supporting evidence in existing studies on gender in the media is often drawn from content analyses based on two criteria. The first is a quantity-based criterion, sometimes labeled as *recognition*, which focuses on the frequency that a certain demographic group appears in the media relative to a comparison group or population mean. The second is a quality-based criterion, sometimes labeled as *respect*, which focuses on how the demographic group is treated or portrayed (Clark, 1972). Examples of both criteria are found in the following description of American women as portrayed on TV in the late 1970s:

> Females constitute 27.7% of the U.S. population. Half of them are teenagers or in their 20s. They wear revealing outfits, jiggle a lot, but don't do much else. More than a third are unemployed or without any identifiable pursuit or purpose. Most others are students, secretaries, homemakers, household workers, or nurses. (U.S. Commission on Civil Rights; cited in Sapiro, 1999, p. 243)

Across media types, recognition criteria point to the continued underrepresentation of women relative to men. Women are underrepresented among characters in TV programming and big-screen films, among newscasters, among the subjects of newspaper stories, and among athletes in sports magazines. However, the degree of underrepresentation appears to have lessened since the late 1960s, with women gaining increasingly more media coverage relative to that of men. For example, Signorielli and Bacue (1999) found that the proportion of prime-time TV characters who are female rose from 24% in 1967 to 38% in 1998.

Across media types, respect criteria point to the portrayal of women in more passive and subservient roles, whereas men are portrayed in active and dominant roles. Furthermore, the media places more emphasis on the physical appearance of women than that of men. In TV and films, women are younger than men, and women are more likely to play roles in comedies, whereas men are more likely to play roles in action-adventure programs.[1] Similarly, news sources tend to marginalize female athletes with the depiction of weak character traits and less focus on their athletic ability. For example, Kinnick (1998) found that in their coverage of the 1996 summer Olympics, leading U.S. newspapers were more likely to discuss the good looks, marital status, and emotionality of female athletes than male athletes.[2] Through their suggestive messages, advertisements perpetuate female stereotypes with their focus on women's interests in appearance, housework, and romance. Demographic targeting also influences the content of advertisements. For example, Craig (1992) found that TV commercials that air during the weekend afternoon sportscasts, when the audience is primarily male, tend to portray men in situations featuring escape from household obligations.[3] There are some indications of favorable changes in the 1990s relative to earlier decades, with females in the media engaged in more activities outside of the home, in fewer stereotypical occupations, and in more assertive roles.[4]

Because news magazines are used extensively in classrooms as instructional supplements, this chapter also contributes to a broader research agenda on gender bias in the classroom. Sex bias in scholarly materials has important ramifications for several reasons. In the United States, textbooks are subject to Title IX of the Education Amendments Act of 1972, which

---

1. In the slasher-film genre, "respect" criteria related to sexuality indicate that female characters who do not survive a slasher attack are more likely to exhibit sexual traits relative to male characters. Slasher films then help to reinforce the detrimental link made in the media between female sexuality and violence (Cowan & O'Brien 1990).

2. Cross-country evidence reviewed in Crossman, Hyslop, and Guthrie (1994) indicates that underrepresentation and trivialization of female athletes in sports coverage are widespread.

3. In related work, Thomas and Treiber (2000) argued that the status of men and women is portrayed differently in print advertisements across popular magazines that differ in their target audience. Commercials during children's TV programming also contain extensive sex-role stereotyping, particularly in single-sex commercials (Larson, 2001; Smith, 1994).

4. For instance, in the last decade, sex-role stereotyping has become less extensive in advertising in the United States, Great Britain, New Zealand, and Canada (Furnham & Farragher, 2000; Zhou & Chen, 1997).

prohibits sex discrimination in federally funded educational institutions. This legislation has made sex bias in instructional materials a legal issue. A growing number of academic organizations have adopted guidelines for achieving greater gender balance in the curriculum. Within economics, in 1991, the AEA's Committee for Race and Gender Balance in the Economics Curriculum adopted a set of guidelines for recognizing and avoiding sexist biases in economics, including the pejorative or stereotypical labeling of women. Feminist scholars are leading current calls to devise solutions for sex-bias problems in the curriculum across disciplines and educational levels, from secondary school to the university (see Feiner, 1993).

For younger children, the reading materials chosen by elementary-school teachers overlap with those chosen by parents and preschool teachers who read aloud to young children. Just as the act of reading to young children yields well-documented benefits, the content of the reading materials matters for the development of children's views of society.[5] With their choices of textbooks and children's picture books, teachers and parents are effectively influencing the attitudes that children have about self-image and sex roles. In general, instructional material with sexist content contributes to attitudes based on sex stereotypes, whereas material with more neutral content contributes to more balanced attitudes toward sex roles (Schau & Scott, 1984). Numerous studies on sex bias in the text and pictures of children's literature have shown that females are underrepresented relative to males, particularly among the main characters of books. The problem is more severe for females of color. Children's books tend to depict females as passive, caring, and emotional, whereas males are depicted as aggressive, competitive, and independent. Few females are shown in occupational roles (see Evans & Davies, 2000; Ramirez & Dowd, 1997). Gender-focused content analyses of pictures and photographs in teaching materials at the university level are far less common than at the primary-school level, although many higher level textbooks and supplementary materials contain pictures.[6]

---

5. Leibowitz (1977) and Zuckerman and Kahn (2000) argued that reading aloud to children is the most significant determinant of the development of children's verbal and literacy skills. Reading to children also improves school performance and labor market outcomes (Lynch, 2000).

6. A few content analyses of textbook photographs—reviewed in Low and Sherrard (1999)—have been conducted in the psychology, human development, and human sexuality fields.

The sample contains a cross-section of all issues in the year 2000 of *Business Week*, *The Economist*, the *Far Eastern Economic Review*, *Newsweek*, and *Time*. These magazines are chosen because they are national and international in coverage and distribution, they are considered to be leading competitors, and they publish many pictures. *The Economist* is edited in the United Kingdom and printed in multiple countries, the *Far Eastern Economic Review* is published in Hong Kong, and the remaining magazines are published in the United States. To examine trends, a time-series sample is constructed from all issues of *The Economist* in every even-numbered year from 1982 to 2000.[7] The beginning year marks the first complete year following *The Economist*'s switch in its publication format from a newspaper to a glossy magazine.

Both the cross-section and time-series samples include all photographs and cartoon pictures accompanying feature articles. Pictures on cover pages are also included. Advertisements, maps, graphs, charts, and pictures accompanying short news briefs (commonly one paragraph in length) are excluded from the sample.[8] No single picture is double counted even if it appears more than once in an issue. All pictures are classified according to female or male status of the individual(s) in focus, and according to sexual content. Pictures containing both males and females are counted separately, as are pictures featuring objects or nonidentifiable individuals. Sexual content includes frontal nudity, rear nudity, partial breast exposure, provocative clothing, or a suggestive pose. These criteria for sexual content are arguably subjective. To help limit subjectivity bias, most instances of

---

7. The time-series sample is limited to *The Economist* because it is the most international in scope, with the greatest focus on economic and political analysis (as opposed to entertainment). Some year-end double issues contain days in the first week of the new year. For example, the December 24, 1983, issue of *The Economist* covers dates through January 6, 1984. Overlap issues are included in the sample if a portion of the issue date coincides with the sample period.

8. This exclusion applies to, for example, *The Economist*'s News Briefs section; the *Far Eastern Economic Review*'s Regional Briefing and Business Briefing sections, *Time*'s Notebook, People, and Milestones sections; *Newsweek*'s Periscope, Cyberscope, and Newsmakers sections; and *Business Week*'s Readers Report and Up Front sections. Special editions published in addition to the regular weekly issues, such as *Time*'s Winter 2000 Year in Review and its Spring 2000 issue on Earth Day, are excluded to ensure comparability in magazine coverage.

nudity and partial nudity are included in the sexual content categories even if the apparent intent of the magazine article may not be to convey sexuality. Provocative clothing is form-fitting or revealing, while a suggestive pose is one that conveys sexual intent. In general, if a questionable picture relates directly to the content of the article and arguably cannot be substituted with an alternative picture showing more complete body coverage, that picture is excluded from the sexual content categories. For example, pictures of nude persons from poor countries and pictures of athletes in tight or skimpy uniforms are considered to contain no sexual content if they are used in the appropriate context.

This classification strategy produces 10 categories:[9] (a) just female, with sexual content; (b) just female, with no sexual content; (c) just male, with sexual content; (d) just male, with no sexual content; (e) both female and male, with female sexual content; (f) both female and male, with male sexual content; (g) both female and male, with female and male sexual content; (h) both female and male, with no sexual content; (i) unidentifiable individual(s), with male or female status not clear; and (j) object, including buildings, animals, and art pieces.[10] For classifying pictures as just female, female status must be clearly identifiable for all individuals who are in focus, and similarly for classifying pictures as just male. For the combined female and male pictures, female status must be clearly identifiable for at least one individual in focus, and male status must be clearly identifiable for at least one individual in focus. Pictures contain-

---

9. Pictures of people holding babies are classified according to the gender of the adult only. Back issues of The Economist differ noticeably from the other news magazines in the use of pictures of males in drag clothing. Because these pictures were not revealing male sexuality or male body parts, we excluded them from the category of male with sexual content. The number of pictures of males in drag clothing averages about three per year. Among other magazines in the sample for the year 2000, only Newsweek contained one image of a male in drag clothing.

10. Pictures with both objects and people are coded as "object" if the object is considerably larger than the person and it is the focus of the picture. The art review sections of the news magazines sometimes contained pictures featuring portraits of nudes. We noted the editors' seemingly frequent use of female nudes, rather than say landscapes or male nudes to illustrate articles. To avoid potential controversy for classifying nudes as sexually explicit material, we included all pictures of portrait nudes that appeared in the art review section in the nonpersonified category.

ing sexual content are further categorized according to the type of sexual content, the topic of the accompanying article, and whether the picture is directly related to the topic.[11]

RESULTS

Results from the cross-section analysis indicate that all magazines publish far fewer pictures featuring just females relative to pictures featuring just males, and even relative to pictures of objects. Table 7.1 presents results for the total number of pictures by category—along with the share of each category in the total—for each magazine in 2000. *Business Week* is by far the most picture-intensive, with almost 5,400 pictures for the year, or about 108 pictures in a typical issue. The *Far Eastern Economic Review* publishes the fewest, with about 2,400 pictures for the year, or about 46 pictures per issue. Of the total pictures, the two foreign-based magazines (*The Economist* and the *Far Eastern Economic Review*) publish proportionately the fewest pictures featuring just females with no sexual content. Less than 7% of *The Economist*'s pictures and less than 9% of the *Far Eastern Economic Review*'s pictures feature just females, compared with about 10% to 13% in the American-based magazines. An average single issue of *The Economist* or the *Far Eastern Economic Review* contains only 4 to 5 pictures featuring just females with no sexual content, compared with 10 to 12 in the others. At the other extreme, *The Economist* and the *Far Eastern Economic Review* publish proportionately the most pictures of just males with no sexual content. About 52% to 55% of their pictures feature just males, compared with 44% to 50% in the other magazines. All of the magazines publish proportionately more pictures of objects than pictures of just females. For example, 23% of pictures in *Time* feature objects, compared with 13% that feature just females with no sexual content.

All of the news magazines include sexually suggestive material in the pictures that accompany their feature articles. Perhaps not surprising given their relatively larger emphasis placed on entertainment news, *Newsweek* and *Time* publish proportionately more pictures containing sexual content for females. In particular, about 2% of all pictures in *Newsweek* and *Time* contain sexual images of females, including those found in pictures of both males and females. This share amounts to roughly two pictures in a typical issue of *Newsweek* and *Time*. In all magazines, just half a percent of all pictures or less contain sexual images of males.

---

11. Sample pictures are available from the author on request.

Table 7.1. Picture Categories by Total Number and Share for Year 2000

CATEGORY	BUSINESS WEEK		ECONOMIST		FEER		NEWSWEEK		TIME	
	TOTAL	SHARE	TOTAL	SHARE	TOTAL	SHARE	TOTAL	SHARE	TOTAL	SHARE
Just female: sexual content	15	0.3%	23	0.7%	5	0.2%	43	1.0%	55	1.2%
Just female: no sexual content	523	9.7%	227	6.5%	209	8.7%	521	12.1%	605	12.9%
Just male: sexual content	7	0.1%	10	0.3%	4	0.2%	14	0.3%	17	0.4%
Just male: no sexual content	2695	49.9%	1904	54.8%	1244	51.9%	2105	48.8%	2053	43.9%
Female & male: female sexual content	15	0.3%	10	0.3%	6	0.3%	39	0.9%	29	0.6%
Female & male: male sexual content	0	0.0%	1	0.0%	1	0.0%	0	0.0%	2	0.0%
Female & male: both sexual content	0	0.0%	7	0.2%	2	0.1%	5	0.1%	9	0.2%
Female & male: no sexual content	513	9.5%	404	11.6%	330	13.8%	620	14.4%	704	15.1%
Unidentifiable individual	267	4.9%	262	7.5%	147	6.1%	126	2.9%	148	3.2%
Object	1362	25.2%	627	18.0%	451	18.8%	838	19.4%	1054	22.5%
Total pictures	5397	100.0%	3475	100.0%	2399	100.0%	4311	100.0%	4676	100.0%

Table 7.2 reports further sample statistics comparing the representation of males and females across magazines. A startling set of figures emerge: In *The Economist, Newsweek,* and *Time,* about 8% to 9% of pictures featuring just females contain sexual images of females. Hence, given a picture featuring just a woman in these magazines, there is an 8% to 9% chance that she will be depicted in a sexual manner. In contrast, across magazines, less than 1% of all pictures featuring just males contain sexual images of males. Also of note, *Newsweek* and *Time* publish three times as many pictures featuring just females with sexual content compared with just males with sexual content. Across magazines, pictures showing females and males together are far more likely to illustrate females in a sexual manner than males. At the upper extreme, 6% of all combined female and male pictures in *Newsweek* contain sexualized images of females, compared with 0% for males.

For pictures that feature just females or just males without sexual content, *The Economist* has the lowest representation of female pictures. For every 100 pictures featuring a single sex, there are only 11 pictures focusing on a female. At 23%, *Time* has the greatest female representation among pictures featuring a single sex. Given that these magazines devote most of their coverage to business, economic, and political news, it is illuminating to compare women's representation in the magazines with their overall representation in the labor market and politics. Among legislators, senior officials, and managers, the percent female is 45% in the United States, 33% in the United Kingdom, and a little over 20% in a number of higher income East Asian economies.[12] Similarly, among professional and technical workers, the percent female is 53% in the United States, 45% in the United Kingdom, and over 40% in numerous East Asian economies. Only figures for women's share of the very top political positions—14% in the United States and 17% in the United Kingdom—are comparable to figures in Table 7.2 for women's representation in the pictures of magazines covering the world of business and politics.

To describe the nature of sexuality found in the news magazines, Table 7.3 divides the subsample of sexually oriented pictures into various categories ranging from frontal nudity to suggestive pose. Overall, *Newsweek* and *Time* publish the most pictures containing sexual content. These magazines each published over 100 sexual pictures in 2000. The *Far East-*

---

12. Descriptive statistics on female shares in broad occupation groups are from United Nations Development Programme (2001).

Table 7.2. Female and Male Comparisons for Year 2000

CATEGORY	BUSINESS WEEK	ECONOMIST	FEER	NEWSWEEK	TIME
PICTURES OF JUST FEMALE OR JUST MALE					
Female sexual/female total	2.8%	9.2%	2.3%	7.6%	8.3%
Male sexual/male total	0.3%	0.5%	0.3%	0.7%	0.8%
Female sexual/male sexual	214.3%	230.0%	125%	307.1%	323.5%
Female no sexual/total no sexual	16.3%	10.7%	14.4%	19.8%	22.8%
Male no sexual/total no sexual	83.7%	89.3%	85.6%	80.2%	77.2%
PICTURES OF FEMALE AND MALE TOGETHER					
Female sexual/combined total	2.8%	2.4%	1.8%	5.9%	3.9%
Male sexual/combined total	0.0%	0.2%	0.3%	0.0%	0.3%
Both sexual/combined total	0.0%	1.7%	0.6%	0.8%	1.2%
Female sexual/male sexual	15:0	0.4173611	0.2506944	39:0	29:2

Table 7.3. Number of Pictures Containing Sexual Content, by Category, in Year 2000

CATEGORY	BUSINESS WEEK	ECONOMIST	FEER	NEWSWEEK	TIME
JUST FEMALE: SEXUAL CONTENT					
Frontal nudity	0	5	0	0	1
Partial breast exposure	7	11	0	23	24
Rear nudity	0	1	0	0	1
Provocative clothing	8	5	5	19	27
Suggestive pose	0	1	0	1	2
JUST MALE: SEXUAL CONTENT					
Frontal nudity	0	2	0	0	1
Rear nudity	0	0	0	0	0
Provocative clothing	6	8	4	14	16
Suggestive pose	1	0	0	0	0
FEMALE AND MALE: FEMALE SEXUAL CONTENT					
Frontal nudity	0	0	1	0	0
Partial breast exposure	5	5	0	17	14
Rear nudity	0	0	0	0	0
Provocative clothing	9	3	5	18	13
Suggestive pose	1	2	0	4	2
FEMALE AND MALE: MALE SEXUAL CONTENT					
Frontal nudity	0	0	0	0	1
Rear nudity	0	0	0	0	0
Provocative clothing	0	1	1	0	1
Suggestive pose	0	0	0	0	0
FEMALE AND MALE: BOTH SEXUAL CONTENT					
Frontal nudity	0	0	1	0	0
Rear nudity	0	2	0	1	1
Provocative clothing	0	3	1	1	8
Suggestive pose	0	2	0	3	0
TOTAL PICTURES WITH SEXUAL CONTENT	37	51	18	101	112

ern *Economic Review* publishes the fewest sexually oriented pictures. *The Economist* publishes more frontal nudity in its female pictures than the other magazines combined, and it also publishes disproportionately more pictures with partial breast exposure than the other magazines. Like *Time*, *The Economist* publishes more female sexuality in pictures that focus on just females, compared with pictures that feature females and males together. Across magazines, the majority of pictures containing female sexual content depict either partial breast exposure or otherwise provocative clothing.

How are these sexually oriented pictures used? The magazines appear to be selling the news with occasional pictures of sex as attention-grabbing devices. Across magazines, the sexual pictures most often accompany articles on related topics such as pornography, travel, entertainment, and health. Placement of a sexually oriented picture in a leading political or economic news article is less common. Pictures containing sexually oriented images of entertainers are most prevalent in *Newsweek* and *Time*, given that these magazines have entire sections devoted to entertainment, whereas *Business Week*, *The Economist*, and the *Far Eastern Economic Review* are more likely to include sexually oriented pictures with special-interest articles. All magazines tend to place the sexually oriented pictures toward the back of the issue rather than the front. In some cases, the news magazines covered the same topic, but used pictures with varying degrees of sexuality to illustrate the article. For example, several of the magazines carried stories on the release of Sony's PlayStation 2.[13] *Business Week* published a picture of a bare-chested and well-toned male fighter. *The Economist* published the same picture, but also added a picture of a scantily clad female fighter showing ample cleavage. *Newsweek* devoted its cover story to the topic. The cover featured the same image of the male fighter, and pictures accompanying the article included two sexual images of females and no sexual images of males.

The Economist stands apart for its frequent use of sexual pictures to accompany articles on unrelated or semirelated topics, where the primary link between picture and topic is a pun or a metaphor in the caption. Among numerous examples, one picture showed a woman exposing most of her breasts in a strip tease—with the caption "The Thrust of Technology"—and accompanied an article on technological change. Another picture showed a woman holding two beverages while wearing a bikini with a gun taped to it—with the caption "Guns and Molls, as Ever"—and accompanied an ar-

---

13. *Business Week* (March 20, 2000, p. 58); *The Economist* (Feb. 26, 2000, p. 71); *Newsweek* (March 6, 2000, cover, p. 54, p. 61).

Guns and molls, as ever   **Growth indicator**

Figure 7.1. Sample pictures from *The Economist* with sexual content and pun.
(L) Photograph courtesy of *The Economist*. (R) Photograph courtesy of Stephen Wayda.

ticle on gun control. Another picture showed a bikini-clad woman revealing ample cleavage—with the caption "Growth Indicator"—and accompanied an article on statistical measures of growth. Another picture showed three female beauty-contest winners in skimpy bathing suits and high heels—with the caption "Pick Your Regulator"—and accompanied an article on the market for regulation.[14] Two of these examples are depicted in Figure 7.1. When used in this manner, *The Economist*'s sexually oriented pictures even appear in the leading political and economic news stories. These sexualized portrayals of women in *The Economist*, particularly when they are linked to an unrelated article through a pun in the caption, may reflect the "page-three girl" phenomenon at work. This idea describes the common trend among British tabloids to include a picture of a topless woman, typically on the third page, to promote sales. *The Economist* does not adhere to this practice literally because sexually oriented pictures are not limited to the third

---

14. Nov. 21, 1998, p. 15 (survey); May 16, 1992, p. 31; Aug. 3, 1996, p. 49; and March 7, 1998, p. 82.

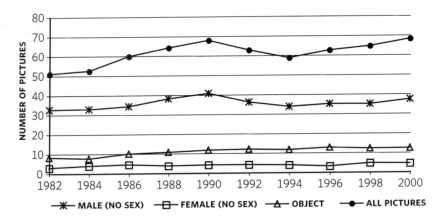

Figure 7.2. Number of pictures per issue in *The Economist*.

page of its issues. Despite its self-promotion as "one of the world's most authoritative and influential publications," this particular practice of regularly publishing nude and seminude women aligns *The Economist* more closely with the tabloid press.[15]

Thus far, results suggest that among news magazines, *The Economist* stands out for its low representation of females with no sexual content and its high representation of female frontal nudity. Are these patterns representative for *The Economist* in earlier years? Figure 7.2 shows that, although *The Economist*'s total number of pictures per issue has risen since 1982, the number of pictures featuring just females with no sexual content has remained stagnant at about four to five pictures per issue. This incidence is well below that of just males and also below that of objects in all years. Figure 7.3 shows that pictures with frontal nudity are a long-term feature of the magazine, particularly for females. Panel A shows the incidence of pictures depicting sexual images of females (found in pictures of just females as well as combined female–male pictures), and Panel B reports the corresponding results for males. For females, in all years there were at least three pictures containing full breast exposure; also, the frequency of publishing partial breast exposure has risen since 1994. The overall incidence of female sexual images has also risen steadily since 1994. For males, the incidence of sexually oriented pictures fluctuated during the 1990s, but exceeded that of the 1980s. The use of puns in captions to link these sexual pictures to the article also extends back in time for both female and male nudity. Furthermore,

---

15. This promotion statement is taken from www.economist.com.

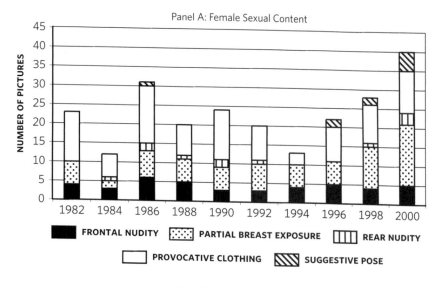

Panel A: Female Sexual Content

FRONTAL NUDITY   PARTIAL BREAST EXPOSURE   REAR NUDITY

PROVOCATIVE CLOTHING   SUGGESTIVE POSE

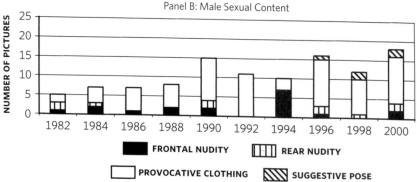

Panel B: Male Sexual Content

FRONTAL NUDITY   REAR NUDITY

PROVOCATIVE CLOTHING   SUGGESTIVE POSE

Figure 7.3. All pictures containing sexual content in *The Economist*.

captions with sexual innuendo for pictures containing no explicit sexual material are also a long-term feature of the magazine.[16]

CONCLUSIONS

This chapter has found a striking underrepresentation of females in the pictures published in leading international news magazines. Although the sample's foreign-based magazines have a particularly low representation of

---

16. For example, a picture containing a fully dressed male miner—with the caption "Hands Off My Rocks"—accompanied a 1982 article on the mining industry.

females relative to males in their pictures, the American-based magazines record proportions that are not much higher. For example, in the *Far Eastern Economic Review,* less than 9% of all pictures feature just females, compared with 52% for pictures that feature just males. In a representative American magazine, 12% of all pictures in *Newsweek* feature just females, compared with 49% for pictures that feature just males. Not only are females underrepresented relative to males, but also relative to the female share of legislative, managerial, and technical jobs that are often the topic of these magazines.

All of the international news magazines sampled publish pictures containing sexual images. Among pictures with sexual content, females are overrepresented relative to males in all magazines. The overrepresentation is highest in *Newsweek* and *Time,* which have a whole section devoted to entertainment news that often carries pictures with sexual content. Most sexual content involves images with partial nudity or provocative clothing. Many of the indicators presented suggest that, compared with other news magazines, *The Economist* publishes disproportionately more images of females with full nudity. These findings are consistent with existing research on other types of mass media: "Recognition" criteria indicate that women are underrepresented, and "respect" criteria point to the focus on women's physical appearance and their subservience to men. Images of women in popular culture have become increasingly sexualized, particularly in the tabloid press, in magazines aimed at women, and in magazines aimed at men. This study has argued that even the relatively highbrow publishing domain of economic and political news analysis is not free from overt sexualization. Given that the international news magazines already have a low representation of women compared with their presence in professional occupations, it is a concern that up to 10% of pictures featuring women contain sexual content.

Broader research on the role of the media strongly suggests that this portrayal of females in news magazine photographs influences the way readers perceive women. Pictures containing derogatory images of women perpetuate stereotypes of women as sexual objects, with potential real repercussions in how women and girls are treated in labor markets, schools, homes, and communities around the world. For example, the hiring decisions of men in positions of power in the business world may be influenced by images they see in their news magazines containing sexually explicit material. Furthermore, a large number of professional economists and students regularly read news magazines as a supplementary source of economics information. Professors assigning articles in class from news magazines or encouraging their students to read these economics news magazines are then helping to perpetuate sexual stereotypes of their female students. Further research on reader responses to news magazine photographs would help us to better understand the extent to which these suggested impacts actually occur in professional and social settings.

ACKNOWLEDGMENTS

The authors gratefully acknowledge Jill Behnke, Ryan Letourneau, Leisa Meyer, Bill Rodgers, Fredrika Teute, Barry Trott, and participants of the Women's Studies and Black Studies seminar series at the College of William and Mary for their helpful suggestions. We also thank Annette Joseph-Walker and Larry Warren for their technical assistance. This research was conducted while Rodgers was at the College of William and Mary and was supported by a Faculty Research Assignment from the College.

REFERENCES

Clark, C. (1972). Race, identification, and television violence. In G. Comstock, E. Rubinstein, & J. Murray (Eds.), *Television and social behavior: Volume 5. Television's effects: Further explorations*. Washington, DC: U.S. Government Printing Office.

Cowan, G., & O'Brien, M. (1990). Gender and survival vs. death in slasher films: A content analysis. *Sex Roles*, 23(3/4), 187–196.

Craig, R. S. (1992). The effect of television day part on gender portrayals in television commercials: A content analysis. *Sex Roles*, 26(5/6), 197–211.

Crossman, J., Hyslop, P., & Guthrie, B. (1994). A content analysis of the sports section of Canada's national newspaper with respect to gender and professional/amateur status. *International Review for the Sociology of Sport*, 29(2), 123–133.

Dines, G., & Humez, J. (Eds.). (1995). *Gender, race, and class in media*. Thousand Oaks, CA: Sage.

Evans, L., & Davies, K. (2000). No sissy boys here: A content analysis of the representation of masculinity in elementary school reading textbooks. *Sex Roles* 42(3/4), 255–270.

Feiner, S. (1993). Introductory economics textbooks and the treatment of issues relating to women and minorities, 1984 and 1991. *Journal of Economic Education*, 24(2), 145–162.

Furnham, A., & Farragher, E. (2000). A cross-cultural content analysis of sex-role stereotyping in television advertisements: A comparison between Great Britain and New Zealand. *Journal of Broadcasting & Electronic Media*, 44(3), 415–436.

Gilens, M. (1999). *Why Americans hate welfare: Race, media, and the politics of antipoverty policy*. Chicago: University of Chicago Press.

Kinnick, K. (1998). Gender bias in newspaper profiles of 1996 Olympic athletes: A content analysis of five major dailies. *Women's Studies in Communication*, 21(2), 212–237.

Larson, M. (2001). Interactions, activities and gender in children's television commercials: A content analysis. *Journal of Broadcasting & Electronic Media, 45*(1), 41–56.

Leibowitz, A. (1977). Parental inputs and children's achievement. *Journal of Human Resources, 12*(2), 242–251.

Low, J., & Sherrard, P. (1999). Portrayal of women in sexuality and marriage and family textbooks: A content analysis of photographs from the 1970s to the 1990s. *Sex Roles, 40*(3/4), 309–318.

Lynch, L. (2000). Trends in and consequences of investments in children. In S. Danziger & J. Waldfogel (Eds.), *Securing the future: Investing in children from birth to college* (pp. 19–46). New York: Russell Sage Foundation.

Ramirez, M., & Dowd, F. (1997). Another look at the portrayal of mexican-american females in realistic picture books: A content analysis, 1990-1997. *MultiCultural Review, 6*(4), 20–27.

Rhode, D. (1999). Media images, feminist images. In A. Kesselman, L. McNair, & N. Schniedewind (Eds.), *Women: Images and realities* (pp. 90–94). London: Mayfield.

Sapiro, V. (1999). *Women in American society: An introduction to women's studies.* London: Mayfield.

Schau, C., & Scott, K. (1984). Impact of gender characteristics of instructional materials: An integration of the research literature. *Journal of Educational Psychology, 76*(2), 183–193.

Signorielli, N., & Bacue, A. (1999). Recognition and respect: A content analysis of prime-time television characters across three decades. *Sex Roles, 40*(7/8), 527–544.

Smith, L. (1994). A content analysis of gender differences in children's advertising, *Journal of Broadcasting & Electronic Media, 38*(3), 323-337.

Thomas, M., & Treiber, L. (2000). Race, gender, and status: A content analysis of print advertisements in four popular magazines. *Sociological Spectrum, 20*(3), 357–371.

United Nations Development Programme. (2001). *Human Development Report 2001.* New York and Oxford: Oxford University Press.

Zhou, N., & Chen, M. (1997). A content analysis of men and women in Canadian consumer magazine advertising: Today's portrayal, yesterday's image? *Journal of Business Ethics, 16*(5), 485–495.

Zuckerman, B., & Kahn, R. (2000). Pathways to early child health and development. In S. Danziger & J. Waldfogel (Eds.), *Securing the future: Investing in children from birth to college* (pp. 87-121). New York: Russell Sage Foundation.

CHAPTER EIGHT

Women's Public Image at the Crossroads

Negotiating Pieties and Paganism in a Southern City

LEANNE STUART PUPCHEK
QUEENS UNIVERSITY OF CHARLOTTE

S TATESVILLE, NORTH CAROLINA, a city of about 22,000 people, is located in the rolling piedmont of the Blue Ridge Mountains. Summers are lush green and hot, and winters are dusty gray and mild, punctuated irregularly by ice and snow. Statesville emanates from the crossroads of Interstates 77 and 40, an "X" on the map about an hour's drive north of Charlotte. Its population is small enough to have relied on its size and geography to provide it with a sense of community for 250 years.

But a small population pays small taxes. In the dusk of the 20th century, Statesville's matter-of-fact civic and business leaders found themselves seeking strategies to leverage the economic boom of the 1990s to put their city on the map of economic development.

The crossroads at Statesville has a long commercial history. Two Native American trade routes met here. The area began attracting European settlers about 1753 (Greater Statesville Chamber of Commerce, 2004). By 2001, the Chamber of Commerce was selling Statesville to potential business investors as a "mecca of modern business," the "Number One small town in America for new industrial growth," one of the "Best Cities for Business in North Carolina," and "home to some of the most notable names in commerce today" (Greater Statesville Chamber of Commerce, 2000, stale Web site text, files of author). Such adjectival phrases could have described one of any number of small cities in the region, and therein lay the difficulty: How was Statesville any different from other towns and cities in the United States vying for the same business investment dollars?

Somehow civic leaders had to brand Statesville in the marketing sense of the word; they had to identify and publicize features of the city that would differentiate it from like locales and provide it with a competitive advantage when compared with other potential business venues. The challenge for civic leaders was to devise a way to characterize the city's charms for potential external investors while promoting civic pride and community spirit for the population, both native and new. The Statesville brand would distinguish it from the encroaching sprawl of Charlotte and allow the city to grow its population and tax base to achieve the economic prosperity that its history demanded.

In 1997, the city took two major steps toward a profitable and bright future. First, Statesville applied for and attained the designation "All-American City." Second, it purchased the land for a civic center. Civic leaders identified the entryway of that new civic center as the place to make a public statement about their community. They commissioned one-time resident Ben Long, an artist with an international reputation, to envision their community in images—not simply to paint a historical mural, but to create a world-class work of public art that would draw attention to the town and its potential. Long responded by creating the fresco *Images at the Crossroads*, which he completed amid controversy in January 2001. The controversy regarding the fresco revealed intersections of a number of separate discourses, including historical, art historical, and religious. The historical context evokes women's mythologized Southern Belle role, complicated by woman's historical and contemporary role in the Southern Baptist Church, and the Christian church's relationship with images. The art historical context, too, recalls visual art's importace in religious observance and celebration, enhanced by the confrontations and questions of feminist art criticism.

This chapter examines how the creation of the fresco *Images at the Crossroads* and the controversy it generated have clearly identified Statesville in a historical moment of transition: moving from its past as a city of neighbors to a future as a city of citizens. To discuss how this work of public art has revealed the community negotiating this transition, I first describe the fresco; second, I outline the controversy; and third, I analyze the controversy by examining historical, art historical and religious discourses that intersect in discussions about it. Finally, I reveal how rhetoric offers a way to understand and mitigate, if not reconcile, the oppositional logics that emerge.

The time of transition in which Statesville finds itself presents a significant opportunity for its people to discuss the future they envision for their city. Statesville is awakening from being a taken-for-granted town with a relatively insulated monolithic culture of assumed (if not actual) common interests to being a reflective settlement that will have to work hard at constructing a community by identifying and negotiating beliefs and values common to an increasingly outward-looking, disparate population with divergent interests. Ben Long's work of public art, *Images at the Crossroads*, has forced Statesville to examine long-standing social assumptions and renegotiate its community beliefs and values to fashion a civic identity that everyone in town can embrace.

THE FRESCO

In 1997, the city of Statesville commissioned Ben Long, a "distinguished portrait painter" (Beck, 2001, p. 14A), to paint a fresco on the wall of the lobby of the city's new civic center. The city council offered him $325,000 and expenses, raised from private sources, to "create his best fresco ever" (Marshall, 2000, para. 3). Raised in Statesville, Long had left decades before to study art, first at the University of North Carolina, then at the Art Students League of New York, and finally in Italy, apprenticing to the world-renowned fresco painter Pietro Annigoni, who was once the official painter of Elizabeth II of England.

Long was drawn to the art of the Italian Renaissance. He had "meticulously rejected" popular artistic styles such as abstract expressionism and pop art that made rich men of artists like Pollock, Warhol, Lichtenstein and Rauschenberg, but appeared "to deny the power and spirit of nature and the natural world to which he is entirely devoted" (Beck, 2001, p. 14A). Rather, he "sought to perpetuate" the art and technique of fresco, "with considerable sacrifice"—after all it took a lifetime to master, and there was not much call for it. But master it he did, as he demonstrated in churches in Italy, Charlotte, and the mountains of North Carolina, as well as in Charlotte's cathedrals of business, notably the Bank of America Corporate Center and the Monumental Dome of Transamerica Square. A Ben Long fresco is what Statesville wanted.

Fresco is a technique distinguished from traditional painting because the artist applies paint to wet plaster rather than to a dry surface. Prevalent in the Renaissance, it requires unique confidence and skill because the artist must complete the painting fast before the plaster dries. Fixing mistakes is time-consuming and labor-intensive; the artist must chip plaster supporting the mistake away from the wall, then quickly plaster the wall again and repaint it.

In November 2000, Ben Long's design for the fresco called *Images at the Crossroads* was made public. The design reflected the "crossroads" theme that civic leaders had discussed with the artist. The theme addressed both Statesville's geographic location and its moment in history, looking back and looking forward. Central to the design's composition, in the foreground against a background reflecting the local landscape of rolling hills and green pastures, stands the figure of Hecate, the three-headed Roman goddess of the Crossroads.

Hecate dominates the image, looking out, ahead, and behind. She stands just right of center (Plate 8.1, p. 279). Traditionally, her three faces would allow her to simultaneously portray classical womanhood's three aspects of Maiden, Mother and Crone. However Long's 21st-century Hecate exposes one aspect to the three directions—perhaps maiden, perhaps mother. She stands serenely, "her hand to her breast . . . an ancient signal of greeting—a sign of arrival" (City of Statesville, 2003, para. 1).

Directly in the center of the image stands a signpost that travelers arriving from each of the four compass points would perceive as a cross (Plate 8.2, p. 279). The word for God appears on the signs at the top of the post, in a distinct ancient language for each of the four directions. Framing the image of Hecate, Long depicts groups of people interacting in moments representing "everything from whimsy to horror, as life itself does" (Livingston, 2001, pp. 1–4A):

> There are lovers, workers, craftspeople, a lone dark figure on the hill that Long said could represent anything from Paladin, a knight of the middle ages, to a lost friend. And then there is the sow with the gloves on. This grotesque vignette is based on an actual story. In a French village in 1457 it happened that a huge sow killed a child and ate on it. The townspeople were so horrified that they didn't just slaughter the animal, but anthropomorphized it by placing gloves on its trotters. Then they hanged it as they would a human. A child's skull can be seen in the sow's mouth.

As Mayor Marshall (2000) told the City Council, "You can see phases of life. You can see justice and injustice. You see people cooperating and people walking alone. You see wealth and poverty" (para. 4).

Many of the faces are portraits. One face in the background belongs to a local artisan who has helped Long on many of his projects. Long's brother appears in one place. Long's sons play in front of his wife and new baby. These family depictions resonate particularly because the classical Hecate protected children and women in childbirth; Long's wife was pregnant when he began the final phase of the project, and she was able to pose with their new child as the painting was finished. Long makes a cameo appearance in the fresco, like Alfred Hitchcock in his films, as the face of the broken bust of a Confederate solder, lying on its side among fallen leaves in the lower right corner of the composition, chained as if toppled by force like a bust of Lenin or Saddam Hussein, the rejected remnants of domination.

Mayor Marshall (2000) emphasized:

> The word "crossroads" has always been important to this project. Ben caught on to the word in our first session and came back to us with an idea of a maiden, based on mythology, to symbolize the theme of "crossroads." Much like the sculptor for the Statue of Liberty used the Roman goddess *Libertas* as a model for the statue in New York Harbor, Ben used the goddess of the crossroads as a model for our maiden. Ben is very well read and loves classical literature and mythology. Ancient tales and myths can be found throughout the fresco—which really is about what happens when one's life is at a crossroads. (para. 4)

Long's design was accepted, and he began to work.

THE CONTROVERSY

For more than 2 months, Ben Long worked in the public space of the lobby of the Statesville civic center. The wall section that accepted the fresco plaster was 21 feet high and 19 feet wide. He completed the imposing *Images at the Crossroads* on January 9, 2001.

As his work progressed, the fresco's visual elements took shape, texture, dimension, and color. Increasingly, the images were discussed and interpreted in public. Indeed *Images at the Crossroads* caught the attention of local Christian leaders, who began to express their misgivings about the idea of an image of Hecate characterizing their community.

Protesters evoked the separation of church and state in public buildings. One chided, "We could not have a picture of Christ in there, I know. . . . But Hecate is a religious figure herself. She's well known as a leader of witches" (Wrinn, 2000, para. 4) The *Statesville Landmark and Record* published more than 40 letters to the editor on the topic, "some rather detailed in their denunciations" (Livingston, 2001, p. 4A). *Worthy News*, an online Christian news magazine, published a report that noted, "Though many evangelical ministers in the community of 22,000 are objecting to the work, the stalwart champion of the First Amendment, the ACLU, is nowhere to be found" (Boggs, 2000, para. 2). The report concluded, "If nothing is done [by the ACLU], they will reveal that it is not so much the separation of church and state that motivates them, rather it is specifically the separation of Christianity from the state they desire" (para. 11).

Pastor Ken Hudson of Landmark Church of God in Statesville expressed an opinion that reflected those of many of his local colleagues. He stated,

The subject matter [of the fresco] is a religious figure that is actively worshipped today in this country and even in this area. Hecate or The Goddess of The Crossroads is the central goddess worshipped by those who practice witchcraft. It is an active religion that is recognized by the U.S. government.... It was a mistake, it was a breach of law and it is a moral error. (personal communication, 2001)

Pastor Hudson, like Boggs (2000), used electronic sources to collect some of his information. He noted,

If you do a little search on the World Wide Web you will find that there are sites dedicated to [Hecate's] worship and there are followers who actually believe that she lives. Beyond the web, if you go to a local bookstore located in the mall you'll find two shelves of books instructing readers how to become a witch and all of them recognize Hecate as an object of worship. (personal communication, 2001)

Perhaps he had visited the Web site of the Sisters of the Craft, which attributed official Christian opposition to Hecate to her empowerment of women in the early Christian era and the threat that female power posed to hierarchical organizations. Although since recomposed, while Long was painting the fresco and for months afterward, the Web site published material contending,

The goddess Hecate is also known as the *liberator of women*, as she sets women free. *That is why the Christian Church* put Hecate down and created her as the Goddess of evil and destruction. (italics in original, stale Web text, files of author)

At a city council meeting, one Christian leader stated, "For [the fresco] to have such a prominent place in the city, it should be more representative of who we are. . . . We're going to have something divisive in this building that should unify us" (Wrinn, 2000, para. 11). Protesters noted that Hecate was antithetical to the values and beliefs for which Statesville stood. She was a pagan goddess at best, Satanistic at worst. She was not only anciently but also currently worshipped by Wiccans and practitioners of witchcraft (see e.g., Conway, 1994; Lady Hecatemoon, 2004; Sisters of the Craft, 2003; Von Rudloff, 1996). Her depiction and prominence in the fresco glamorized witches; it was tantamount to goddess worship and incompatible with God's admonition that there be no God but Him. They agreed that the image of Hecate was patently inappropriate for public display in a Christian community and certainly no way to characterize Statesville.

Expressing his own opinions grounded in this orientation, Pastor Hudson (personal communication, 2001) noted:

> I have real concerns as to the message [the fresco] is sending to the world regarding Statesville. Do we embrace witchcraft as a viable religion? Are we ready to accept and allow it to be practiced by the next generation? Young people are being bombarded by temptation and outright enlistment efforts by witches to join in their worship. . . . I personally believe witchcraft is wrong. Therefore I believe it is morally wrong to put an image in a prominent spot that represents something that I believe is wrong. There is so much more that could have been used besides a three-headed goddess that represents darkness and fear. I suppose the Wicca organization with over 600,000 members in the US alone will be happy to know that.

ANALYSIS

Technological advances have changed the environment in which audiences view visual images. In fact as is the case with many kinds of texts, visual images are often viewed by publics that do not know, understand, or appreciate the tradition within which they emerge, whether that tradition be artistic, religious, economic, or some other. Bryson (2003) clarified that in the last century, "Electronic reproduction enhanced the velocity of images, shortened their half-life, and rendered them weightless and decontextualized, radically detached from whatever place they had originally been made" (p. 229). The controversy regarding the fresco stems from the way different interlocutors have contextualized it.

That is not to say that among people who ascribe meanings to images some must be right and others wrong. Receiver-focused studies such as de Certeau (1984), Jenkins (1992), and Radway (1991) and have shown how creative and important alternative readings can be. Burke (1969) directed our attention to the intersections of multiple discourses, identifying them as "mediatory ground that makes . . . communication possible" (p. 25). Thus, if, as feminist art historian Griselda Pollock (1988) asserted, "Art which engages with the social world is political, sociological, narrative. . ." (p. 14), then we can look to very breadth of the discussion triggered by this work of public art and the narratives that emerge to locate opportunities for social change in the crossroads of political, sociological, and historical spheres. In terms of this study, reviewing the context of alternative readings and their intersections can provide productive suggestions for social change.

As Pollock (1988) emphasized, "Artists do not passively reproduce dominant ideology; they participate in its construction and alteration. Artists work in but also on ideology" (pp. 46–47). Ben Long illustrated Pollock's point in the strength of the central image of Hecate and when he assigns his Confederate soldier a place on the ground at her feet. Hecate's strength and domination of the image and her confident confrontation of the viewer challenge the rhetorical construct of southern femininity known as the Southern Belle (and, once married, the Southern Lady).

According to historian Alexis Brown (2000), the traditional, perhaps iconic, image of the Southern Belle characterizes a pre-Civil War white woman of the elite class embodying submissiveness. The Southern Belle reveals her superior status in her:

> delicacy, gentility, and hospitality within the domestic sphere of the household. . . .The highest roles to which a southern woman could aspire were those of nurturing mother, dutiful wife, and social moral pillar. Men, in contrast, operated in a public sphere, where they provided for their families and property and carried on business. These separate spheres constituted an unwritten contract between men and women, where women remained domestic and atop their pedestals, and men protected them. (p. 759)

Further, Sarah Gleeson-White (2001), reviewing the image of the Southern Belle in southern writing, notes in Carson McCullers' writing the emergence of "descriptions of ideal femininity" emphasizing "cleanliness and smallness, suggesting that the female body is both inherently dirty and in need of containment" (p. 113). Clean women were untouchable, and small women were easily overpowered and required protection.

Thus, as Brown (2000) noted,

> Southern society demanded that women remain under the protection of fathers, husbands, brothers, and even sons. Women could not even own property that was not inherited. Under the law of *coverture*, derived from English common law, a wife had no legal identity of her own. (p. 760)

While weighing the relative important of class, race and patriarchy, Jones (1989) confirmed,

> it is the peculiar relation of patriarchal attitudes toward women with the development of a hierarchical slave society that produced, in the early 19th century, both the South's most intense period of self-definition and the refinement of the images of the lady as the slaveholder's ideal—and the dominant ideal of the South. (p. 1529)

Religion in the South played a paradoxical role, both empowering women in one way and hobbling them in another. Brown (2000) noted that renewed religious commitment in the 1800s strengthened "the notion of piety and morality as important requirements of gentility, particularly in women" (p. 761). By contrast, women found the increasingly popular revival meetings to be "a religious outlet" that almost subversively "became an important part of women's growing sense of self-awareness." Said Brown, "the revival . . . provided a rare opportunity to become loud and rambunctious without violating the prescribed ideals of the belle." Women could be seen and heard in the context of church independent of their patriarchal keepers, who they "frequently referred to in words used for God: Lord and Master" (Scott; cited in Brown, 2000, p. 761).

Berkin (1989) acknowledged that history has questioned the mythology of southern women:

> Since the serious study of American women began in the 1970s, the southern woman has become a troublesome figure. . . . If she is white, she simply will not stay on her pedestal. . . . If she is black . . . . she is not content to be the linchpin of the planter's "domestic patriarchy," but is sometimes a fierce opponent of the peculiar institution. (p. 1519)

The requisite, yet complicit, silence of southern women made it difficult to learn that, "Each element of the image—leisure, passivity, dependence, sexual purity, submission, ignorance (with the possible exception of piety) failed to correspond to the reality of women's lives" (Jones, 1989, p. 1530). Indeed the strength, endurance, and independence of white women during the Civil War did little to mar their impression as Southern Belles: domestic, protected and subordinate.

Yet the social consequences of the image endured. As late as 2002, the Southern Baptist Convention, "the official 'established' church of the South" (Leonard, 1989, p. 1331), codified the submissiveness of the southern wife and inadmissibility of women pastors among their proscriptions for the feminine role. Yohn (2002) noted that, "Recent statements by denominational leaders that women should withdraw from public life are reiterations of a conservatism that has characterized much of Southern Baptist history" (p. 990).

As the evangelical critics recognized, Ben Long's Hecate is no Southern Lady. She is the anti-Belle: public, not private; dominant, not submissive; earthy, not sublime; gigantic, not small; powerful, not passive; knowledgeable, not ignorant; responsible, not innocent. She confronts the spectator directly, eye to eye, a woman subject "not available to the viewer's controlling, possessing or fantasizing gaze" (Pollock, 1988, p. 175.) Pollock asserted that "iconic quality of many of these images . . . resides in the particular combination of physical loveliness and a remote look" (p. 126). Long's Hecate can be inserted into this tradition. Such an icon might disconcert an institution, indeed a social system, that bases its legitimacy on patriarchy. The image of such a women, illustrating attitudes or behaviors that do not match the proscribed status of southern women, toys with social balance by questioning hierarchical, paternalistic (i.e., patriarchal) assumptions, and "threaten[ing] disorder" (p. 32).

To tread a slippery slope, if patriarchal assumptions are not safe, then the foundation on which the Christian church is based is called into question. This inevitable logic explains one aspect of the reaction from evangelical community churches to the image. On a basic level, the uproar reveals the disjunction between women and the archetypical patriarchal institution of the Christian church.

Indeed once Christianity began to dominate Western Europe in the first millennium, it denounced many other religious beliefs, especially colloquial and women-centered practices, as pagan. As early as the Middle Ages, Hecate and her associations with witchcraft were vilified by the Christian church as The Sisters of the Craft articulated earlier. She was a floating goddess in a sea of monotheism. Further, she was deemed an evil one. She was the Queen of Witches, associated with fire and dragons. She was the superior of the three weird sisters in *Macbeth* and even made an appearance in the play. Think of black-horned Malificent in Disney's *Sleeping Beauty*, who calls herself "Queen of Evil" and "Queen of Hell" as she transforms into a dragon, spewing fire and looming over the hero. Now envision her with three heads. These and similar images, promoted for hundreds of years by Western society, fund Pastor Hudson's characterization of Hecate worshippers as not only un-Christian and alien, but also dark and ultimately Satanistic.

Contrary to the assumptions of this bad PR, the 21st century's "New Goddess" does not lord over an organized religion per se. As Lefkowitz (1993) revealed:

> Unlike goddesses in the other religions we are familiar with, the New Goddess is worshipped primarily by women. Her cult has no designated places of worship or ordained clergy or official iconography. Rather, the Goddess is believed to reside in all females and can thus be present in any individual or any gathering of women. She is the central cult figure of the New Witchcraft and plays an increasingly important role in feminist theology. (p. 262)

The Statesville fresco's audience can be forgiven for thinking of the civic center image in the context of religious art, and not only because of Hecate's role as goddess. Interested viewers have been encouraged to place the Hecate in that tradition by virtue of the technique in which she is rendered: fresco. In the brochure available onsite or in stories on the Web or in the newspaper, interested viewers can learn fresco's connections to churches: It is a Renaissance technique. Michelangelo—perhaps the most familiar creator of religious images—used it on the Sistine Chapel ceiling; Ben Long has used it in churches both in Europe and North America.

In addition to such prompting, the Statesville fresco is linked to religious images because its look evokes the artistic style and traditional iconography of mass-produced devotional images that viewers might recognize. Despite theological arguments and institutional schisms that might suggest the contrary, religious imagery is important in the daily lives of religious faithful. As Morgan (1998) found, "Middle-class men and particularly women rely on devotional images to make the home a sacred space in a secular age that posits a disenchanted, demythologized universe" (p. 45). So the fresco stands at the crossroads of many conversations; art, religion, ideology, and sociopolitical narrative, all speaking to issues of confirming or questioning ideological constructions of gender, race and class. A lot of history and geography separates today from the Roman era, when Hecate was revered as goddess of the crossroads. Today in Statesville, Hecate's ability to disconcert can be found in the meanings ascribed to the representations of women, the social conventions of women's roles in the South and the Southern Baptist church, and the 2,000-year evolution of the reputation of Hecate.

DISCUSSION

Rhetoric, specifically Burke's theory of identification and division, offers a way to understand and mitigate, if not reconcile, the oppositional logics that emerge from the Statesville controversy. Analyzing the discussion prompted by the fresco reveals that the rhetoric of identity lies at the heart of the controversy.

For one thing, the controversy that surrounds the fresco illustrates the *rhetorical power* of the visual image—the capacity to promote identification and division—that contributes to the cultural meanings attached to particular images. The meanings associated with a particular image at any given time, what Burke (1969) called "pieties," have evolved with their historical use in the conversations of a society's communication.

Burke (1984) observed that at any given point in history, most of a society's members share a fundamental orientation or dominant mode of signifying and interpreting the meanings of symbols and events in social conversation. When conflicting orientations operate simultaneously at a given time and place, the result can be ambiguity, confusion, or conflict on the part of social actors.

Such conflicts may lead to attempts to compromise or merge different symbols so that certain symbols may encode meanings and imagery that draw from the different orientations. One of Burke's (1984) primary metaphors for this kind of symbolism is the "gargoyle," which literally combines two different kinds of mythic symbols such as an animal and a demon or an animal and a person. A gargoyle symbol can transcend the meanings that made it. The "realm of gargoyles" (p. 69) is a transitional state that Burke calls "perspective by incongruity," a rhetorical move that violates accepted symbolic associations or pieties to reveal relationships where previous orientations permitted none. Burke saw radical art movements such as surrealism and dadaism as attempts to forge symbols that represent and reflect times of radical change and conflict, combining symbols that mean differently in competing systems of meaning. It may be hard to remember that the Renaissance was a radical art movement when it swept from Italy to England from the 15th to 17th centuries. Visual and literary artists recovered and renewed the classical mythology and art of the Greeks and Romans. In painting, the transition from flat depiction to natural perspective embodied an astoundingly different artistic paradigm. The form and themes of *Images at the Crossroads* evoke the Renaissance confrontation of classical and Christian. The once evocative symbolic associations that revealed startling relationships between orientations may still be rich, but in the intervening centuries they have transcended and thereby lost their incongruity. Except, perhaps, in Statesville.

As we have seen, Ben Long's Renaissance-informed image serves as a sort of rhetorical crossroads where competing orientations and competing claims to interpret the image intersect. Long's artistic, poetic, metaphoric orientation providing the rich associations carried by the image of Hecate have resurrected patriarchy in provoking the unintended interpretation of Hecate as goddess and Wicca as the practice of witchcraft.

The challenge facing Statesville is how to redeem the image of Hecate as a gargoylish figure whose meanings transcend (ironically in an almost goddess-like fashion) those assigned to it now. Reading Hecate as a religious rather than a mythological or historical representation evokes irrational fear of the unknown and a passionate emotional conflict without any winners. Speakers who promote competing orientations—Christianity versus paganism and/or classical mythology, patriarchy versus feminism, secularism versus religiosity—cannot communicate with one another in any meaningful way because they participate in separate conversations. The underlying assumptions of their positions are irreconcilable. The result is confusion and conflict, anathema to the kind of understanding required to build community.

To communicate, competing orientations must find common ground; they must identify a conversational framework within which the two sides can communicate. One framework that has emerged in the fresco controversy is that of the First Amendment, charging the separation of church and state. Indeed Christian leaders in Statesville have evoked the First Amendment. Pastor Hudson illustrated the position when he argued that the U.S. constitution "guarantees that no religion will be given priority over another." He noted that the First Amendment serves as the basis for regular lawsuits that sue:

> to remove Christian symbols and objects from public owned places. I am confused as to why it is OK to use public money (hotel-motel tax revenues . . .) to create a piece of art in a very high profile place in a public owned building that is clearly an object of worship by an actively government recognized religion ([the] armed forces recently hired a witch as a chaplain). I am convinced that it is a violation of the U.S. Constitution as blatantly as if it were a fresco of Jesus or Abraham. (personal communication, 2001)

In the United States, where people may be divided by the freedom to hold divergent opinions and worship in different ways, they do hold their legal residence and probably their citizenship in common. Their rights are protected by the U.S. Constitution. Evoking the First Amendment to the Constitution by disputing Statesville's civic government's role as the ostensible patron of the image makes the issue resolvable. The context of the U.S. Constitution provides the common orientation required for negotiating the meaning of the civic center image and healing the rift in the community.

The U.S. Constitution is a document designed to be interpreted. The framers of the Constitution created the U.S. Supreme Court to serve as the location for the negotiation and interpretation of the Constitution's meanings. That does not mean that to resolve the issues the case will have to be considered by the Supreme Court. Statesville's civic leaders must make their case as part of a public dialogue to strategically purge the image of any religious context.

If the image of Hecate is legally purged of a religious context and recognized as an artistic rendition, it cannot serve as a catalyst for the disunity that has emerged in the community since the fall of 2000. Evoking the constitutionality of the fresco demands community negotiation of the interpretation of the image in a way that redeems it from the emotional ambiguity and confusion of the alternative conversation

Any acknowledgment of the artwork's imputed religiosity essentially equates the depiction of religious subjects with the construction of idols, and therefore would shut down state-sponsored museums of art in the United States that carried European art from Roman times to the 20th century. Even if the Supreme Court agreed to consider the case, it is unlikely it could deliver such a ruling. Otherwise, that would mean that all national, state, and city-funded art museums would close. The Supreme Court would be hard-pressed to legislate a definition of art at all, let alone defining all depictions of religious subjects as de facto objects of worship.

Perhaps part of the issue is that the richness of Hecate's associations has been lost with disuse—a victim of the decline of liberal education. Perhaps the popularity and power of New Age and feminist orientations that have permeated a great deal of society contribute to empower the image. The controversy suggests the conflict dramatized in the Scopes trial of 1925. The interesting thing about comparing these two transitional moments in which competing orientations negotiate meaning with Christianity is that the Scopes trial took place less than 70 years after Darwin published *The Origin of Species*, whereas the Statesville controversy takes place now 600 to 400 years after the Renaissance seemingly resolved the competing orientations.

The vigor of the reconfrontation of the orientations of Christianity and classical mythology, patriarchy and feminism, church and state illustrates the dynamic nature of the interplay between identification and division: the inevitability of competition between permanence and change. However successfully Renaissance imagery may have transcended or merged competing meanings since the 15th century, constant flux characterizes the symbol systems of contemporary society. Burke acknowledged that symbols are nearly always forged as compromises or gargoylish mergers between a social group's old orientations and new meanings. The meanings are largely acts designed to persuade the majority of group members toward a new perspective advanced by a minority of members hoping for political change or renewal. The controversy also illustrates how, no matter how orientations may shift, merge, or transcend traditional meanings associated with an image, the image can rarely shed all of its previous associations.

The controversy allows us to examine the way that the meanings of symbols become attached and interpreted by diverse members of a society, the way certain symbols are negotiated among different orientations. Long's fresco occupies a cultural space between "old" and "new," between bucolic and sophisticated, traditional and New Age, hierarchical and feminist, past and future.

CONCLUSION

Kenneth Burke saw society's communication as a whole system that out of necessity performed all of the psychological and social tasks required to promote social cooperation, perform socialization, and enable social change for the betterment of its members (Payne, 1995). In such a vision, aesthetic expression in all of its varieties contributes to that communication system, helping to invent new modes of thought and new language both to accommodate us to change and forge new relationships.

Visual images have become part of a greater system of meanings that serve to orient us toward the context and significance of these works. Ben Long's use of classical themes to express civic qualities of Statesville, North Carolina, illustrates how art is not insulated in a self-referential system of meaning, but can become involved in the larger political and institutional rhetorics of government, commerce, and religion. Further research may identify examples of images that have been so redeemed and suggest a strategy by which Statesville can approach the redemption of *Image at the Crossroads*.

Acknowledging that societies can transform themselves justifies why this moment of transition is so important to Statesville and provides it with opportunities to negotiate its future path(s). Of course orientations do not have to shift. In fact the conception of orientations as static actually helps to maintain a particular culture or society. Yet accepting Burke's premise regarding the dialectic of identification and division acknowledges that, where there is permanence, there also is change. Indeed an important corollary of identifying the old-fashioned nature of the fresco controversy is the recognition that the baseline assumptions of much of North American culture have shifted so much with regard to women that the Statesville controversy seems strange.

Mitchell (2002) called on critics to recognize visual culture as a dialectic that travels a tension between nature and culture:

A dialectical concept of visual culture cannot rest content with a definition of its object as the social construction of the visual field, but must insist on exploring the chiastic reversal of this proposal, *the visual construction of the social field*. It is not just that we see the way we do because we are social animals, but also that our social arrangements take the forms they do because we are seeing animals. (p. 171)

The Statesville controversy illustrates what can happen when the visual contributes to constructing the social field.

When Ben Long started working on his fresco, Statesville was a community taken for granted. The introduction of *Images at the Crossroads* has sparked self-reflection: A civic identity once silently defined by broad common interests of geography, economics, and monoculture is being publicly renegotiated according to values, assumed and professed. Statesville is growing up from a place where everybody knows your name to a place where the networks of relationships will become more and more complex, and it will become more and more difficult to find common ground. Statesville, like the maiden, is at a crossroads, looking back at the city it was, looking out at the city it is becoming, and looking ahead to the community it can be.

According to Mayor John Marshall (2000), "The fresco will be criticized and it will be praised. And without a doubt, it will do what art does—regardless of its form—it will invoke reflection and response" (para. 8). The good news is that the neighbors have something to talk about.

REFERENCES

Beck, J. (2001, January 19). Long fresco distinguishes Statesville. *Charlotte Observer*, p. 14A.

Berkin, C. R. (1989). Womens' life. In C. R. Wilson & W. Ferris (Eds.), *Encyclopedia of southern culture* (pp. 1519–1526). Chapel Hill: University of North Carolina Press.

Boggs, K. (2000). Civic center's pagan fresco raises question of "ACLU, where are you?" *Worthy News*. Retrieved March 20, 2003 from http://worthynews.com/news-features/aclu-civic-center.html

Brown, A. (2000). The women left behind: Transformation of the Southern Belle, 1840-1880. *Historian, 62*(4), 759–778.

Bryson, N. (2003). Visual culture and the dearth of images. *Journal of Visual Culture, 2*(2), 229–230.

Burke, K. (1969.) *A rhetoric of motives* (3rd ed.). Berkeley: University of California Press.

Burke, K. (1984). *Permanence and change: An anatomy of purpose* (3rd ed.). Berkeley: University of California Press.

City of Statesville. (2003). *Statesville fresco site* (online). Available: http://www.ci.stateville.nc.us/fresco.htm (Nov. 30, 2003).

Cole, M. (2002.) The demonic arts and the origin of the medium. *Art Bulletin, 84*(4), 621-640.

Conway, D. J. (1994). *Maiden, mother, crone: The myth and reality of the triple goddess.* St. Paul, MN: Llewellyn.

de Certeau, M (1984). *The practice of everyday life* (S. Rendall, Trans.). Berkeley: University of California Press.

Gleeson-White, S. (2001). Revisiting the southern grotesque: Mikhail Bakhtin and the case of Carson McCullers. *Southern Literary Journal, 33*(2), 108–123.

Greater Statesville Chamber of Commerce. (2004). *History and culture* (online). Available: http://www.statesvillechamber.org/ (Mar. 20, 2004).

Jenkins, H. (1992). *Textual poachers: Television fans and participatory culture.* New York: Routledge.

Jones, A. G. (1989). Womens' life: Belles and ladies. In C. R. Wilson & W. Ferris (Eds.), *Encyclopedia of southern culture* (pp. 1527–1530). Chapel Hill: University of North Carolina Press.

Lady Hecatemoon. (2004). Crone turns witch. *Hecate's cauldron* (online). Available: http://www.hecatescauldron.org/Crone%20Turns%20Witch.htm (Jan. 19, 2004).

Lefkowitz, M. R. (1993). The new cults of the goddess. *American Scholar, 62*(2), 261–269.

Leonard, B. (1989). Religion: Southern Baptist convention. In C. R. Wilson & W. Ferris (Eds.), *Encyclopedia of southern culture* (pp. 1330–1331). Chapel Hill: University of North Carolina Press.

Livingston, M. (2001, January 9). Fresco finito: Final strokes made on contentious civic center artwork. *Statesville Record and Landmark,* p.1, 4A.

Marshall, J. (2000). *Remarks by Mayor John Marshall made during the Dec. 4, 2000 city council meeting.* Statesville Fresco Site (online). Available: http://www.ci.stateville.nc.us (Dec. 2, 2003).

Mitchell, W.J.T. (2002). Showing seeing; a critique of visual culture. *Journal of Visual Culture, 1*(2), 165–181.

Morgan, D. (1998). Domestic devotion and ritual: Visual piety in the modern American home. *Art Journal, 57*(1), 45–54.

Payne, D. (1995). Kenneth Burke and contemporary criticism. *Text and Performance Quarterly, 15,* 333–347.

Pollock, G. (1988). *Vision and difference: Femininity, feminism and the histories of art.* London: Routledge.

Radway, J. (1991). *Reading the romance: Women, patriarchy and popular culture.* Chapel Hill: University of North Carolina Press.

Sisters of the Craft. (2003). Understanding Hecate and her history. *Hecate—Beneath the Veil* (online). Available: http://www.hecate.awebspider.com (Dec. 2, 2003).

Von Rudloff, R. (1996). Hekate in early Greek religion. *The Horned Owl Library* (online). Available: http://www.islandnet.com/~hornowl/library/hekate.html (May 2, 2001).

Wrinn, J. (2000, December 4). Goddess in fresco evokes cries of paganism: Ben Long's art upsets hometown of Statesville. *Charlotte Observer* (online). Available: http:www.charlotte.com/1205fresco.htm (Mar. 5, 2001).

Yohn, S. (2002). All that fits a woman: Training Southern Baptist women for charity and mission, 1907–1926 (Book Review). *Journal of Southern History, 68*(4), 990–991.

SECTION III
RHETORICAL INNOVATORS
AND VISUAL TECHNOLOGIES

CHAPTER NINE

Visual Rhetoric as Indices of Political Change

A Sketch of a Conceptual, Technical Approach to
Benjamin Franklin's Pictorial Representations
Portraying British America

LESTER C. OLSON

UNIVERSITY OF PITTSBURGH

EIGHTEENTH-CENTURY VISUAL RHETORIC circulated through diverse media. Pictorial messages circulated on almost every extant medium in British America, Britain, and France throughout the Revolutionary era. Visual images were distributed widely on the preponderance of mundane objects and highly refined art in public and private life. Symbolic designs appeared on metal and paper currency, medals, paintings, statues, architectural elements, flags, drums, powder horns, illuminated displays, imprinted textiles, housewares, and, above all, illustrations in magazines, pamphlets, almanacs, newspapers, and broadsides. Sometimes displayed exclusively among intimate friends in the home, other times ubiquitous in public life among all ranks of people, pictorial images were employed by partisans to express and advocate political commitments throughout the Revolutionary era. In the colonies, for example, portraits and statues were commissioned and displayed prominently in praise of leaders who had defended America's interests, whereas portraits and statues of other opprobrious individuals were removed from public forums and destroyed. Engraved, etched, and woodcut illustrations circulated as frontispieces and satirical prints inside pamphlets, magazines, and almanacs or, in other cases, as mastheads on major newspapers. While newspapers and paper currency were the predominant means of visual rhetoric in British America, broadsides were the most pervasive form in which allegorical prints circulated in Britain, where the golden age of caricature was developing in the aftermath of William Hogarth's widely admired engravings. Images of British America as one body politic were distributed widely during the decades before the American revolution—not only through art objects, currency, and reading materials, but also through objects displayed or used on a daily basis in the home: commemorative medals, imprinted textiles, and housewares such as creamware, porcelain, or china pitchers, plates, and bowls (Olson, 1991, pp. 4–14).

Benjamin Franklin was typical of 18th-century polemicists in his recognition of visual rhetoric as a powerful means to influence beliefs and actions. My recently published book entitled *Benjamin Franklin's Vision of American Community: A Study in Rhetorical Iconology* focuses on the pictorial images that he designed to represent those British colonies in the America that became the United States (Olson, 2004; see also Olson, 1987, 1990). He invented at least one such image during each decade from the 1750s to the 1780s. In 1754, "JOIN, or DIE" represented the colonies as a segmented snake in a woodcut designed to promote unity among the British colonies during the French and Indian War (Fig. 9.1). A decade later, "MAGNA *Britannia: her Colonies* REDUC'D" portrayed the colonies as the severed arms and legs of Britannia in a political cartoon designed to advocate imperial unity during the Stamp Act controversy of 1765 and 1766 (Fig. 9.2). In 1776,

Figure 9.1. "JOIN, or DIE," *Pennsylvania Gazette* [Benjamin Franklin], Philadelphia, May 9, 1754, p. 2, col. 2. Publisher: Benjamin Franklin and David Hall. Medium: newspaper woodcut, size: 2" × 2⅞". Photograph courtesy of the Prints and Photographs Division of the Library of Congress.

Figure 9.2. "MAGNA *Britannia: her Colonies* REDUC'D" [Benjamin Franklin, London, 1765-1766]. Medium: engraved print on a card, size: 4⅛" × 5⅞". Photograph courtesy of the Library Company of Philadelphia.

"WE ARE ONE" designated the United States as 13 interlinked rings on the continental currency to suggest unity among the states during the initial war years (Fig. 9.3). Finally, in 1783, *Libertas Americana* depicted the United States as the infant Hercules strangling two serpents on a commemorative medal issued near the Revolution's conclusion (Fig. 9.4). No other American colonist's pictorial representations designating the emerging nation were more original or influential in their time than those by Benjamin Franklin.

Figure 9.3. "One Sixth of a DOLLAR" [Benjamin Franklin], Philadelphia, 1776. Printer: [David] Hall and [William] Sellers. Medium: colonial paper currency, size: 3¼" × 2½". Similar designs were printed on "One Third," "Half," and "Two Thirds of a DOLLAR." Photograph courtesy of the Rare Books Division of the Library of Congress, the Thatcher Collection.

Figure 9.4. *Libertas Americana,* obverse and reverse, proposed and commissioned by Benjamin Franklin, executed by Augustin Dupré, environs of Paris, 1783. Medium: gold, bronze, and silver medals, size: 1¹⁵⁄₁₆" diameter. Photograph courtesy of the British Museum, Department of Coins and Medals.

These four pictorial representations of British America are connected by more than their similar subject of the British American colonial community. All can be classified as belonging to the same general kind of visual rhetoric based on three particular features that they shared: (a) a pictorial representation, (b) a motto in the vernacular or Latin, and (c) a resulting moral or lesson. As visual rhetoric, they were derived from an aesthetic tradition of emblems and devices that had spanned centuries in Europe and Britain. Although many varied and sometimes subtle distinctions were drawn between emblems and devices before the 18th century, during the era of the American Revolution, some individuals used the terms *emblem* and *device* interchangeably or in the combination *emblematical device* (Sommer, 1961). A pseudonymous author, "Clericus," outlined essential features that emblems and devices had in common: "An emblematical device, when rightly formed, is said to consist of two parts, a *body* and a *mind*, neither of which is compleat [sic] or intelligible, without the aid of the other. The figure is called the *body*, the motto the *mind*." These comments, published initially in the *Pennsylvania Gazette* of September 20, 1775 (p. 1, col. 1), and reprinted with minor typographical changes in the *Pennsylvania Magazine* of December 1775 (vol. 1, p. 561), neither specified whether a human, animal, plant, or architectural form could be used for "the figure" or pictorial element of the design, nor did they mention whether the motto should be in Latin, a foreign language, or the vernacular.[1] This article by "Clericus" has sometimes been attributed to Franklin (Newman, 1983, pp. 2272–2273; see also Lemay, 1986, pp. 122–124; Stansbury, circa 1776). But the attribution is uncertain, however, simply because Franklin never used the expression "emblematical device" in any of his other known prose.

Franklin's comments about and use of emblems and devices reveal that he did not distinguish between them based on either the subject matter depicted in the pictorial image or the language of the motto, as did some earlier authorities on such messages during the 16th and 17th centuries in France (Russell, 1985, pp. 142–160). Historically, one commonplace distinction was that devices conveyed particular ideas in Latin, whereas emblems were for ideas applicable to everyone and were expressed in the vernacular. Nor did he adhere to the common practice of distinguishing as *emblems* those pictorial messages that employed representations of the human form,

---

1. The explanation was later published in an almanac for 1777, to judge from a citation for it in *The Historical Magazine and Notes and Queries* (1861, March), 5, 71-73. The explanation was also reprinted in Phillips (1865–1866), 2, 251-256.

verses *devices*, which did not (Russell, 1985, p. 145; Sommer, 1961, p. 58).[2] In these respects, he was typical of most American colonists in using both terms interchangeably.

Whether the mottos of Franklin's pictorial representations were in Latin or the vernacular was rhetorically consequential because of the messages' accessibility to various audiences. But his choices of language did not necessarily reveal his political commitments, such as a democratic impulse, because his use of Latin mottos recurred regularly throughout his entire career (for an alternative account, see Lemay, 1987, esp. pp. 473, 475, and 494). He used them in his emblems and devices for the Associator flags in 1747, for the Continental currency in 1775, again for the various medals commissioned to honor military victories during the American Revolution, and yet again for *Libertas Americana* in 1783. This lifelong pattern of using Latin mottos makes it unlikely that he sought fundamentally to make emblems and devices democratic, especially because he never explicitly identified himself as having such political commitments. His use of Latin or the vernacular depended, above all, on rhetorical considerations of the audience and their generic expectations for the particular type of message. Such considerations may have taken priority over adhering to familiar conventions distinguishing emblems or devices.

Franklin's language choice may have depended on a combination of factors, including not only the conventions for a specific medium, such as

---

2. Benjamin Franklin's (henceforth BF) article about the Associator flags in 1747, for instance, employed the term *devices*, with reference to a list of 10 designs, some of which portrayed animal forms and others that depicted human forms (Franklin, 1959–2004, vol. 3, pp. 267–269). Further, although the image on "JOIN, or DIE" depicted the British colonies in America as a snake, not a human, and although the motto was expressed in the vernacular, not Latin or a foreign language, BF employed the word *emblem* to describe it in BF's letter to Richard Partridge (vol. 5, p. 273). Three decades later, in 1776, when BF chaired a committee charged by Congress "to prepare Devices for a Great Seal" of the United States, he proposed an image that portrayed the destruction of the Pharaoh's army in the Red Sea. Other committee members, Thomas Jefferson and John Adams, also proposed images with human forms (vol. 22, p. 563). BF used the term *device* in a letter to his sister, Jane Mecom, on May 30, 1757, when he commented on designs to be placed on "the papers" and "the crown soap" after objecting to Peter Mecom using "the Franklin arms" on the latter. BF seems here to have employed the term, *device*, as a synonym for a *mark*, which would identify the maker of a product (vol. 7, p. 222).

the honorary medals, but also the principal audience's level of education. "JOIN, or DIE" and "WE ARE ONE" were both widely distributed among Americans of all backgrounds, the former in newspapers such as the *Pennsylvania Gazette* in 1754 and the latter on the Continental currency's fractional notes in 1776; both had vernacular mottos (Matthews, 1908; Olson, 1987). In contrast, toward the end of his career, *Libertas Americana* was the title of the commemorative medal that he presented in 1783 to prominent political figures in France and the United States: King Louis XVI, Queen Marie Antoinette, the ministers in the French court, and the president and representatives in the American Congress (Olson, 1990). Franklin used Latin in this instance because most of these leaders would have had the classical education necessary to comprehend the message. One notable problem with this hypothesis about adjusting to audiences, however, is that Latin mottos accompanied the designs on the Continental currency that circulated widely among the American people in 1775. The same is the case for the emission of paper money the following year in 1776, with the exception of Franklin's fractional note design ("WE ARE ONE") and the $40 bill printed in English. Perhaps the use of Latin on the rest of the currency reflected the committee's deliberations, not Franklin's judgments.

The choice of Latin for a motto also had rhetorical ramifications for an author's persona. Franklin was aware of this, to judge from a humorous commentary in *The New England Courant* on February 11, 1723, when it was published under Benjamin Franklin's editorship instead of his older brother James'. The *Courant* commented,

> Gentle Readers, we design never to let a Paper pass without a Latin Motto if we can possibly pick one up, which carries a Charm in it to the Vulgar, and the learned admire the pleasure of Construing. We should have obliged the World with a Greek scrap or two, but the Printer has no Types, and therefore we intreat the candid Reader not to impute the defect to our Ignorance, for our Doctor can say all the Greek Letters by heart. (Franklin, 1959-2004, ongoing, vol. 1, p. 50)

Franklin's contemporaries certainly regarded the use of Latin for the mottos as a means of making an author appear well educated. "A. B.," a pseudonymous respondent to "Clericus" in the *Pennsylvania Magazine*, offered amusing commentary *"On the Use and Abuse of MOTTOS."* In the *Supplement to the Pennsylvania Magazine for the Year 1775*, "A. B." generalized that, "Writers of essays, pamphlets, & c. are very fond of mottos. . . . It must be confessed there is sometimes a good reason for this; for, perhaps, the motto is the only thing that shews the author's learning; the work itself being insufficient for this purpose" ("A.B." [pseud.], ([1775]), p. 588, col. 1).

This chapter provides an overview of one technical, conceptual approach to research on Franklin's visual rhetoric as indices of political change while recognizing that any such approach only articulates a shorthand for scholars who are endeavoring to understand visual communication under specific circumstances in highly variable cultures, not an altogether objective or universally applicable orientation to scholarship concerning visual rhetoric. The chapter highlights the broad outlines of one approach for treating Franklin's visual rhetoric as indices of political change, although other approaches are certainly possible and desirable. The contribution of this chapter is a technical, conceptual orientation that sketches in necessarily broad terms one scholarly sensibility for investigating visual rhetoric. It is not concerned with reporting the results of the scholarship concerning Franklin's pictorial messages as a sustained example—for that it would be necessary to consult the resulting book (Olson, 2004).

Although Franklin's experience with the production of emblems and devices was extensive, it is the four pictorial representations depicting British America that are the most important of his designs for understanding his emerging nationalism between the early 1750s and mid-1780s because, in varied ways, they envisioned the British colonies as one body politic. Therefore, these four images constitute the central focus of my recent book, which investigated these pictorial images as elements in Franklin's communication about the nature of colonial union—not only because they are a vehicle to explore his evolving vision of a British American community, but also because they reflected and promoted changes in American culture throughout the Revolutionary era. These images, designed with American audiences in mind, are useful indices of transformations in American culture. In addition, they reveal changes in his vision of a British American community because in every instance Franklin modified the depictions of unity among those disparate colonies that became the United States.

Although Franklin directed all of the pictorial images to Americans, the study of his visual communication is international in scope because he also directed most of them to audiences in Britain and at least one to a French audience. Franklin was a representative in the Pennsylvania Assembly in 1754, a colonial agent in Britain at London in the mid-1760s, a representative in the Continental Congress at Philadelphia in 1776, and the United States' *ministre plénipotentiaire* to France in 1783 when he lived in Paris. At these moments, roughly a decade apart, his political and social roles as an American colonist differed significantly. In 1754 and again in 1776, for example, he was well situated as a representative in Pennsylvania to participate directly in the formation of colonial policies. Yet in the mid-1760s and again in 1783, he was located on the periphery of the forums for exercising political power and social privilege—first in the British Parliament and then the French ministry.

Researchers have devoted essays to discussing the iconography of each image designed by Franklin to represent British America, but we have yet to study the images collectively as indices of cultural and personal change. Albert Matthews (1908) investigated the iconography of "JOIN, or DIE" by describing the dissemination of the segmented snake in newspapers throughout Pennsylvania, New York, and Massachusetts between 1754 and 1776 (see Olson, 1987, 1991). Referring to "JOIN, or DIE," Philip Davidson (1941) underscored that Franklin "was a propagandist" who "was the first to see the real possibilities in the use of cartoons" (pp. 14–15). Frederic R. Kirkland (1949) and Edwin Wolf II (1955) researched "MAGNA *Britannia*" to document the numerous variants of this image, which were reproduced subsequently in Britain, Holland, France, and America throughout the American Revolution (see also Olson, 1987). David P. McBride (1979) and Eric P. Newman (1966) investigated the image of the interlinked rings on the continental currency to conclude that it, too, was of widespread significance because the design was used on currency, military flags, and housewares produced in the United States, Britain, and China. Finally, Carl Zigrosser (1957) and Winfried Schleiner (1976–1977) focused on *Libertas Americana* to specify the iconographic and textual traditions that informed the design of the commemorative medal (see also Olson, 1990). This image was distributed in the United States, France, Malta, Germany, and Italy in the form of medals, engraved broadsides, book illustrations, textile designs, terra cotta plaques, and poetry.

The existing studies are helpful because they identified several germane artifacts, described the iconography of each motif, and provided ample evidence that Franklin's images of America merited a systematic study. However, they failed to account for fundamental differences between the images; they ignored the relationship of the images to Franklin's career, objectives, and evolving outlook as his sensibility changed over the decades; and they neglected altogether the relationship of the images to the prevailing ideologies and partisan interests of the contemporaneous audiences in America, Britain, and, on occasion, France. A more intellectually satisfying account may be articulated by broadening our focus from the discrete motifs to include the designer and culture by foregrounding Franklin's rhetorical practices in the visual communication with which he engaged others. Such an approach is appropriate for Franklin's visual rhetoric because it comports with what R. T. H. Halsey (1936) described as Franklin's pragmatic view of the arts. Franklin regarded the arts as a means to influence public beliefs and actions. In this respect, his use of pictorial images was thoroughly rhetorical. Despite extensive research on Franklin, including Charles Coleman Sellers' study on 18th-century portraits of him (Sellers, 1962; see also Bailyn, 2003; Craven, 1993; Miles, 1993), no previous book has focused on his proposals in the visual arts.

Benjamin Franklin's Vision of American Community describes the transformations in his vision of America as expressed in his rationales for each pictorial image representing America, and it also articulates underlying transformations in American culture as suggested by his contemporaries' changing reactions to these images. For example, rather than initially symbolizing protest or rebellion within the British Empire, the snake device on "JOIN, or DIE" dramatically symbolized the need for well-orchestrated action against the outside threat posed by the French and Indians in 1754. Franklin's idea of union at the time was not radical in its implications for the British Empire. Instead it was a practical, military necessity consistent with the expressed wishes of the British government's Board of Trade as conveyed in a circular letter to the governors of several colonies. Even so, a decade later, during the Stamp Act controversy of 1765 and 1766, American protestors appropriated this image in the Constitutional Courant to urge colonial opposition to the British law. In 1776, Franklin sought to counter this radical use of the image by distributing "MAGNA Britannia: her Colonies REDUC'D" among Americans to underscore the vital nature of imperial unity and among parliamentarians to advocate moderate political policy as they considered enforcing the legislation with military force. Despite his efforts tacitly repudiating his own earlier visual rhetoric that had been appropriated for other uses by radical protestors in British America, the snake device took on a life of its own in American politics: Loyalists sought to connect the image with the biblical traditions, wherein the serpent represented guile, deceit, and treachery, whereas Patriots countered those efforts by associating the image with eternity, vigilance, and prudence (Olson, 1991, pp. 21–74). Toward the Revolution's conclusion, Franklin was once again associated with the snake's image when Joseph-Siffrède Duplessis' portrait of him featured a rattlesnake's image carved on the gilt wooden frame (Fig. 9.5).

Figure 9.5. "Benjamin Franklin," Joseph-Siffrède Duplessis, Paris, 1778. Medium: oil portrait on canvas with a gilt carved wooden frame featuring rattlesnake, oval 28½" × 23". Photograph courtesy of the Metropolitan Museum of New York, Michael Friedsam Collection.

Each of the pictorial images representing the British colonies in America were details in much broader campaigns. Because the meanings of these images were shaped not only by the palpable form of the messages, but also by the points of view of the audiences and the political circumstances surrounding their distribution, it was necessary for me to interpret these images in light of the ephemeral, rhetorical understandings and public address of the period. In this respect, I agree with Douglas Anderson (1997), who commented in *The Radical Enlightenments of Benjamin Franklin* that a study of the meanings of his prose must take into account that "the social conditions of writing are inevitably an ingredient in meaning" (p. 36). The same insight applies to his pictorial messages. Every one of the pictorial compositions had an enduring, but changing, significance throughout the Revolutionary era, as contemporary partisans appropriated them for a range of reasons and uses in Britain, France, America, Holland, Germany, Spain, Italy, and elsewhere as far away as China.

Although each image portraying a British American community took on a life of its own internationally at the time, each was admittedly a small part of Franklin's extraordinary life. In fact the pictorial images were of such slight importance as details in his life that even Franklin's best biographers ordinarily mention only one or two of them—typically the most famous of the images, "JOIN, or DIE," but seldom many others (Brands, 2002, pp. 234, 369, and 373; Isaacson, 2003, pp. 159, 225, 228, plate 19; Morgan, 2002, p. 237; Wright, 1986, p. 89, and illus. following p. 66). Even Carl Van Doren (1938), who set the standard for subsequent biographies with his Pulitzer Prize-winning *Benjamin Franklin*, mentioned only three of them, omitting as he did the designs for the Continental paper currency in 1776 (pp. 220, 491–492, and 628). But small details though these visual images certainly were in Franklin's life, I argue that careful attention to them throws into high relief fundamental changes in Franklin's sensibility concerning British America, especially his political commitments as he changed from being an American Whig to a republican.

In my research, I have focused individually on each of Franklin's emblems of American community. My discussions concentrate on the rhetorical dynamics of each major motif by investigating the production, dissemination, and reception of one of his pictorial images representing British America. First, there is an analysis of the circumstances surrounding the production of a particular pictorial message by identifying the factors that Franklin considered when he developed it. Examples of such factors include the design's specific audiences and concerns, his expressed objectives whenever he was explicit about them, and the techniques entailed in production insofar as all these factors illuminate the visual appeals as instruments for persuasion. Of course drawing any inferences about motivation from expressed objectives is such a fallible undertaking that it cannot be an altogether adequate ground for rhetorical interpretation, but attention to them gives us some sense of his mode of operation and his depictions of his own rhetorical sensibility. The ramifications of his social and political roles emerge as significant factors in the rhetorical analysis, as well as his position vis-à-vis political institutions, such as the Parliament in London and the French ministry in Paris, because institutions enable and circumscribe some varieties of human agency while excluding most people altogether.

Patterns of dissemination for the designs surfaced in attention to the diverse media through which each motif was distributed among the audiences typically in British America, Britain, and France, not only as used by Franklin, but also as redistributed by others who often had different political agendas. The discussion details acts of appropriation, subversion, and redefinition of the pictorial images by partisans as the motifs from Franklin's visual works were reproduced internationally on currency, medals, paintings, statues, flags, textiles, housewares, and illustrations in magazines, pamphlets, almanacs, newspapers, and broadsides. As evidence of patterns in the reception of the designs by the principal audiences, I consider other designs featuring the motif on various media as well as written comments concerning the designs in Franklin's contemporaries' diaries, letters, poetic verses, newspapers, magazines, and pamphlets. The extant evidence of active interaction with Franklin's messages is inevitably fragmentary and may, in some instances, say more about the viewpoints of the commentators than about Franklin or his messages. Hence, each discussion of reception provides background concerning the commentators' social roles, partisan concerns, and uses of the motifs. My claims about the reception are meant to be suggestive, not conclusive of how contemporaries actively interacted with Franklin's pictorial compositions to make them meaningful in a range of different circumstances or to blunt their political import on occasion.

Examples of the factors and issues, which I have considered throughout this process, include the value of diverse media for reaching various segments of the audiences; the role of conventional motifs and genres in the formation of the pictorial compositions and in interpretations of the images' meanings during the period; and the underlying political factors impinging on the diverse, contemporaneous audiences' reception of the message and on its occasional appropriation by rival groups. Of course the specific meanings of the motifs were multiple and highly varied in the specific circumstances and cultural contexts of their circulation among partisans of the period. The best available evidence consists of the pictorial and verbal messages that commented directly on each pictorial representation of the united British colonies. Yet in some instances, I found it necessary to draw on Franklin's and his peers' contemporaneous ideas concerning union to suggest possible interpretations and understandings of the images simply because they provided best available evidence.

In attempting to synthesize the rhetorical usage of each of the pictorial images, I have employed a classical vocabulary for organizing both the analysis of the message's role in its time and the analysis of the major appeals to the principal audiences during the Revolutionary era. The classical terms for types of persuasive messages in civic forums—deliberative, judicial, and ceremonial rhetoric—were salient genres during the 18th century, especially among political leaders who ordinarily had the benefit of a classical education. As such these genres are useful for organizing an interpretation of the visual rhetoric in these specific forums during that time. Well-educated, economically privileged, and politically powerful men in 18th-century patriarchal British and American colonial cultures would have been familiar with these types of persuasive discourse in public life, corresponding as they did to highly visible, public activities in the legislatures, courts, and ceremonial occasions. Dating back historically to classical Greece, the types of persuasive speeches in these forums were identified and detailed in treatises on rhetoric, especially Aristotle's *Rhetoric*. Each type of public speech had corresponding commonplace lines of public argument (or *topoi*), which recurred in appeals to specific audiences for consensus on the decisions concerning the expediency or inexpediency of future policies, the justice or injustice of past deeds, or the current praiseworthiness or blameworthiness of individuals or institutions. Early writers on emblems and devices drew on classical treatises on rhetoric to develop their commentaries about the visual arts (Russell, 1985, pp. 149–150).

At the same time, I have employed these classical terms for kinds of discourse under certain strictures, such as an emphatic recognition that they were not adequate for understanding broad, popular forms of participation in the rhetorical life of the community. Those without political power and economic privilege often resorted to types of rhetorical appeals in various mundane objects, such as textiles and housewares, as well as popular forums, such as public demonstrations featuring effigies, illuminated displays, and symbolic processions. Such people often relied on metaphor and allegory, as I have argued at length in my earlier book, *Emblems of American Community in the Revolutionary Era* (1991), because these were relatively indirect, but nonetheless robust means to assert their views. The utility of the classical terms is ultimately circumscribed in the present study—not only through emphatic strictures on their use in relationship to specific types of decision making in certain public forums, but also through a conscious broadening of the forms of rhetorical appeal through an examination of common objects used for persuasion in public life: paper money, military flags, textile designs, medals, terra cotta plaques, housewares, and the like.

The thesis that I discerned by examining the differences among his pictorial representations of British America as one body politic was that the distinctive pictorial images each decade reflected his complex process of rejecting Britain's constitutional monarchy and ultimately endorsing republicanism as a form of government in the United States. Initially, he veered toward increasing the monarch's power in British America before he repudiated that political system altogether and embraced republicanism. This transformation resulted from his active engagement with diverse, intercultural influences and his dramatically changing political circumstances. The portrait of Franklin emerging from close attention to his visual rhetoric over the decades is that of a man whose capacity to reconsider his own most fundamental beliefs resulted in his dramatically changed political commitments over the decades. Franklin's visual rhetoric indices these basic changes in his political commitments.

REFERENCES

"A. B." [pseud.]. ([1775]). *On the use and abuse of* MOTTOS. *Supplement to the Pa. Mag. for the Year 1775*, pp. 587–589.

"A. B." [pseud.]. (1861, March). *On the use and abuse of* MOTTOS. *Historical Magazine and Notes and Queries*, 5, 71–73.

Anderson, D. (1997). *The radical enlightenments of Benjamin Franklin*. Baltimore: Johns Hopkins University Press.

Bailyn, B. (2003). Realism and idealism in American diplomacy: Benjamin Franklin in Paris, Couronné par la Liberté. In *To begin the world anew* (pp. 60–99). New York: Knopf.

Brands, H. W. (2002). *The First American: The life and times of Benjamin Franklin*. New York: Random House.

"Clericus" [pseud.]. (1775, September 20). *Pennsylvania Gazette*, p. 1, col. 1.

"Clericus" [pseud.]. (1775, December). *Pennsylvania Magazine*, 1, 561.

Craven, W. (1993). The American and British portraits of Benjamin Franklin. In J. A. Leo Lemay (Ed.), *Reappraising Benjamin Franklin: A Bicentennial perspective* (pp. 247–272). Newark: University of Delaware Press.

Davidson, P. (1941). *Propaganda and the American Revolution*. Chapel Hill: University of North Carolina Press.

Franklin, B. (1959–2004, ongoing). *The papers of Benjamin Franklin* (Vols. 1-36, plus forthcoming). New Haven, CT: Yale University Press.

Halsey, R. T. H. (1936). Benjamin Franklin: His interest in the arts. In *Benjamin Franklin and his circle: A catalogue of an exhibition* (pp. 1–16). New York: Plantin Press for the Metropolitan Museum of Art.

Isaacson, W. (2003). *Benjamin Franklin: An American life*. New York: Simon & Schuster.

Kirkland, F. R. (1949). An unknown Franklin cartoon. *Pennsylvania Magazine of History and Biography*, 73, 76–79.

Lemay, J. A. L. (1986). *The canon of Benjamin Franklin, 1722-1776*. Newark: University of Delaware Press.

Lemay, J. A. L. (1987). The American aesthetic of Franklin's visual creations. *Pennsylvania Magazine of History and Biography*, 111, 465–499.

Matthews, A. (1908). The Snake Devices, 1754-1776, and the *Constitutional Courant, 1765. Publications of the Colonial Society of Massachusetts, 11,* 409–453. Cambridge: John Willson and Son.

McBride, D. P. (1979, November). Linked rings: Early American unity illustrated. *Numismatist, 92,* 2374–2393.

Miles, E. G. (1993). The French portraits of Benjamin Franklin. In J. A. L. Lemay (Ed.), *Reappraising Benjamin Franklin: A Bicentennial perspective* (pp. 272–289). Newark: University of Delaware Press.

Morgan, E. S. (2002). *Benjamin Franklin.* New Haven, CT: Yale University Press.

Newman, E. P. (1966, December). Continental currency and the *Fugio* cent: Sources of Emblems and Mottos. *Numismatist, 79,* 1587–1598.

Newman, E. P. (1983, November). Benjamin Franklin and the chain design. *Numismatist, 96,* 2271–2284.

Olson, L. C. (1987). Benjamin Franklin's pictorial representations of the British colonies in America: A study in rhetorical iconology. *Quarterly Journal of Speech, 73,* 18–42.

Olson, L. C. (1990). Benjamin Franklin's commemorative medal, *Libertas Americana*: A study in rhetorical iconology. *Quarterly Journal of Speech, 76,* 23–45.

Olson, L. C. (1991). *Emblems of American community in the Revolutionary era: A study in rhetorical iconology.* Washington DC, and London: Smithsonian Institution Press.

Olson, L. C. (2004). *Benjamin Franklin's vision of American community, 1754-1784: A study in rhetorical iconology.* Columbia: University of South Carolina Press.

Phillips, H., Jr. (1865–1866). *Historical sketches of the paper currency of the American colonies: Prior to the adoption of the federal constitution* (Vols. 1–2). Roxbury, MA: W. Elliot Woodward.

Russell, D. S. (1985). Differences between the emblem and the device. In *The Emblem and Device in France* (pp. 142–160). Lexington, KY: French Forum.

Schleiner, W. (1976–77). The infant Hercules: Franklin's design for a medal commemorating American liberty. *Eighteenth-Century Studies, 10,* 235–244.

Sellers, C. C. (1962). *Benjamin Franklin in portraiture.* New Haven, CT: Yale University Press.

Sommer, F. H. (1961, Spring). Emblem and device: The origin of the great seal of the United States. *Art Quarterly, 24,* 57–76.

Stansbury, J. (circa 1776). Loyalist rhapsodes (Ser. 8D, No. 90, Reel 49). Peter Force Collection, Manuscript Division, Library of Congress.

Van Doren, C. (1938). *Benjamin Franklin.* New York: Viking.

Wolf, E. II. (1955). Benjamin Franklin's stamp act cartoon. *Proceedings of the American Philosophical Society, 99,* 388–396.

Wright, E. (1986). *Franklin of Philadelphia.* Cambridge, MA.: Harvard University Press.

Zigrosser, C. (1957, December). The medallic sketches of Augustin Dupré in American collections. *Proceedings of the American Philosophical Society, 101,* 535–550.

CHAPTER TEN

Free Guns and Speech Control
The Structural and Thematic Rhetoric of
Bowling for Columbine

BRIAN J. SNEE
STATE UNIVERSITY OF NEW YORK AT POTSDAM

> Congress shall make no law respecting an establishment of religion, or pro-
> hibiting the free exercise thereof; or abridging the freedom of speech, or of
> the press; or the right of the people peaceably to assemble, and to petition the
> Government for a redress of grievances.
>
> —First Amendment, U.S. Constitution

> A well regulated Militia, being necessary to the security of a free State, the
> right of the people to keep and bear Arms, shall not be infringed.
>
> —Second Amendment, U.S. Constitution

O N THE MORNING OF APRIL 20, 1999, Eric Harris, Dylan Klebold, and
an arsenal of assault weapons headed for Columbine High School in
Littleton, Colorado. By day's end the body count had reached 15: 1 teacher
and 14 students had been killed, including the teen shooters, who eventually
turned their guns on themselves. Just days later, Charleton Heston and the
NRA arrived in nearby Denver to hold a pro-gun rally. The actor best known
for portraying Moses opened the event with characteristic drama: Hoisting
an antique musket above his head, he challenged an unseen enemy with
these words: "From my cold, dead hands!"

The irony was not lost on writer and documentary filmmaker Michael
Moore, who was inspired by the remarkable juxtaposition of these events to
make a film that would raise profound questions about the deadly and, he
argues, uniquely American cultural combination of uncontrolled guns, unwarranted fears, and unparalleled violence. When he announced his intention to make what would become *Bowling for Columbine,* Moore was already
a best-selling author and award-winning filmmaker armed with a carefully
constructed public persona that had him looking like a working-class com-
moner, but sounding like a leftist intellectual elite.

Yet few knew that Moore had yet another side to reveal. The Michigan native was in his teens an award-winning marksman. He remains a member of the NRA and claims to have considered challenging Heston when he first sought the NRA's top office—not to dismantle the institution from within, as one might suspect, but because at the time Moore sincerely believed that the NRA was capable of making a productive contribution to American society. In the end, Moore never threw his hat into the ring, but guns remained very much on his mind, right up until the day of the Columbine killings. What resulted from Moore's prolonged meditation is a fascinating, frustrating, and, some contend, flawed commentary on modern America.

But it is more than that. The film raises serious questions about the evolving relationship between the First and Second Amendments to the U.S. Constitution. In our increasingly violent society, how many guns are too many guns? In our increasingly mediated society, how much speech is too much speech? This centuries-old debate frames the historical, political, and ideological context in which Moore's film insists on being understood. However, it is not the goal of this analysis to use Moore's film to ask how we might begin to bridge the divide between our First and Second Amendment freedoms. Such a discussion is badly needed, but first one must determine what the rhetoric of Moore's film contributes to that ongoing discussion, and that is no easy task given the apparently incompatible perspectives the film both explores and exploits.

This chapter examines from a rhetorical perspective the structural and thematic composition of *Bowling for Columbine* and arrives at three conclusions. First, despite a fragmentary style that might be labeled *postmodern*, Moore's film is identified as a hybrid of two traditional modes of documentary representation: expository and participatory.

Second, the film left many reasonably confused about what to blame for the epidemic of violence in the United States: guns or the media? This chapter asserts that understanding the film's ideological position requires more than a casual viewing of its content and, in fact, demands a sophisticated understanding of the modes of representation utilized by Moore as he ponders both possibilities—a demand few viewers are capable of meeting (hence their confusion). Moore begins with the premise that too many guns are the cause of the violence. Yet after studying the heavily armed, but relatively peaceful, Canadian culture, Moore moves on to suggest that the U.S. news media bears a greater responsibility because it makes otherwise peaceful people afraid of one another—especially persons of color. However, after this evolution in its argument, the film concludes with two memorable sequences that seem misplaced. In these closing scenes, we find Moore reverting to his discarded thesis that guns ultimately are to blame, despite his effective discrediting of that position throughout the film.

This chapter contends that, despite the film's concluding sequences, its consequential use of participatory and expository rhetoric in fact tips the scales toward blaming the media. Thus, as the film's content drifts back toward its initial indictment of guns, its structural composition continues to concentrate its sharpest argumentative focus on the news media. Many viewers left theaters aware that a grave problem existed, but uncertain of its cause or their course of action.

Finally, it is asserted that the form and content of Moore's text create an ironic contradiction in that the film accuses the U.S. news media of creating a culture of fear that leads to violence, all the while the film appropriates several major themes that define modern news coverage. In other words, the film seems to incriminate itself unknowingly and unintentionally by becoming the very sort of visual text that it identifies as destructive to American culture. *Bowling for Columbine* frightens its viewers as a means of persuading them to be wary of unwarranted fear.

CRITICAL AND SOCIAL RESPONSE

As is always the case with Moore, *Bowling for Columbine* uses humor to great effect even as it explores its deadly serious subject. In the very first scene, Moore visits a rural Michigan bank that hands out a free rifle to anyone opening a checking account. When he asks the bank's employees if handing out guns in banks is a sane idea, one senses that the question had never before occurred to them. Even the title of the film reflects its dark humor. After Columbine, some critics searching for an explanation for such senseless violence were quick to point a finger at the usual suspects: violent movies, videogames, song lyrics, and other forms of popular culture. Moore contends—at least initially—that this is fallacious reasoning. He notes that Harris and Klebold did not begin their killing spree until after first period because they did not want to miss their favorite class: bowling. With tongue firmly in cheek, Moore asks via voice-over narration: What is it about bowling that drove these otherwise peaceful kids to kill? His point, of course, is that Marilyn Manson's music wasn't to blame anymore than bowling.[1] Just

---

1. Ironically, after first pointing to weak gun control as an explanation for America's violent epidemic, Moore goes on to propose that the news media, which he believes makes people afraid of one another, may bear an equal, if not greater, burden. Why it is laughable to suggest that music could inspire one to kill, but

who or what is to blame is a matter that is difficult to resolve not just in life, but on screen as well.

Despite its controversial style, or perhaps because of it, *Bowling for Columbine* received numerous honors and awards. It was, for example, the first documentary in 46 years to be entered in the Cannes Film Festival, where it received the coveted Palme d'Or. The film also earned Moore an Academy Award for Best Documentary Feature.[2] The list of other awards and critics choice designations that it was given is far too long to detail. Whatever one's interpretation of the First and Second Amendments, few argued that Moore had not created an influential social text.

Perhaps the central issue on which audiences and critics were divided was whether *Bowling for Columbine* merely raises questions, as Moore has insisted, or whether it truly asserts a causal argument regarding the relationship between guns, fear, violence, and the media in the United States. If the latter is true, as this chapter suggests, the text seems schizophrenic when it comes to the matter of placing blame. Certainly the film suggests that the United States suffers from a level of gun violence unmatched in the international community. Certainly the film suggests that both guns and the media are part of the equation. Yet the relationship between these two all-important elements is not readily apparent. Moore's interview with Professor Barry Glassner figures prominently in the film, implying that, like Glassner, Moore may believe that guns do not kill people, but rather that the media scares gun owners into killing people. However, the film's historical and contextual sections seem to contradict Glassner's (and, at times, Moore's) thesis, charging that guns and gun owners are in fact the primary problem. Clearly both cannot be the *primary* problem. Unfortunately, most of the film's critics sidestepped this and other related issues, and a few even celebrate the film based (oddly) on their conviction it advances no argument whatsoever.

For instance, one critic asserted that, "Moore's picture is not a treatise, it's not a presentation, it's not even really a single, coherent argument. Instead, Moore provokes, he searches, he even pokes fun" (Chihara, 2002). It is true that Moore searches and pokes fun, but it is a mistake to conclude

---

plausible that TV news coverage can, is an issue Moore never takes up in any satisfying way.

2. Moore's acceptance speech included a frank and, some insisted, inappropriate antiwar statement that included a scathing critique of the Bush administration, especially its foreign policy. For a complete list of awards earned by the film, see http://www.bowlingforcolumbine.com/reviews/festivals.php.

that the film does not include a coherent argument. Another reviewer contended: "there are no easy answers and often no answers at all, just a number of very uneasy questions."[3] A third like-minded reviewer concluded:

> Those looking for insight into "why" Columbine happened should look elsewhere. Moore avoids that perhaps impossible question by consistently widening his focus to broader issues. The shootings happened in unincorporated Jefferson County, and Moore points out that defense industry mainstay Lockheed Martin is one of the principal employers in the area. Moore reminds us that on the day of the Columbine shootings, the U.S. was bombing Kosovo. To his credit, Moore doesn't make facile claims for these links; he just raises them as points worth discussing. (Giltz, 2002, p. B4)

This analysis respectfully disagrees and asserts that the alternating modes of representation employed throughout the film at times conceal and consistently complicate the causal argument suggested by its structure. Unfortunately, those critics who recognized the film's unusual structure seemed content simply to applaud its complexity, as opposed to analyze it consequences.

> Moore . . . [builds] his thesis that the media—particularly television— conspire to stoke a year-round climate of fear, convincing ordinary folks that their death or maiming is probably around the corner unless they arm themselves to the gills. . . . Moore targets and indulges in specious reasoning about just what makes so many Yanks so violent. Is Moore objective? Absolutely not. But he has pertinent axes to grind and the sparks fly, thanks to his patented blend of curveball research, expedient juxtaposition, genuine satire and bottomless chutzpah. (Nesselson, 2002, p. 24)

Said another:

> Michael Moore is the documentary filmmaker that movie critics hate to love. *The Los Angeles Times* calls his new movie, "scattershot," "haphazard" and "all over the map." *The New York Times* accuses him of "slippery logic, tendentious grandstanding and outright demagoguery." And yet, with almost no exceptions, the critics heartily recommend *Bowling for Columbine*. (Chihara, 2002)

---

3. The precise source of this quotation is unclear. The film's web site, "bowlingforcolumbine.com," attributes this review to *The Hollywood Reporter*. However, the review is not available in the *Hollywood Reporter*'s online archive or through Lexus Nexus. To read the review at the film's site, go to http://bowlingforcolumbine.com/reviews/2002-05-17-hollywood.php.

However, a few critics have recognized the profound consequence of the film's competing rhetorics. One reviewer, whose politics is not aligned with Moore's, wrote, "One moral ill leads to another leads to another leads to another, in a causal string that anyone just a few clicks to the right [of Moore's far-left politics] can't help but poke holes in" (Horwich, 2003, p. A7).

> Moore has a different thesis. Over archival footage of far-flung genocide, Moore asks how we can forgive our country for the murderous overthrow of elected governments from Chile to Iran yet express shock when affluent children resort to guns to resolve their disputes. His point is that all these things—conspicuous consumption, intractable racism and military misadventures—are connected. Although the film is a departure for the admittedly perplexed Moore in that it eschews easy answers, his reasoning resonates. (Williams, p. D5)[4]

Indeed it does. One of the fundamental axioms of rhetorical studies is that a syllogism can be at once valid and untrue. Truth, in this case, may exist only in the eye of each individual beholder. Yet examining the film's validity—the internal logic of its argument—requires that one look at the structuring of its modes of documentary representation. There we find an answer to the question "What is he suggesting?" that might surprise even Moore.

STRUCTURAL RHETORIC: IDENTIFYING MODES OF REPRESENTATION

To read a film rhetorically is to attend to the viewing process and subsequent meanings that the text may be said to encourage through the concerted development of its cinematic devices and narrative content. Although issues of external context (such as the controversy that this film created) are an important part of any rhetorical analysis, the primary focus remains on the text. Thomas W. Benson and Carolyn Anderson (1989) explained what such a perspective encompasses:

> [F]ilms are social constructions and as such invite shared experiences. The rhetorical critic inquires into that shared experience, not by surveying audience response, and not simply by reporting the critic's subjective, impressionistic responses, but by interrogating the film itself, regarding the film as a constructed invitation to a complex experience of thoughts and feelings.

---

4. Interestingly, this review is available on the press page of the official *Bowling for Columbine* Web site (www.bowlingforcolumbine.com), but the beginning of the title has been changed from "Ambush Documentarian" to simply "Michael Moore."

At best, the film is an "invitation" rather than a "cause" of its viewer's response. . . . Properly executed, however, a rhetorical criticism, in identifying both the experience of the film and the way in which the film brings about that experience, may open the film to discussion in a way audiences and filmmakers might find useful. (p. 3)

A structural approach to the rhetorical criticism of film is even more complex and involves "understanding how it [the film] creates the structures that invite audiences to make meaning in a multi-layered approach to the film as entertainment, art, and social text" (Benson, 2003, p. 9). A structural, rhetorical analysis of *Bowling for Columbine* reveals that most of the film's critics have misunderstood its argumentative design.

Stylistically, *Bowling for Columbine* intoxicates the viewer with what *Time* magazine called, "a Molotov cocktail of interviews, cartoons, news footage and righteous rabble-rousing" (Corliss & Sachs, 2002, p. 89). With its erratic editing and cartoon interludes, it owes more to Oliver Stone's *Natural Born Killers* than Errol Morris' *The Thin Blue Line*. Moore's film is remarkable and effective due to the disjunction between its competing rhetorics. Although the fast-paced montage style of the film places it closer on the dial to MTV than PBS, it is essentially a hybrid of two traditional modes of documentary representation (Plate 10.1, p. 280).

In his *Ideology and the Image* (1981), film scholar Bill Nichols (1981) described various types of direct and indirect address commonly employed throughout the history of documentary film. Julianne Burton (1990) expanded Nichols' work and created a systematic four-part typology of dominant organization patterns, which Nichols (1991) later adopted and expanded into a six-part typology. What has resulted from this evolution of thought and analysis is a clear and extremely useful set of dominant structural patterns that not only describe how documentary films are organized, but also explain how those structural patterns are rhetorical, exerting an influence on the viewer's experience of and reaction to the film regardless of its specific subject matter.

Nichol's six-part typology includes the following modes: poetic, expository, observational, participatory, reflexive, and performative. Moore's film is a hybrid of expository and participatory modes; its 20 major sequences repeatedly alternate between them as the 2-hour film unfolds (see appendix).

Expository Mode

The "expository text addresses the viewer directly, with titles or voices that advance an argument about the historical world" (Nichols, 1991, p. 34). An example of exposition in *Bowling for Columbine* is the footage of the Columbine shooting accompanied by Moore's voice-of-authority narration. Despite its inherently rhetorical nature, exposition tends to create "the impression of objectivity and of well-substantiated judgment" (Nichols, 1991, p. 35).

This is often the most influential rhetorical form in any medium: persuasion that purports not to persuade, but merely to inform. In *Bowling for Columbine*, this is achieved largely, although not entirely, due to the absence of the filmmaker on the screen during key expository sequences. Although Moore's influence on the text is both heard (through narration) and felt (through editing), he is not seen interacting with his subjects—the style for which he is best known—when the film is in expository mode (Plate 10.2, p. 280).

The key to understanding how the viewer's expectations are managed through exposition in documentary film is found in the surprising relationship between the spoken narration and the film's images.

> Expository documentaries rely heavily on an informing logic carried by the spoken word. In a reversal of the traditional emphasis in film, images serve a supporting role. . . . The commentary is therefore presumed to be of a higher order than the accompanying images. It comes from some place that remains unspecified but associated with objectivity or omniscience . . . like the authoritative manner of news anchors and reports, [it] strives to build a sense of credibility from qualities such as distance, neutrality, disinterestedness, and omniscience. (Nichols, 2001, p. 107)

Thus, *Bowling for Columbine*'s expository sequences, such as a brief history of U.S. involvement in the illegal and violent overthrow of foreign leaders and even its outrageous cartoon history of fear and racism, accrue a sense of authority due to their formal properties and not due to their treatment of the subject matter.[5]

Participatory Mode

The participatory documentary revels in its own subjectivity and "gives us a sense of what it is like for the filmmaker to be in a given situation and how that situation alters as a result" (Nichols, 2001, p. 116). In *Bowling for Columbine*, participatory sequences range from the infamous Heston interview (in which the subject reveals something that, if not for the interview, likely

---

5. The irony of utilizing a mode of representation that is newslike in a film that suggests that news coverage is at least partly to blame for American violence is explored in the final section of this chapter.

would never have been known—namely, that Heston believes that America is violent due to racial "mixing"), to the ambush of Kmart (in which Moore and two boys injured at Columbine convince, or rather coerce, the company into a pledge to stop selling bullets).

The participatory style is known as *cinéma vérité*, or "film truth," which "emphasizes that this is the truth of an encounter rather than the absolute or untampered truth" (Nichols, 2001, p. 118). In other words, this mode is unabashedly subjective (Plate 10.3, p. 281). "When we witness participatory documentaries we expect to witness the historical world as represented by someone who actively engages with, rather than unobtrusively observes, poetically reconfigures, or argumentatively assembles that world" (Nichols, 2001, p. 116). Unlike exposition, in which the narrator's commentary provides the film's primary argument, in participatory mode, "[t]extual authority shifts toward the social actors recruited: their comments and responses provide a central part of the film's argument" (Nichols, 1991, p. 44).

In terms of viewer expectations, participatory sequences differ from expository sequences in at least one significant way: The former are unapologetically rhetorical, whereas the latter "tend to mask . . . the tangible process of enunciation, the saying of something as distinct from that which is said" (Nichols, 1991, p. 56).

STRUCTURAL RHETORIC: INTERPRETING MODES OF REPRESENTATION

Bowling for Columbine is able to balance these two different organizational structures and modes of address largely because of its strategic use of two key elements: evidentiary editing in expository mode and interviews in participatory mode.

Evidentiary Editing

> Editing in expository mode generally serves less to establish a rhythm or formal pattern . . . than to maintain the continuity of the spoken argument of perspective. We call this evidentiary editing. Such editing may sacrifice spatial or temporal continuity to rope in images from far-flung places if they help advance the argument. (Nichols, 2001, p. 107)

Because evidentiary editing does not follow basic laws on continuity, films that make use of it can employ rapid and apparently random transitions without confusing the viewer. In the case of *Bowling for Columbine*, this includes not only the random mixture of content, but also the many transitions from expository mode to participatory mode and back again. The editing style allows Moore to act as social actor in certain sequences and authoritative narrator in others without distraction, but not without consequence. By occupying two different, but unequal, positions in the same text, Moore manages to articulate two different arguments, each apparently plausible, although ultimately incompatible.

The Interview

The film also makes extensive use of a staple of the nonfiction film: the interview. Its power in *Bowling for Columbine*, which features no less than seven extended interviews, cannot be overestimated. Nichols distinguishes between the rhetorical contribution interviews make in expository versus participatory documentaries:

> When interviews contribute to an expository mode of representation, they generally serve as evidence for the filmmaker's, or text's, argument. When interviews contribute to an interactive [i.e. participatory] mode of representation, they generally serve as evidence for an argument presented as the product of the interaction of filmmaker and subject. (Nichols, 1991, p. 50)

Although Moore's film combines both modes in one text, his interviews are uniformly participatory. In every one, we either see Moore or at least hear his questions.[6] The result is a subtle, but significant, hierarchical relationship between Moore's competing arguments that a proliferation of guns has caused the epidemic of violence in the United States (which is articulated primarily in participatory sequences, including some interviews) and that the media has caused an epidemic of fear that led to violence in the United States (which is articulated primarily in expository sequences, usually by Moore's voice-of-authority commentary).

THE STRUCTURED RHETORIC OF *BOWLING FOR COLUMBINE*

The theoretical relationship between the film's two modes of documentary representation could not be more clear: The expository argument trumps the participatory argument—not because the evidence is more compelling, but rather because of the rhetorical structure and authoritative dynamic created and sustained by each. As Nichols (1991) noted, expository com-

---

6. Expository interviews feature only the subject's responses and offer no sense that an interviewer was involved, although viewers will assume that some question asked by someone likely prompted the response they are witnessing.

mentary "made by or on behalf of the filmmaker clearly subordinates the [participatory] interviews to the film's own argument" (p. 50).

Bowling for Columbine actually uses both modes of representation to promote both arguments. What is consequential, however, is Moore's decision to first use exposition to indict guns (Sections 4, 5, 6, and 8; see appendix), only to turn that authoritative mode over to the exclusive pursuit of his other argument—that the media is to blame (Sections 9, 11, 12, 13, 16, and 17). Meanwhile, participatory mode is first used to investigate guns (Sections 1, 2, and 3); it is then used to explore the media theory (Sections 7, 10, 14, 15, and 18) and eventually returns to guns for the film's conclusion (Sections 19 and 20). Thus, although the less compelling participatory mode alternates between promoting each possibility, the more compelling expository mode abandons one premise (guns) in favor of another (the media). Moore's subjects and even some of his own commentary may blame guns, but the structure of his film places the news media in the crosshairs.

Moore may not have intended this result, but the structuring of his modes of discourse determined the argument that his film ultimately would advance. By vacillating between one mode that professes objectivity (expository) and one that celebrates its subjectivity (participatory), the film was sure to confuse its audience's expectations and understanding regarding its rhetorical trajectory. Despite the many merits of the film, it is in this regard not a masterful means of intellectual and emotional manipulation, but rather a text that appears to the casual viewer to succumb to contradiction and ambiguity. Although Moore seems unable to decide which is the greater cause of violence in the Unites States—guns or the media—Moore's film (structurally) does decide.

THEMATIC RHETORIC: NEWS, FEAR, AND IRONY

There is a clear element of irony associated with the tone and style of the film insofar as it exhibits many of the qualities associated with contemporary news coverage. In most of its participatory sequences, *Bowling for Columbine* holds guns, gun owners, and gun advocates primarily responsible for the culture of violence in the United States. Yet in its expository sequences, the film identifies the media as cause and violence as consequence (Plate 10.4, p. 281). Ironically, the film appropriates in these (expository) sequences the thematic structures that define modern American news coverage—the tactics that they indict as culturally destructive. Thus, close scrutiny of the thematic rhetoric of Moore's film reveals it to be a prime example of the sort of visual text that the film suggests is harmful to American culture.

Kathleen Hall Jamieson and Karlyn Kohrs Campbell (2000) argued that a relatively small number of common "themes are woven into the very nature of newsgathering in the United States" (p. 51). They are appearance versus reality, little guys versus big guys, good against evil, efficiency versus inefficiency, and unique versus routine.

Bowling for Columbine appropriates at least four of these themes and does so to great rhetorical effect. The first—appearance versus reality—is especially significant in that it "reflects an emphasis on conflict and the 'objective' role of skeptical newsgatherers who uncover hypocrisy" (Jamieson & Campbell, 2000, p. 51). The film's review of the U.S. government's involvement with the illegal and violent overthrow of foreign dictators is a perfect illustration of *Bowling for Columbine*'s use of this theme. Its creation of the appearance of objectivity—that is, of nonargumentativeness—in its expository sequences is essential.

The second theme—little guys versus big guys—is the one for which Moore is best known. One of his earlier films, *Roger & Me*, is a classic example of how Moore, armed with a camera and thus the upper hand, effectively casts himself as a David battling a more powerful Goliath. *Bowling for Columbine* employs this theme repeatedly, including Moore's siege on Kmart and his interview with Heston.

The third theme—good against evil—also accurately describes the dynamic established in the scenes at Kmart and Heston's home, as well as many others in which the benevolent and socially conscious Moore butts heads with an uncaring foe. Curiously, Heston, the physical embodiment of evil in the film's closing sequence, has made use of this thematic structure, and he did so for purposes similar to Moore's. In 1999, Heston made headlines after he delivered a speech entitled "Winning the Cultural War" at Harvard University, in which he criticized American culture for being too politically correct (see McCroskey, 2001). Pitting himself against the media giant Warner Brothers, Heston told the crowd that one brave man can make a difference so long as he defends that which is good and right. Heston's argument resonated with Moore's in remarkable ways. Addressing the relationship between the First and Second Amendments, Heston suggested that violent movies and song lyrics, as opposed to guns, were contributing to the destruction of American values.

Finally, and most ironically, the last theme—unique versus routine—is employed by Moore's film in its depiction and characterization of how the mainstream U.S. media covers violence, especially gun violence. By contrasting what U.S. news outlets always do (routine) versus the novel approach taken by news outlets in less-violent Canada (unique), Moore indicts U.S. news coverage as a contributing factor in its problem with violence for employing the same dramatic themes appropriated by Moore in documenting that coverage. *Bowling for Columbine* thus reveals itself as, at least thematically, a prime example of the sort of visual text that is supposedly bad for America and that makes Americans bad to one another.

CONCLUSION

It is the function of speech to free men from the bondage of irrational fears.
—Justice Louis D. Brandeis *Whitney v California*
(1927; Cited in Tedford & Herbeck, 2001, p. 56)

"I don't have all the answers," Moore insists in the film and in countless interviews since its release (Chihara, 2002). But his film presumes that it does. Although the narrator (Moore) at times insists that a causal argument cannot be made because the elements in the equation that the film sets up are too numerous and too complex for such simplification, this analysis of the film's structural and thematic rhetoric reveals that in fact two competing arguments articulated in two different modes of documentary representation are advanced within the same text. The first suggests that guns and gun owners are primarily responsible for violence in the United States. The second suggests that the media is in fact the problem. This analysis further reveals that the film's consequential use of expository and participatory modes creates a perhaps unintended imbalance, ultimately charging that guns do not kill people, but rather the media occasionally scares gun owners into killing one another.

In addition, this analysis has found that Moore's attempt to hold the media accountable borders on the ironic. *Bowling for Columbine* charges that U.S. news coverage is a contributing factor in its problem with violence for employing such dramatic themes as appearance versus reality, little guys versus big guys, good against evil, and unique versus routine. The text is identified as ironic because, in the process of documenting the problem with the media, it appropriates these same themes attributed to the allegedly destructive media.

Certainly one can further investigate the claims advanced by Moore's text and find fault, whatever one's politics, with its logic. For instance, viewers are positioned to conclude that the relationship among violence, videogames, music, and movies is nonexistent. Even the film's title pokes fun at this apparently illogical conclusion. Yet Moore equivocates by asserting that sensational news reports do contribute to the climate of irrational fear that results in such violence, without explaining how news differs from other forms of mass media. But *Bowling for Columbine* has succeeded in starting a national debate about the relationship among guns, fear, violence, racism, and the media that can only be good for our too-violent culture.

Unfortunately, as the film withdraws from its original charge—that guns are the problem—it takes up a second charge that, although plausible, fails to distinguish between sensationalism and the responsible exercise of free speech. Moore has said:

> If anything, the way to honor those deaths [resulting from 9/11] is to have more freedom now, is to have more openness, more liberty. . . . What better way to show the rest of the world that this is what we truly believe in than by having more democracy, not less? . . . America is about asking questions, and the freedom to think, and to dissent. There's nothing more American than that. (cited in Kaltenbach, 2002, p. 2E)

Moore may believe this in his heart, but his film tells a different story. Although the issue of censorship is never raised explicitly, it hovers like a darkening cloud as Moore continues his broad indictment of the news media in particular and society in general. Two hours after setting out to rid the nation of its weapons, Moore's film concludes by prescribing a remedy for what ails us that has less to do with banks handing out free guns and more to do with the selective exercise speech control.

APPENDIX

FILM SEQUENCE	EXPOSITORY MODE	PARTICIPATORY MODE
1. Michigan Bank		X
2. James Nichols		X
3. Lockheed Martin		X
4. Violence in United States	X	
5. Columbine footage	X	
6. NRA rally	X	
7. Matt Stone		X
8. Violence in schools	X	
9. Media frenzy	X	
10. Marilyn Manson		X
11. Violence in Europe	X	
12. Cartoon history of United States	X	
13. News media	X	
14. Barry Glassner		X
15. COPS TV show		X
16. Violence in Canada	X	
17. Tamara Owens	X	
18. Dick Clark		X
19. Kmart		X
20. Charleton Heston		X

REFERENCES

Benson, T. W. (2003). Mother and monster: The rhetorical structure of Alfred Hitchcock's *The Man Who Knew Too Much*. Unpublished manuscript.

Benson, T. W., & Anderson, C. (1989). *Reality fictions: The films of Frederick Wiseman*. Carbondale: Southern Illinois University Press.

Burton, J. (1990). *The social documentary in Latin America*. Pittsburgh: University of Pittsburgh Press.

Chihara, M. (2002, October). Michael Moore asks big questions. AlterNet.com. http://www.alternet.org/story.html?StoryID=14296

Corliss, R., & Sachs, A. (2002, October 7). Blood bath and beyond: Guerilla filmmaker Michael Moore takes aim at American gun culture, and makes a terrific movie. *Time*, p. 89.

Giltz, M. (2002, May 17). *Columbine* scores at Cannes: Moore documents culture of fear. *Denver Post*, p. B4.

Horwich, J. (2002, November 30). Columbine movie, aiming at America's flaws, exposes the Left's instead. *Courier-Journal*, p. A7.

Jamieson, K. H., & Campbell, K. K. (2000). *The interplay of influence: News, advertising, politics, and the mass media* (5th ed.). Belmont, CA: Wadsworth.

Kaltenbach, C. (2002, June 2). French hail their new hero; step aside Jerry Lewis— Cannes goes wild for Michael Moore and his film, *Bowling for Columbine*. *Baltimore Sun*, p. 2E.

McCroskey, J. C. (2001). *An introduction to rhetorical communication*. Boston: Allyn & Bacon.

Nesselson, L. (2002, May 27–June 7). *Bowling for Columbine*. *Variety*, p. 24.

Nichols, B. (1981). *Ideology and the image: Social representation in the cinema and other media*. Bloomington: Indiana University Press.

Nichols, B. (1991). *Representing reality: Issues and concepts in documentary*. Bloomington: Indiana University Press.

Nichols, B. (2001). *Introduction to documentary*. Bloomington: Indiana University Press.

Tedford, T. L., & Herbeck, D.A. (2001). *Freedom of speech in the United States* (3rd ed.). State College, PA: Strata.

Williams, J. (2002, October 24). Ambush documentarian takes his best shot at firearms. *St. Louis Post Dispatch*, p. D5.

CHAPTER ELEVEN

Rural Electrification Administration
A Rhetorical Analysis of the Lester Beall Posters, 1937–1941

SUSAN B. BARNES
ROCHESTER INSTITUTE OF TECHNOLOGY

R HETORICAL ANALYSIS HAS BEEN APPLIED to the examination of visual communication (Foss, 1982, 1993; Foss & Kanengieter, 1992) including advertising (Hope, 1999; Meister, 1997; Mullen & Bauman, 2001), photography (Erickson, 2000; Finnegan, 2000), cartoons (Benoit, Klyukovski, McHale, & Airne, 2001; Bruce, 2001), and illustrations (Olson, 1983; Peterson, 2001). Although scholars have examined a variety of visual texts, rhetorical techniques have not yet been applied to the analysis of graphic design. Critiques of graphic design tend to be written from a practical perspective that examines design principles, rather than the messages conveyed through the visual elements (Heller & Pomeroy, 1997; Meggs, 1989; Tufte, 1990). In contrast to exploring design principles, this study examines the rhetorical messages communicated through a series of posters created by graphic designer Lester Beall for the Rural Electrification Administration. The purpose of these posters was to communicate the benefits of electricity, and the visual and verbal rhetoric was designed to convince rural Americans to adopt electrical technologies.

In ancient Greek culture, rhetoric described oral communication. As newer communication technologies emerged, rhetorical principles were updated and applied to electric and visual forms of communication. For example, Kathleen E. Welch (1999) discussed TV and Web sites in terms of classical rhetorical techniques to argue that these methods can help people better understand contemporary "electric rhetoric." Similarly, Sonja Foss (1982, 1993) wrote articles that apply rhetorical techniques to the examination of visual texts. Foss' methods have been adopted by other scholars and used to study illustrations (Peterson, 2001) and advertisements (Mullen & Bauman, 2001). Foss and Kanengieter (1992) described three steps in the process of understanding visual messages. These steps are: (a) identification of the presented elements, (b) processing of the elements, and (c) formulation of the message.

In the first step, identification of presented elements—the elements that compose the images—are named and sorted. These include the objects depicted along with the shapes, lines, angles, textures, rhythms, and text. An examination of the elements within the layout of a design is the first step in becoming visually literate. According to Dondis (1973), the objective of visual literacy is similar to the aim "of written language: to construct a basic system for learning, recognizing, making, and understanding visual messages that are negotiable by all people" (p. x). Identifying, sorting, and naming basic elements in a graphic design builds a vocabulary that can be applied to an analysis of the visual messages communicated through the design.

During the second step, the elements identified in Step 1 are grouped and organized. "The viewer looks for interactions among various suggested elements—how they relate to each other, how they can be grouped, and the tensions among them" (p. 315). The arrangement of elements on a page can create visual stress and balance (see Dondis, 1973). For instance, symmetrical and asymmetrical shape arrangements evoke feelings of balance or imbalance in the viewer. In *The Sense of Order*, E. H. Gombrich (1979/1984) stated that the arrangement of patterns in visual works "appeal to our sense of balance, our feeling for scale, our search for the familiar in the unfamiliar" (p. 302). The organization of elements in a visual text conveys messages through unconscious feelings and conscious symbols. Thus, visual organizations can evoke emotional feelings. Feelings often occur on an unconscious level. In contrast, symbolic messages are understood through conscious awareness. For instance, red-and-white stripes combined with a blue rectangle often communicate the idea of an American flag. In his analysis, Gombrich also utilized *gestalt theory*, which argues that the whole image is different from the sum of its individual elements parts, to understand meanings conveyed through visual symbols (also see Arnheim, 1954). For example, two dots, a circle, and a curve placed in the proper arrangement become a smiley face. The proper arrangement of these four elements can be easily understood on a conscious level.

According to Barry (1997), "Our cognitive system developed from our perceptual system" and visual information is first processed on an unconscious level before rational thought occurs (p. 24). For this reason, images can make us feel a certain way before the message is rationally understood. Step 2 identifies the larger meanings associated with combined elements in the design. Moreover, it helps the viewer better understand the emotional balances and tensions being communicated through the arrangement of elements in a visual layout. Because visual imagery does not have a fixed grammatical structure, Foss (1993) contended there is a certain amount of ambiguity associated with a visual message: Images "do not express a thesis or proposition in the way that verbal messages do—the thesis [message] is usually uncertain and ambiguous" (p. 213). Ambiguous visual messages attract the viewer on an unconscious level through the use of technical novelty: "Some dimension of the form, structure, or construction technique of the image stands out as exception or extraordinary" (Foss, 1993, p. 215). Technical novelty captures the viewer's attention and requires the viewer to resolve the ambiguity on a conscious level to find meaning in the image.

On a conscious level, Messaris (1997) argued that pictures have the ability to suggest rather than state meanings, which adds to the persuasive use of visuals in graphic design and advertising. Commercial images have the "ability to imply something in pictures while avoiding the consequences of saying it in words" (p. xix). Additionally, Suh (1999) stated that when visual images are incorporated into persuasive messages, they "make a message more attention-getting, and reinforce [verbal] message arguments" (p. 9). Images imply messages, support textual statements, and add to the overall persuasiveness of a message. To summarize Step 2, objects in a visual text both capture the attention of the viewer and create messages that are greater than their individual meanings.

In the final step, the viewer devises a message. According to Dewey (1934), "Works of art, like words, are literally pregnant with meaning" (p. 118). Intellectual meanings are carried over from past experiences, and emotional excitations occur when looking at colors and objects. Visual messages are understood in relationship to cultural experiences and individual interpretations. "The *material* out of which a work of art is composed belongs to the common world rather than to the self, and there is self-expression in art because the self assimilates that material in a distinctive way to reissue it into the public world in a form that builds a new object" (p. 107). During the creation process, the artist must vicariously become the viewing audience. A rhetorical triadic relationship exists among the artist, the visual object, and the audience. This relationship occurs within particular cultural contexts. As a result, visual messages are often social constructions that reflect the times in which they are created. For example, Marchand (1985) argued that early advertising reinforced ideologies that already existed within American culture, such as support for a capitalistic economy and the myth of the American dream.

Interpreting visual messages involves both a personal reaction to the objects arranged in the design and an understanding of the symbolic messages being communicated. Because the artist works within a cultural context, a more complete understanding of a visual message requires a historical examination of the period in which the message was constructed. In the case of the Beall posters, they were created at a time when American culture was filled with rhetorical themes designed to persuade the public to use electrical products (Marchand, 1985; Nye, 1985, 1990). In this study, a historical rhetorical component is being added to the three steps identified by Foss and Kanengieter. Prior to analyzing the posters, research was conducted on the history of the electrification of America, the history of graphic design, and the history of advertising messages. Thus, the model has been revised as follows: (a) conduct historical research to better understand the context in which the work was created, (b) identify the basic objects, (c) organize the objects into meaningful relationships and messages, and (d) examine the meaningful relationships and messages within their cultural context. The following sections provide a historical overview of graphic design and examine the rhetorical themes associated with the electrification of the United States.

THE RHETORIC ASSOCIATED WITH ELECTRIFYING AMERICA

Central to the social adoption of a new technology is the visual and verbal rhetoric used to describe, promote, and support its acceptance (see Rogers, 1995). A historical survey of the electrification of the United States (Nye, 1985, 1990) reveals four rhetorical influences occurring in American culture during the time Beall designed his posters for the Rural Electrification Administration (REA). These influences fall into the categories of cultural ideals, social needs, electrical advertising messages, and modernist design.

Theme 1: American Cultural Ideals

Cultural ideals include the utopian narratives written and illustrated about electrical futures. In the United States, its electrical future was promoted through public expositions and fairs, such as Buffalo's Pan-American Exposition and the Chicago World's Fair. In the late 1800s and early 1900s, Americans transformed electrification into civic pride. According to Nye (1990), electrical terms began to permeate common American speech, and these terms emphasized connectedness. "After 1881 all fairs emphasized dramatic lighting and many made illuminated towers their symbols: Buffalo's Electric Tower, San Francisco's Tower of Jewels, and New York's Trylon and

Perisphere in 1939 are obvious examples" (Nye, 1990, p. 35). The fairs made a visible relationship between electricity and the American ideology of progress. For a city or home to be considered modern, it needed electric lights.

Electricity ushered in a brilliant future for Americans. By illuminating cities, electricity created a new spectacle of brightly lit buildings, window displays, and electric advertising signs. Entire city skylines were now aglow from powerful beams of light. Streetlights became commonplace, and electric trolleys transported people between the city and the country. Trolleys made it easier to send goods to remote places and "easier for residents in these regions to travel to central markets" (Nye, 1990, p. 119). People could now live in the countryside and commute to the city. Additionally, mail-order stores could get their products to larger groups of customers.

Moreover, the widespread use of electricity made it a marketable commodity. Private companies were formed around the United States to sell and distribute it. "Led by the electrical industry, between 1890 and 1920 businessmen defined electricity as a commodity rather than as a public service" (Nye, 1990, p. 169). Private utilities dominated the electric industry and they eventually overwhelmed smaller public systems. In addition to being a source of profits, electricity helped to define modern progress and social well-being in the United States. However, the commercial distribution of electricity excluded farmers from the new utopian ideals of electrical progress and modernity. Private electrical companies did not want to incur the cost of running electrical lines to rural areas with a limited number of customers. As a result, rural areas tended to be left off the electrical grid.

Theme 2: Social Needs

As cities and suburbs throughout the United States adopted electricity, rural areas lagged behind. The electrification process started with streetlights in the 1880s and the domestic adoption of electricity after 1910. By the early 1930s, farms still did not have electricity. As a result, a social need developed to electrify rural communities in the United States. Because commercial electrical companies would not spend the money to electrify rural America, the government stepped in to bring electricity to rural farm communities by enabling them to set up electrical cooperatives. During the 1930s, electricity was no longer a luxury because it became a necessity. In May 1936, President Roosevelt signed a national law establishing the REA to loan money to local cooperatives because private companies saw little profit in electrifying the farm. The purpose of the REA was to get electrical transmission lines to the rural areas, such as Appalachia.

The REA loaned money to help grassroots organizations build their transmission lines and operate electrical services. To make these local cooperatives profitable, the REA turned to General Electric and Westinghouse for help. A committee was formed to prepare and distribute booklets on wiring installations, and inexpensive lighting packages were developed. Federal agencies developed promotional materials, including sample talks, filmstrips, publicity, and posters. "After 1936 a half century of electrical technology arrived on the farm all at once" (Nye, 1990, p. 319). In addition to publishing educational materials, the REA developed advertisements depicting the benefits of electricity.

Theme 3: Electrical Advertising Messages

Electricity and electrification became the subjects of national advertising campaign efforts. Electrification introduced a new set of electric lights, appliances, and tools. After 1900, advertisements for electrical gadgets appeared in national American magazines, such as *Harper's Magazine* and the *Saturday Evening Post*. Major corporations, such as General Electric, dominated the electrical industry. Their domination was ensured through extensive advertising and the promotion of brand names. For example, General Electric spent hundreds of thousands of dollars advertising their products to various audiences throughout the United States (Nye, 1985). Starting with the light bulb, "utilities and electrical corporations adopted an informational form of advertising, with extensive text emphasizing the social improvements made possible through new products and services" (Nye, 1990, p. 183).

On the farm, electricity could make the tasks of pumping water, churning butter, and washing and ironing clothing much easier. Washing machines, electric pumps, and irons would greatly ease the burden of the farmwoman. A variety of additional electrical products were developed specifically for farm use, including an electric plow, cream separator, thresher machine, corn husker, and electric pumps. Although reluctant to incur the expense of rural electrification, manufacturers such as General Electric and Westinghouse were anxious to reach the farm market to sell their products. In 1925, General Electric created a series of magazine advertisements targeted toward the rural market; they appeared in *Capper's Farmer, Farm Life,* and *Southern Agriculturalist.* These advertisements described how electrical products could modernize farm life and help farmers increase their production. In contrast, city and urban advertisements were focused on the consumption of electricity through the use of electrical products as a symbol of modernity and the use of mass transportation. For example, farmers read nothing about transportation because electric trolleys and subways were irrelevant to them. City dwellers needed to rely on mass transportation, which led to the rise of suburbs. For the same reason, city dwellers did not "read about how to prolong the day artificially in hen houses during the winter and thus raise egg production" (Nye, 1985, p. 128). Urban and rural residents did not read the same magazines. As a result, different advertising messages could be developed to reach specific audiences. Although messages were different, the underlying purpose of electrical advertising remained the same. The advertisements encouraged Americans to adopt electrical technology, buy electrical products, and increase their electrical consumption.

The rural and urban uses of electricity were very different. In the cities, subways and trolley cars brought people to work and families to the amusement park on the weekends. Trolleys began to replace the horse as a major form of transportation. In contrast, electrification of the farm greatly eased the work burden of the farmwoman. No longer did she have to carry buckets of water into the house to do laundry or take a bath. Moreover, electrification led to the improvement of farming practices. Although different audiences, electricity helped people in both the urban and rural areas through modernization and an improved farm life.

When electrical advertisements portrayed farm life, the farmer in the ads displayed "just as much interest in modern goods and styles as did city folk" (Marchand, 1985, p. 68). Building a relationship between progress and electricity reinforced advertising's goal to promote modernity. According to Marchand (1985), "Advertising men [and women] were modernity's 'town criers.' They brought good news about progress" (p. 1). People learned about the benefits of modern technologies through advertisements placed in national magazines. Electric lights, vacuum cleaners, washing machines, and refrigerators were necessary appliances in the modern home. Advertisements directed toward urban families depicted an elegant lifestyle facilitated by the use of refrigerators and vacuum cleaners. For example, an advertisement for a Hoover cleaner shows four elegantly dressed women surrounding the machine. Similarly, an advertisement for Crosley refrigerators illustrates two couples in evening clothes around an open refrigerator door. It is interesting to note that illustration rather than photography was the method of visual communication applied to many consumer advertisements. Illustrations tended to glamorize and idealize the use of modern electrical appliances.

In stark contrast to the elegant urban lifestyles portrayed in consumer advertisements for electrical products is a series of advertisements created by the REA that utilized photography to show electricity in use. An advertisement called "Electrical Lighting in the United States" consists of a montage of photographic images that show electrical use in homes, schools, office settings, public streets, baseball parks, transportation systems, and stores. These images portray a more realistic view of how electricity changed the urban environment. "Rural Electrification in the United States" is a second advertisement directed toward farm life. It also used the photographic montage technique to communicate messages about how electricity improves farm work and housework in rural areas. Although the visual styles and messages communicated in the REA and consumer advertisements were different, all of these advertisements communicate the underlying message that modern American life was based on the use of electricity and electrical products. To be modern Americans, people had to have and use electricity in their homes. However, on the farm, electricity improved basic living conditions, and it was not a luxury item.

Theme 4: Graphic Design and the Modernist Movement

Paralleling the rise of electrification in the United States was graphic design. In addition to advertisements designed to sell electrical products as a symbol of modernity and progress, a new graphic design style emerged in American culture that communicated the same ideology. Modernism was a style developed during the 20th century. Along with the rise of modernism came the growth of graphic design professionals and mass media. Commercial artists, including illustrators, boardmen, and letterers, were in great demand to produce print-based media, including books, posters, journals, and advertisements (see Heller, 1998). According to Heller (2001), the term *graphic designer* was coined in 1922 by William Addison Dwiggins in his book, *Layout in Advertising*. With the rise of mass communication, many artists became interested in forms of graphic design directed toward mass rather than elite audiences (see Carroll, 1998).

In Europe, predominantly left-wing artists argued that the commercial world offered them an opportunity to democratize art. Social mass art, such as advertising and poster design, was viewed as an art form that could shape the visual habits of the public. For example, Russian constructivist artists renounced the idea of "art for art's sake" and encouraged artists to use posters as a means of social expression. Heller (2001) stated: "As the modern movements sought to redefine the place of art and the role of the artist in society, advertising was seen not only as a medium ripe for reform, but as a platform on which the graphic symbols of reform could be paraded along with the product being sold" (p. 296).

Designers rallied around the *modernist style* of graphics, which was influenced by the German Bauhaus Art School (see Whitford, 1984; Wingler, 1969). The Bauhaus reformed art education by replacing Romantic ideas of artistic self-expression with rational quasi-scientific approaches to design. Form was related to function. By erasing the boundaries between fine and applied art, the Bauhaus attempted to bring art into a close relationship with life through design. Design was perceived to be a vehicle for social change and cultural revitalization. The modernist graphic design movement originated in Europe and then moved to the United States. The following artists are associated with the modernist style: Gyorgy Kepes, Laszlo Moholy-Nagy, Walter Gropius, and Herbert Bayer.

While working as a commercial illustrator in Chicago, Lester Beall was introduced to Bauhaus and constructivist design through European avant-garde magazines and a colleague named Fred Hauck, who had lived and painted in Paris (see Remington, 1996). After seeing these works, Beall began to experiment with form, black-and-white silhouettes, dynamic angled typography, and indexical arrows as recurring themes in his designs. According to Remington (2002), Beall developed a new visual language that "involved the use of graphic elements (color, form, texture, lines, gridded frames, geometric shapes); implied spatial structures (receding perspective lines, strong foreground/background relationships); typographic forms (bars, arrows, pointing fists, boldly mixed type styles, angled lines of type, masses of type set to conform to shapes)" (p. 13). Additionally, he incorporated photomontage into his work: "Photomontage became a natural way for him to combine his interests in photography, typography, art, and printing with the revolutionary ideas about typographic form and page layout being propounded by El Lissitzky, Moholy-Nagy, Herbert Bayer [along with other European designers]" (p. 13). Beall's complex style "sought visual contrast and a rich level of information content" (Meggs, 1983, p. 362).

During the late 1920s and 1930s, Beall "almost single-handedly launched the modern movement in American design" (Meggs, 1983, p. 432). Of special significance were the series of posters that he designed for the REA. The purpose of these posters was to convince rural farmers in the United States to adopt electricity. During the 1930s, illustrators were hired by corporations to redesign or create new trademarks for a variety of new electrical products. The stylized lightning bolt streaked its way across numerous trademarks of manufacturers: "A fist grasping a lightning bolt, a physical impossibility, was the perfect visualization of man's conquering the elements" (Mendenhall, 1983, p. 3). Many of these designs used traditional illustration techniques, mythological figures, and symbols. For instance, William Blake's *Angel of Revelation* was transformed into a trademark for James H. Rhodes & Company (see Mendenhall, 1983).

Traditional images of electricity reinforced the American ideals of industrial progress and power. In contrast to traditional techniques, Beall's modernist style combined strong bold shapes with contemporary symbols and photography. Beall's style supported the idea of progress and communicated the message of modernity, which was largely associated with electrification. He designed within a rhetorical environment that promoted the use of electricity through public events, corporate logos, and advertising messages. Beall designed promotional materials for radio companies such as the Columbia Broadcasting System (CBS). George Bijur, who was in the advertising department at CBS, hired Beall to design a promotional booklet for CBS Radio. Bijur later recommended Beall to Bill Phillips, an information officer of the REA. In 1937, Beall was hired by Phillips to design a series of posters to encourage rural farmers to adopt electricity.

POSTER ANALYSIS

Beall designed three series of posters for the REA between 1937 and 1941. Six sets of images are included in each series. In 1938, Series 1 was featured in a one-man show of Beall's work exhibited at the Museum of Modern Art in New York City. Prior to the Beall exhibit, the museum had presented an exhibition called "New Horizons in American Art," which featured Federal Art Project artists. Its goal was to promote the achievements of federally funded art projects to the American people (see Harris, 1995). Similarly, the Beall exhibition championed the posters commissioned by the government's REA. Achievements in American design and technological progress were themes running throughout the Beall exhibit. The REA posters gained Beall national and international recognition. Remington (1996) stated: "The posters are icons in the history of graphic design" (p. 74). As icons, these posters reflect a period of technological change in American culture (Table 11.1).

Series 1

The first REA poster series includes the following designs: "Farm Work," "Heat . . . Cold," "Light," "Radio," "Running Water," and "Wash Day" (Plate 11.1, p. 282). Looking at these images, one is immediately struck by their strong use of symbols and graphic simplicity. Simplicity was necessary because the target audience for these posters was rural farmers, and some had limited reading skills. Simple shapes are combined to create the impression

Table 11.1. Series 1 Basic Objects in Images

CATEGORY	OBJECTS
FARM WORK	rectangles triangle thick line two thin lines generator large blue rectangle large white rectangle large red rectangle Rural Electrification Administration Beall
HEAT . . . COLD	two black medium lines two black thin lines white line + circle = thermometer large red rectangle large blue rectangle Rural Electrification Administration Beall
LIGHT	four black rectangles five thin white lines three white squares light bulb large red rectangle large blue rectangle Rural Electrification Administration Beall
RADIO	four black rectangles six white squares one white rectangle three white arrows blue five-sided shape red five-sided shape Rural Electrification Administration Beall
RUNNING WATER	six black arrows faucet yellow/green rectangle blue rectangle Rural Electrification Administration Beall
WASH DAY	four black rectangles five white arrows white washing machine blue rectangles yellow/green rectangle Rural Electrification Administration Beall

of a farmhouse at night with light, running water, electric appliances (radio, washing machine), and heating. Words (*light, radio, running water, wash day*) make a direct connection between the farm and symbol in the design. Viewers of these posters would be cognizant of the fact that electricity is required for indoor plumbing, heating systems, and running water. Thus, a simple relationship could be made first between electricity and the modern convenience symbolized. The reading public could then make a second relationship between the advantage of electricity and the REA. Beall's name also appears on all of the posters to identify him as the designer. The senders of the message are clearly identified in all cases.

Color usage in the first series of posters is definitely an American theme, and they further support that the sender of the message is the U.S. government. Visual reinforcement of the governmental role in sending these messages is both denotative and connotative. Red, white, and blue together tend to convey the idea of the American flag, which symbolizes the United States. Additionally, Beall's use of color dramatized the idea of light and electricity through his use of white paper to create the light bulb, lighted windows in the farmhouse, and dramatic arrows knocked out against a dark blue sky. Country or farmland is implied by his use of the color yellow. Strong bold colors combined with white space create a dramatic eye-catching effect, which makes this series of images extremely memorable.

Relating these posters to cultural trends, Remington (1996) stated that there is a resemblance between the first series of images and posters designed by Russian constructivists 20 years earlier. Beall utilized a modernist style to reinforce the concepts of modernity and progress. Progress is often visually depicted as movement. Movement is central to Beall's design style, and arrows are often included to create a sense of movement or flow within the design. The design work of Kurt Schwitters in the 1920s was a strong influence on the directional emphasis placed in the Beall designs. In some cases, such as the radio poster, the directional arrows can be interpreted as radio broadcast signals. However, often the arrows have no direct symbolic meaning and are included strictly as a design element to create movement, which connotes the idea of progress. Internal movement within the designs combined with the modernist style, clearly express the ideas of progress and modernity (Table 11.2).

According to Marchand (1985), modernity and progress, combined with the ideology of consumption, were messages underlying advertising at the time Beall was designing the REA posters. Beall strengthened these cultural messages through his designs in several ways. First, his design

Table 11.2. Series 1 Objects Grouped Into Meanings

FARM WORK	rectangles + triangle = barn thick line + one thin lines = electrical pole generator + electrical pole = electrical generator red + white + blue = American design style is modern, which means progress Rural Electrification Administration reinforces electrical message Message: American farm work can be improved with the use of electrical generators
HEAT . . . COLD	red reinforces the idea of heat blue reinforces the idea of cold thermometer indicates temperature two black medium lines + two black thin lines = power lines red + white + blue = American design style is modern, which means progress Message: Electricity can be used to regulate temperatures
LIGHT	four black rectangles = farm house three white squares = light coming from windows in farm house five thin white lines make a visual connection between farmhouse and light bulb large blue rectangle symbolizes night red + white + blue = American design style is modern, which means progress Rural Electrification Administration reinforces electrical message Message: American electricity lights up the home at night
RADIO	four black rectangles = large two-story house six white squares + one white rectangle = light coming from windows blue five-sided shape + red five-sided shape = hill (house on hill) blue five-sided shape = night (electric light coming from windows) three white arrows + word radio = radio air waves coming to the house red + white + blue = American design style is modern, which means progress Rural Electrification Administration reinforces electrical message Message: American electricity brings radio to the home
RUNNING WATER	six black arrows + faucet = running water reinforced by the words running water blue rectangle = water yellow/green rectangle implies field and/or in-door wall design style is modern, which means progress Rural Electrification Administration reinforces electrical message Message: the Rural Electrification Administration brings running water
WASH DAY	four black rectangles = farm house five white arrows symbolize electricity white washing machine is inside the farmhouse blue rectangle symbolized the sky yellow/green rectangle symbolizes farmland design style is modern, which means progress Rural Electrification Administration reinforces electrical message Message: Electricity brings washday inside the farmhouse.

style is modern and progressive. Second, objects such as the radio, washing machine, running water faucet, and light bulb encourage the use and consumption of electrical products. In contrast to consumer advertisements for electrical products that glamorize the benefits of electricity, these graphics depict advantages to basic living necessities. As a result, the graphics are more informational than glamorous. Bringing light, running water, and washing into the farm home would make basic farm work easier, especially for women.

In summary, the message power of the first series of posters is created through the simplicity of the design and the strong use of color and symbols. Direct relationships are made between the benefits of electricity and the symbols illustrated in the designs. Further identification between electricity and the REA is produced through the use of strong type that clearly identifies the sender of the message, which is also reinforced through the use of color.

Series 2

In the second series, the six posters are titled "Boy and Girl on Fence" (Plate 11.2, p. 282), "Here It Comes," "It's Fine for Us," "Now I'm Satisfied," "Things Look Better," and "When I Think Back." Several major differences can be visually observed between the first and second series of posters. These include the use of captioning and photography. Captioning was suggested by Phillips (1939) at the REA. He believed that placing themes on the images would create a psychological effect similar to listening to a song. The following captioning ideas were sent to Beall in June 1939:[1]

1. Home comfort on the farm
2. Labor saving in farm work
3. Widened horizons for farm people
4. Future of farm young people
5. New opportunities for rural schools
6. Cooperation
7. Better health on the farm (personal letter sent to Beall, June 19, 1939)

Beall experimented with photomontage in the second series, which made the images more complex. Beall did all of the original photography,

---

1. Letter available in the Lester Beall Collection, Rochester Institute of Technology Archives and Special Collections.

and the images were hand-retouched to silhouette the figures and remove the backgrounds. The photographic images of farmers were then placed into abstract backgrounds, which removed specific geographic locations. By replacing the actual backgrounds with abstract shapes, the viewer's attention is drawn to the image of the farmer as a symbol of farm life (Table 11.3).

Table 11.3. Series 2 Basic Objects in Images

CATEGORY	OBJECTS
BOY AND GIRL ON FENCE	four horizontal red stripes four horizontal white stripes blue rectangle photo of boy and girl photo of fence Rural Electrification Administration U.S. Department of Agriculture Beall
HERE IT COMES	two uneven four-sided red shapes yellow bar one uneven four-sided white shape one red arrow one black line photo of electrical worker Rural Electrification Administration U.S. Department of Agriculture Beall
IT'S FINE FOR US	one five-sided uneven blue shape one five-sided uneven white shape white bar three red arrows woman working a machine Rural Electrification Administration U.S. Department of Agriculture Beall
NOW I'M SATISFIED	yellow rectangle white uneven four-sided shape yellow uneven four-sided shape red bar photo of woman sitting in chair doing needlework photo of lamp on table next to chair Rural Electrification Administration U.S. Department of Agriculture Beall

THINGS LOOK BETTER	white four-sided uneven shape green/yellow rectangle red bar red arrow photo of a man photo of a horse Rural Electrification Administration U.S. Department of Agriculture Beall
WHEN I THINK BACK	white rectangle white four-sided uneven shape yellow/brown rectangle three red arrows black bar photo of radio photo of man in rocking chair tuning radio Rural Electrification Administration U.S. Department of Agriculture Beall

In the second series, the type treatment for the REA is no longer a dominant feature in the design. The REA is presented in a more subtle way and set in a serif typeface that resembles a stencil. Additionally, the U.S. Department of Agriculture is added to the text and placed on the posters in a smaller version of the same typeface as the REA. This additional type further identifies the governmental agencies sending the message. Textual captions are dominant elements in the designs, with the exception of the boy and girl on fence. This image is so powerful that it does not need to be reinforced with words. "Boy and Girl on Fence" combines the ideas of "the future of American farm youth" with "widened horizons for farm people" into a single image. Placing the fence on an angle against the striped background creates the impression of a horizon moving into the distance against an American flag. The boy and girl smile as they look up toward the sky or the future. Moreover, the patriotic quality of this image makes it stand out from the other posters in the series. Hope, a bright future, and the American way of life are connotative messages communicated through the design.

Captions incorporated into the second series communicate positive messages about electricity and farm life. "It's Fine for Us," "When I Think Back," and "Now I'm Satisfied" depict improved conditions in the farmhouse. For instance, "It's Fine for Us" shows a woman working an indoor machine, and "Now I'm Satisfied" depicts a woman sitting in a chair doing her sewing with an electric light turned on. "When I Think Back" is a photograph of an older farmer sitting in his rocking chair tuning a radio.

Moreover, the caption "When I Think Back" implies the future by evoking the past. These posters show how electricity can make the farmer's life easier and more enjoyable. In contrast to the three posters described earlier, "Things Look Better" does not include any electrical appliances. The poster communicates the message that electricity will make farm work easier by simply showing a photograph of a smiling farmer who is petting his horse.

Of all the posters in the three series, only one directly tries to show the installation of electrical lines. "Here It Comes" is a photograph of an electrical worker holding or pulling a thin black line. He smiles as he works. The underlying messages communicated through this image are again positive. Bringing electricity to your area is helpful to everyone, and your community should welcome electricity as it "comes" to your area. Additionally, a strong sense of movement is created in the design through the stark contrast between the irregular red shapes and the middle irregular white shape. White surrounded by red is also reminiscent of the American flag. Unlike the first series of posters, the colors in the second series do not communicate as strong a sense of the United States. However, "Here It Comes" and "Boy and Girl on Fence" do communicate a strong American theme. In the second series, a shift occurs in the overall color application from the use of red, white, and blue colors, which are associated with the United States to the use of colors and images that more directly relate to rural farmers (Table 11.4).

Table 11.4. Series 2 Objects Grouped Into Meanings

BOY AND GIRL ON FENCE	the horizontal red+ white stripes strongly resemble an American flag the flag association is reinforced by the blue rectangle the angle of the fence and the gaze of the boy and girl up and toward the right indicate looking toward the future the text (Rural Electrification Administration & U.S. Department of Agriculture) is subtle the reader has to work harder to make a connection between the image and organization Message: the future of American farm youth depends upon the Rural Electrification Administration
HERE IT COMES	uneven red shapes + white shape + red arrow = movement electrical worker + black line = installing electrical lines This idea is reinforced by the caption "Here It Comes" highlighted in a yellow bar The modernistic design style also suggests the idea of progress Installation of electrical lines is associated with the Rural Electrification Administration Message: The Rural Electrification Administration brings you electricity

IT'S FINE FOR US	five-sided uneven blue shape + five-sided uneven white shape = interior walls three red arrows + white bar = movement woman churning butter inside the house implies that electricity makes work easier phrase "It's Fine for Us" reinforces the idea that electricity makes farm work easier Message: The Rural Electrification Administration makes farm work easier because of electricity
NOW I'M SATISFIED	yellow rectangle + white uneven four-sided shape = interior wall and carpet uneven yellow shape + red bar creates the feeling of movement color yellow + lamp = light inside the home photo of woman sitting in chair doing needlework + lamp = electricity makes domestic work easier "Now I'm Satisfied" reinforces the idea that electricity is helpful on a practical level Message: The Rural Electrification Administration makes domestic work easier
THINGS LOOK BETTER	yellow-green rectangle = grass with four-sided uneven shape + horse implies corral red arrow and angled red bar create movement "things look better" + photos of man and horse = things look better on the farm Message: The Rural Electrification Administration makes things look better on the farm
WHEN I THINK BACK	white rectangle + yellow/brown rectangle = interior of house white four-sided uneven shape = interior carpet three red arrows = movement and the idea of radio broadcast signals photo of radio + interior of house = electrical appliances in the home "When I Think Back" + Older male farmer in rocking chair = remembering the past rocking chair = relaxation, life is easier Message: Life was more difficult before the Rural Electrification Administration brought electrical appliances to the farm.

Additionally, replacing symbols with images of actual farmers helps communicate the message about the benefits of electricity more directly. Depicting real people engages the viewer because it is easier to emotionally identify with a photograph rather than an abstract symbol. Similar to the shift in color usage, a change from symbols to photographs communicates the message that electricity helps the farmer execute his or her tasks more easily. An appealing aspect of the second series is the actual representation of farm life. However, the images have been turned into silhouettes and placed within abstract shapes to add a modernistic effect. Thus, the idea of modernity and progress is also communicated. Modern design is further emphasized by the placement of captions in rectangular boxes, which are frequently placed on an angle to add visual movement.

Through a shift in color treatment, the use of photographs, the addition of captions, and the arrangement of abstract shapes, the second series communicates positive messages about the benefits of having electricity on the farm. Moreover, the design style conveys the idea of modernity and progress. The designs created for Series 2 are more complex than Series 1, and many of the visual techniques utilized in the second series are further developed in the third series.

Series 3

In Series 3, Beall further advanced his use of photography and continued to caption the designs. Series 3 was produced in 1947 and includes the posters entitled, "A Better Home" (Plate 11.3, p. 282), "A Turn of the Hand," "Our Lines," "Power for Defense" (Plate 11.4, p. 282), "Power on the Farm," and "Rural Industries." These posters are the most visually complex with angled typography, silhouetted photographs, and patterns of colored stripes and dots (Table 11.5).

Table 11.5. Series 3 Basic Objects in Images

CATEGORY	OBJECTS
A BETTER HOME	white rectangle filled with red dots blue rectangle woman cooking with electric stove baked rolls coming out of oven blue elongated oval shape red rectangle Rural Electrification Administration U.S. Department of Agriculture Beall
A TURN OF THE HAND	Red rectangle thirteen white stripes on an angle twelve blue stripes on an angle blue rectangle white elongated oval shape photo of man turning on water faucet water coming out of faucet into horse trough photo of horse drinking from trough Rural Electrification Administration U.S. Department of Agriculture Beall

OUR LINES	large blue rectangle eleven white stripes on angle eleven red stripes thin blue rectangle red elongated oval shape photo of five men and one woman group is wearing coats & looking at plans one man is writing down information Rural Electrification Administration U.S. Department of Agriculture Beall
POWER FOR DEFENSE	nineteen white stripes on angle nineteen red strips on angle blue elongated oval shape thin blue rectangle photo of an airplane photo of a radio tower blue circle on top of tower photo of an aerial view of land Rural Electrification Administration U.S. Department of Agriculture Beall
POWER ON THE FARM	nineteen white stripes on angle nineteen blue stripes on angle thin blue rectangle red elongated oval shape black uneven four-sided shape photo of a man in overalls operating machine photo of electrical farm equipment Rural Electrification Administration U.S. Department of Agriculture Beall
RURAL INDUSTRIES	fifteen white stripes sixteen red stripes large blue rectangle thin red rectangle blue elongated oval shape photo of a man with hat operating equipment photo of an electrical saw for cutting wood Rural Electrification Administration U.S. Department of Agriculture Beall

Flag-style stripes in blue and white or red and white appear in five of the six posters. These stripes are definitely a reminder of the American flag. In contrast to Series 2, colors used in the third series are all red, white, and blue plus black. Moreover, the shapes of the colors are close to American flag shapes. At the time Beall created these posters, the United States had just entered World War II. As a result, national defense is an underlying message in several of the posters. An overall change can been seen in the message strategy from improving farm life to the importance of electrical *power.* "Power on the Farm" and "Power for Defense" make direct references to the term. Other types of power implied in the series include power in the home, power in rural industries, and power of people to organize. "Power on the Farm" is the caption of one poster and also an implied message in "A Turn of the Hand." Both images show the benefits of electricity in actual farm work because both are photographs of men operating electrical machines.

"Our Lines" breaks from all previous posters and implies the importance of citizen activism to set up a local electrical farm cooperative. It visually portrays a group of local farmers engaged in a planning discussion. One man holds a drawing while another man writes notes on a pad of paper. Of all the posters, this one symbolically depicts the primary purpose of the REA, which is to help local farmers organize to bring electricity to their own local areas. The red-and-white strips combined with the blue rectangle in the design communicate the message of an American flag. Thus, two messages are clearly communicated: the idea of America and the concept of local cooperation.

The use of numerous stripes in these posters also conveys the idea of fast movement and energy, which creates a different, more urgent dynamic in these designs. Jerome Snyder described the Beall posters as: "An expanding world of science, technology, and manufacturing had generated raising expectations that called for a new graphic industry, succinct of statement and visually attend to the increasing velocity of American life" (cited in Remington, 1996, p. 74).

Messages communicated through Series 3 reflect the changing political situation in the United States. The country was at war and everyone at home needed to support the war effort. "Power for Defense" directly sends this message. It is a photograph of an airplane flying over a rural area with a tower placed toward the middle of the design. Through the caption, "Power for Defense," an association is made between the tower and electricity. Implied in this design is the idea that rural areas need electricity to support the war effort. Patriotic feelings are strengthened through the red-and-white stripes placed in the "sky" area of the image and the blue elongated oval shape in which the caption is placed. Positioning the strips on angles creates a sense of urgency that is more dramatic in this poster than the others (Table 11.6).

Table 11.6. Series 3 Objects Grouped Into Meanings

A BETTER HOME	blue rectangle + white rectangle filled with red dots = interior wall
	white rectangle filled with red dots = wall paper
	electric stove places the room as a kitchen
	elongated oval shape creates movement
	"A Better Home" + woman cooking on electric stove = electricity
	    makes a home better
	Message The Rural Electrification Administration helps make a
	    better home by bringing electricity into the kitchen

A TURN OF THE HAND	red rectangle + white stripes + blue stripes = America
	angled stripes + white elongated oval shape = movement
	man turning on water faucet + "A turn of the hand" = the ease of
	    accessing water with electricity
	horse drinking from trough +water coming out of faucet into trough
	    = ease of watering animals
	"A Turn of the Hand" implies an relationship between pumping water
	    versus accessing it with a faucet
	Message: The Rural Electrification Administration helps make the
	    car of farm animals easier.

OUR LINES	large blue rectangle + red and blue stripes = America
	large blue rectangle implies sky + people wearing coats = outdoors
	group of people + picture of plans = a planning committee
	"Our Lines" + writing down information = planning our lines
	    (ownership by the group or community)
	Message: The Rural Electrification Administration helps your
	    community plan and own its own electricity.

POWER FOR DEFENSE	white stripes on angle + red strips on angle= symbolizes American flag
	blue elongated oval shape = movement
	photo of a radio tower + photo of airplane makes a relationship
	    between planes and electricity
	photo of an aerial view of land places the radio tower in a rural area
	"Power for Defense" + radio tower implies the need for electricity to
	    defend the country
	Message: The Rural Electrification Administration brings electricity
	    to rural areas to help defend America.

POWER ON THE FARM	white stripes on angle + blue stripes on angle = America
	black uneven four-sided shape creates the impression of a floor
	red elongated oval shape = movement
	photo of a man in overalls operating machine = farmer operating
	    equipment
	photo of electrical farm equipment= shows equipment in use
	"Power on the Farm" reinforces the idea of electrical farm equipment
	Message: The Rural Electrification Administration brings power
	    tools to the farm.

RURAL INDUSTRIES	fifteen white stripes + sixteen red stripes blue elongated oval shape= movement photo of a man with hat operating equipment= man operating equipment photo of an electrical saw for cutting wood = building "Rural Industries" indicates that the work being done is for an industry rather than private use Message: The Rural Electrification Administration brings electricity to rural areas to build rural industries.

Patriotism, support for the war effort, and the power of electricity are all messages that are explicitly communicated through the final series of posters. The color treatment of red, white, and blue plus black creates an automatic feeling of patriotism. Emphasizing the idea of power visually and verbally makes a strong connection between electricity and the power needed to defend the United States and support the war effort. A dramatic shift in message concept occurs between the second and third series of posters. Instead of emphasizing the benefits of electricity on the farm, this final series highlights the need for power in a time of war.

CONCLUSION

Beall's dynamic modernist designs for the REA encouraged rural Americans to adopt electricity and electrify the farm. Moreover, his style reflected the social changes occurring in American culture. A rhetorical analysis of the REA posters reveals that, in addition to communicating messages commissioned by the REA, Beall was reinforcing cultural messages about technology, modernity, and progress that were also being expressed throughout American culture in expositions and advertisements. Moreover, the final series reflects the needs of a nation at war. Thus, these posters can be viewed as an expression of American social movements designed to embrace electrical products for the purposes of improving the American home, building American industry, and supporting the war effort.

Although improvements in the home made housework easier, especially for the farmwoman, it also required the consumption of electricity. Electrical consumption is an underlying effect of electrification. In urban areas, commercial companies distributed electricity. In contrast, local cooperatives originally funded by government agencies controlled electrical distribution in rural areas. Consumer advertisements tended to glorify the electrical home through elaborate illustrations. In contrast, the REA's advertising and promotional efforts logically showed how electricity could improve living conditions on the farm through the use of running water, heat, and lighting. Beall's approach to convincing people to adopt electricity is to appeal to basic human necessities and conveniences, and he did not glamorize electrical use. Thus, his messages of social persuasion are more direct and down to earth like the audience he was addressing.

REFERENCES

Arnheim, R. (1954). *Art and visual perception: A psychology of the creative eye*. Berkeley: University of California Press.

Barry, A. M. S. (1997). *Visual intelligence: Perception, image, and manipulation in visual communication*. Albany: State University of New York Press.

Benoit, W. L., Klyukovski, A. A., McHale, J. P., & Airne, D. (2001, December). A fantasy theme analysis of political cartoons on the Clinton–Lewinsky–Star affair. *Critical Studies in Media Communication, 18*(4), 377–394.

Bruce, D. R. (2001, June). Notes toward a rhetoric of animation: The *Road Runner* as cultural critique. *Critical Studies in Media Communication, 18*(2), 229–245.

Carroll, N. (1998). *A philosophy of mass art*. New York: Oxford University Press.

Dewey, J. (1934). *Art as experience*. New York: Putnam's Sons.

Dondis, D. A. (1973). *A primer of visual literacy*. Cambridge, MA: The MIT Press.

Erickson, K. V. (2000, June 2). Presidential rhetoric's visual turn: Performance fragments and the politics of illusionism. *Communication Monographs, 67*, 138–157.

Finnegan, C. A. (2000). Social engineering, visual politics, and the new deal: FSA photography in Survey Graphic. *Rhetoric and Public Affairs, 3*(3), 333–362.

Foss, S. K. (1982, January). Rhetoric and the visual image: A resource unit. *Communication Education, 31*(1), 55–66.

Foss, S. K. (1993). The construction of appeal in visual images: A hypothesis. In D. Zarefsky (Ed.), *Rhetorical movement: Essays in honor of Leland M. Griffin* (pp. 210–224). Evanston, IL: Northwestern University Press.

Foss, S. K., & Kanengieter, M. R. (1992). Visual communication in the basic course. *Communication Education, 41*(3), 312–323.

Gombrich, E. H. (1979/1984). *The sense of order*. Ithaca, NY: Cornell University Press.

Harris, J. (1995). *Federal art and national culture*. New York: Cambridge University Press.

Heller, S. (1998). *The education of a graphic designer*. New York: Allworth Press.

Heller, S. (2001). Advertising: the mother of graphic design. In S. Heller & G. Ballance (Eds.), *Graphic design history* (pp. 294–302). New York: Allworth Press.

Heller, S., & Pomeroy, K. (1997). *Design literacy: Understanding graphic design*. New York: Allworth.

Hope, D. (1999, April/May). All that's gold does not glitter: Mystification and demystification in visual rhetoric. Paper presented at the 90th annual Eastern Communication Association Conference, Charleston, WV.

Marchand, R. (1985). *Advertising the American dream: Making way for modernity 1920-1940*. Berkeley: University of Los Angeles Press.

Meggs, P. B. (1983). *A history of graphic design*. New York: Van Nostrand Reinhold Company.

Meggs, P. B. (1989). *Type & image: The language of graphic design*. New York: Van Nostrand Reinhold.

Meister, M. (1997, Summer). "Sustainable development" in visual imagery: Rhetorical function in the Jeep Cherokee. *Communication Quarterly, 45*(3), pp. 223–234.

Mendenhall, J. (1983). *American trademarks 1930-1950: Symbols of power*. New York: Art Direction Book Company.

Messaris, P. (1997). *Visual persuasion: The role of images in advertising*. Thousand Oaks, CA: Sage.

Mullen, L. J., & Bauman, J. D. (2001, May). *A visual analysis of prescription drug advertising imagery: Application of Foss's rhetorical technique*. Paper presented at the International Communication Association Conference, Washington, D. C.

Nye, D. E. (1985). *Image worlds: Corporate identities at General Electric*. Cambridge, MA: MIT Press.

Nye, D. E. (1990). *Electrifying America: Social meanings of a new technology*. Cambridge, MA: MIT Press.

Olson, L. C. (1983). Portraits in praise of a people: A rhetorical analysis of Norman Rockwell's icons in Franklin D. Roosevelt's "Four Freedoms" campaign. *Quarterly Journal of Speech, 69*, 15–24.

Peterson, V. (2001, November). The rhetorical criticism of visual elements: An alternative to Foss' schema. Paper presented at the National Communication Association Conference, Atlanta, GA.

Phillips, W. B. (1939, June 19). Letter sent to Lester Beall (personal correspondence). Lester Beall Collection, Archives and Special Collections, Rochester Institute of Technology.

Remington, R. R. (1996). *Lester Beall: Trailblazer of American graphic design*. New York: W. W. Norton.

Remington, R. R. (2002). *Lester Beall: Space, time & content*. Rochester, NY: RIT Cary Graphic Arts Press.

Rogers, E. M. (1995). *Diffusion of innovations* (4th ed.). New York: Free Press.

Suh, T. (1999). Visual persuasion. *Communication Research Trends, 19*(3), 1–18.

Tufte, E. R. (1990). *Envisioning information*. Cheshire, CT: Graphics Press.

Welch, K. E. (1999). *Electric rhetoric: Classical rhetoric, oralism, and a new literacy*. Cambridge: MIT Press.

Whitford, F. (1984). *Bauhaus*. New York: Thames & Hudson.

Wingler, H. M. (1969). *The Bauhaus*. Cambridge: MIT Press.

CHAPTER TWELVE

The Rhetorical Structure of Marc Riboud's Photojournalistic Books

A Journalist's Changing Attitude in *Three Banners of China* (1966), *Visions of China* (1981), and *Marc Riboud in China: Forty Years of Photography* (1997)

TIMOTHY R. GLEASON

UNIVERSITY OF WISCONSIN, OSHKOSH

A S A PHOTOGRAPHER FOR MAGNUM, one of the best-known and respected photographic agencies in the world, Marc Riboud demonstrated an ability to make works of art as well as socially concerned photojournalism. He is one of the few Western photojournalists to have been allowed repeated access to China from the 1950s through the 1990s. His first visit was in 1957, and he returned in 1965, 1971, 1979, 1980, and 1992 through 1995. From these trips, he produced the books *Three Banners of China* (1966), *Visions of China* (1981), and *Marc Riboud in China: Forty Years of Photography* (1997).[1] The selection and arrangement of photographs presented in Riboud's books tell a riveting tale of modern China and reveal the journalist's changing attitudes toward a country he photographed for more than 40 years. The significance of the books as rhetorical artifacts relies on juxtaposition of subject and meaning, positioning of color and black-and-white image sequencing, and the pairing of images selected and arranged for contextual setting. The rhetorical structure allows readers a glimpse into Riboud's changing attitude toward China. I argue that the structure of his books reveal Riboud's early optimism for communist China, his increasing criticism as witness to the loss of personal freedoms, and his final mourning over the loss of Chinese culture to global commercialism. The techniques of photographic criticism and photojournalism historiography are used to to consider Riboud's photography within its historical context. The goal of this research is to demon-

---

1. There is one other rare book that Marc Riboud produced on China. *Capital of Heaven* (New York: Doubleday, 1990) is a difficult book to find in libraries and is an expensive find at a used bookstore. It contains landscapes and is much less socially concerned than his other books.

strate how a photojournalistic collection presented in a book can be studied using both a qualitative photojournalism historiography and photographic criticism as a methodology to uncover a book's rhetorical structure as a way to understand subtle shifts in the journalist's attitudes.

There is surprisingly little research on Riboud despite his photographic prowess and unwavering humanity. A number of writers have recognized Riboud's work, but overall not in depth. Russell Miller (1999) mentioned Riboud in his book about the Magnum Photo Agency. Riboud's work has been discussed by publications such as *American Photo*, *LIFE*, *Newsweek* and *The New York Times*. Biographical surveys often mention Riboud, but, as is their custom, they do not provide much detail. For example, *20th Century Photography: Museum Ludwig Cologne* (1996) only featured a few pages on Riboud. From this work and the Magnum Photo Agency Web site, it is known that Riboud was born in 1923 in Lyons, France.[2] Magnum reported that Riboud made his first picture in 1937, and that from 1943 to 1945 he was active in the French Resistance. He studied engineering from 1945 to 1948. He then worked until 1951 as an engineer for factories in Lyons. In 1952, Riboud switched his profession and became a freelance photographer based in Paris. He became an associate member of Magnum that year and became a full member in 1955. From 1975 to 1976, he served as Magnum's president. His work has appeared in leading international magazines such as *LIFE*, *Geo*, *National Geographic*, *Paris-Match*, and *Stern*.

Riboud "considers himself 'shy, a poor journalist'" and not even an artist, according to *Newsweek*. "His best pictures, like his glimpse of Hue after the Tet offensive, resemble great paintings: the components fit like a puzzle" (Mullarkey, 1988, p. 71). He told *The New York Times* that, "I am not an analyst. I just collect impressions" (Riding, 1996, p. 15c). Riboud's humility has not kept him from photographing in unlikely places with difficult access, such as China and North Vietnam. He was allowed in such places because of his fairness and his interest in seeing whether revolutions would work. Riboud seems to have been interested in the results of China's revolution, but was not blinded by ideology.

Claude Cookman (1999) studied Riboud's photographic reporting of North Vietnam. He examined photographs published in *Look* picture magazine and also Riboud's original manuscript for *Faces of North Vietnam*. Last,

---

2. http://www.magnumphotos.com/portfolio/rim/rimbio.html. The locations for photographers' bios on the Magnum Web site change often, so this was the last confirmed location within their site.

he interviewed a *Look* editor and Riboud. Riboud's photographs of North Vietnamese peasants and soldiers revealed proud, hard-working people who would not succumb to the enemy. The photographs showed the people's humanity, something not evident in most reporting. For example, in contrast to claims made by American propaganda, the North Vietnamese were able to pursue their religions. Cookman concluded how Riboud's photographs, in conjunction with *Look* editorials and articles, argued that the war could not be won by either side. Cookman demonstrated that Riboud's photography had a political perspective.

This chapter analyzes Riboud's photographs of China over five decades—from the 1950s through the 1990s—to see whether his view of the country and its revolution changed over time. This research contributes to the field of photojournalism scholarship in a number of ways. First, it examines a photographer who has not received much attention from scholars. Second, it builds on previous knowledge of Riboud by studying his work over a period of time. This project gives attention to historical changes in society as well as Riboud's personal evolution as a photographer. Third, it considers photographs as aesthetic statements and not simply visual documents. The research also aids understanding of China by offering an unusual perspective.

METHODOLOGY

The methodology brings together photojournalism historiography and photographic criticism in the analysis of Riboud's work. This is accomplished by using the terminology and practice of photographic criticism when discussing individual photographs. The books are studied from the perspective of photojournalism historiography. A purposive sample of photographs from the books is described and interpreted within the context of the rhetorical structure of each book. Photographers often aim to have their work reproduced in book form because it provides some level of permanence and offers a new form of distribution for their images. Photography critics and historians see great value in photographic books because it allows them to study the images that the photographer selected for inclusion and to speculate on reasons for their inclusion. Images from the books are meaningful because they are Riboud's final statements on his subject. Photographers have greater control over the images that appear in books, unlike newspapers or magazines. A book is a personal statement that enables the photographer to have control over editing, cropping, and toning of photographs. Technical issues can be analyzed because of the high reproduction quality of the books when compared with newspapers and some magazines. Significant to this study is the necessity to structure a book as a complete technical artifact. As the journalist makes choices regarding selection and arrangement of photographs, so the critic chooses those photographs that best serve to make a significant statement about China, about Riboud's photography, and about how the arrangement of images reflect Riboud's attitudes toward his subject. The photographs selected are the best representations of particular themes in Riboud's work. To identify a theme is to take notice of organizational tendencies. The themes include the photographer's tendencies in shooting style, choosing subjects, editing, and organization of photographs in books. Photojournalism historiography is driven by the asking of open-ended questions that lead to additional, often unanticipated questions. Photography historians will ask, in general: How were the images made? How are the images sequenced? What are their political-economic implications? What are their cultural implications? What do these images mean?

The Three Banners of China was Riboud's first documentary book about the country. Photographs in it were the result of two visits—the first in 1957 and the second in 1965. His first visit coincided roughly with the Hundred Flowers Movement, which was a brief loosening of speech restrictions that resulted in criticism of the government and then the purging or jailing of those who made the criticisms. Between then and his next visit in 1965, a number of events happened. China underwent or saw the first People's Commune, the Great Leap Forward, conflict with Tibet and the Dalai Lama escape, the Great Famine, and the Sino-Soviet split (Schoppe, 2000). According to Riboud (1966), ". . . new schools, institutes, and hospitals sprung up. Where there had been wasteland, new neighborhoods and factories had appeared. Despite its early fiascos the Great Leap Forward seems definitely to have brought about concrete facts, visible everywhere" (p. 16). Ultimately, this book represents Riboud's hope for China to improve its condition. He showed this in his representations of labor, travel, children, and politics.

The second book, *Visions of China* (1981), contains photographs taken on Riboud's first visit to China in 1957, and it ends with images from 1980. Some of the events that occurred between the 1965 and 1980 visits were the Cultural Revolution, the creation of China's first hydrogen bomb, entry into the United Nations, President Nixon's visit, Mao Zedong's death in 1976, the normalization of United States–China relations, and the Sino-Vietnamese War, where there was a historical problem over borders (Schoppa, 2000). The book contains some of the same photographs appearing in *Three Banners of China*, so there are natural similarities between them. *Visions of China* is structurally different than its predecessor because it is not broken into sections. Photographs run continuously throughout, with captions placed in the back of the book. Each photograph is accompanied by a few descriptive words, the location, and the year the image was taken. There are no page numbers, but each photograph is numbered. Riboud (1981) tried to explain the ordering, or lack of order, of the photographs in his "Photographer's Note." He said the images are placed intentionally out of any chronological or geographic order because the country was undergoing such massive change. Ultimately, this book focuses on changes within China that Riboud witnessed and photographed.

The third book, *Marc Riboud in China: Forty Years of Photography*, was published in 1997. Riboud visited from 1992 through 1995. During 1992, Deng Xiaoping approved economic reforms, which was a year after the violent suppression of demonstrators at Tian'anmen (Schoppa, 2000). The book is composed of three sections. The first section contains photographs taken during Riboud's early visits to China. The second section contains photographs from the 1950s through the 1990s. The last section contains photographs taken during the 1990s. There are 150 black-and-white photographs and no color images. All of the photographs are identifiable by their page number, and each is paired with a caption at the end of the book. Preceding the photographs are a three-page introduction by Jean Daniel and a single-page commentary by Riboud.

Riboud (1997) prefaced his photographs with the statement that his photographs are "travel notes" that "record more than they analyse or judge" (p. 8). He then cited Walker Evans, the American documentary photographer who recorded the American Depression. "'The eye,' as Walker Evans said, 'traffics in feelings not in thoughts'" (p. 8). Evans is known for his "straight aesthetic" and mastery of black-and-white photography. This information suggests Riboud sees himself as a photographer who works in a similar fashion to Evans. Riboud uses China's past as context for the present condition. Sometimes Riboud is happy with the changes, but he expresses sadness because China is losing its distinctiveness. According to Riboud, ". . . the beauties of an ancient culture seem to be fading before our eyes" (p. 8).

DESCRIPTION AND COMPARISON OF RIBOUD'S THREE BOOKS

This section provides a critical description of each book, presented in chronological order. After the three books have been discussed separately, they are compared to each other. It is assumed that the reader is unfamiliar with these works. A critical description not only provides a basic description of a book's contents, but also allows for critical interpretations to be presented.

The Three Banners of China contains three sections of photography that tell a story when viewed in order. An introductory text before the first section continues throughout the book and across sections. The first of three photographic sections of the book is "The People's Commune," pages 24 to 64. This makes it difficult to follow the text. The second section is "The Great Leap Forward." The last is "The General Party Line."

The division of *The Three Banners of China* into three sections indicates an organizational structure designed to communicate major concepts or themes. Each section leads to the next, but their relationship is not well defined either visually or in the written text. It is the summation of the photographs that gives each section its meaning and *The Three Banners of China* an identity. The pairing of the photographs is less significant or successful in *The Three Banners of China* than in *Visions of China* or *In China*. In the latter two books, placement is important because the meaning of one image is often enhanced by the image adjacent to it that is visually similar or of a contrasting meaning. A similar image placement design does not exist in *The Three Banners of China*. Instead many of the photographs build on each other because of their similar subject matter.

Section 1

In general, *The Three Banners of China* is a snippet of one country's historical process. Section 1 provides context for *The Three Banners of China* to frame Riboud's larger argument and hope for communist China. This context is the transformation of China through, in part, its agrarian practices. Riboud (1966) demonstrated this through a number of photographs of farming. Riboud initially showed rather isolated farmers, but the images show a more communal nature as the section advances. Agrarian life as a background story is further communicated via photographs of Mao's childhood home and paintings of Mao in farmers' homes. These and other images are also illuminating the conditions of peasants. The chapter concludes by shifting its focus to people in movement. The number of photographs is a small, but significant, change because it prepares the readers for "The Great Leap Forward" in the following section. This leap forward required the Chinese to sacrifice in countless ways, including the forced relocation of numerous workers.

Section 2

Section 2, "The Great Leap Forward," starts several pages later, on page 68, after the continuation of the text from the previous section. The text for

Section 2 is continued on page 133. This section emphasizes the vital role of children in achieving the great leap forward. Whereas adults were previously shown toiling in the fields, this section begins by addressing how children contribute to the expected improvement of China. Children are shown in primary school and in college.

The first photo of this section shows a row of girls in the foreground forming a visual diagonal across the page (p. 69). This image represents the conformity expected of students. Conformity to the party line is important because misdirected attention will delay China's success. The girls in the image seem to wait for permission to take one more step forward. They are frozen by the command of someone outside the image's frame. The caption reports that in the village of Kwangsi, there used to be no school. Now there is one, and the children are shown listening to a lesson in patriotism from the teacher. Without the caption, it is difficult to tell what the children are waiting for (pp. 68–69). It is easy, however, to tell that the children are obedient and almost militant in their discipline.

This photo was the first of six color photos leading off the section, all of children and students. The black-and-white photos that follow these are a mix of young and old people. The color images seem almost of out of place after the reader has gone through a number of black-and-white images that reinforce a sense of the past. The combination of color, as a medium, and children, as subjects, promotes the idea of future and newness. It is not a free and playful childhood. The children are shown as orderly, disciplined, and trained. One photo that covers two pages shows children mindlessly marching in step with white wooden guns for discipline training. The caption reports that children of the "Young Pioneer movement" are told they should "Make your own wooden rifles!" (pp. 68, 72–73). The combination of color and content shocks the senses, and it disjoints the natural progression of flipping through the book.

The photos of the girls in line and the marchers are in sharp contrast to the image between them, which is of children in a nursery at a textile factory. On the wall behind them is a painting of children of different races that show "the world is made up of children of all colors" (pp. 68–69, 70–71). There is a distinct contrast between the photos that make the children look militant and those that show children being educated and conducting science experiments. It demonstrates the problem that different people will remember different kinds of images. Sometimes readers latch onto images that contain a similar theme and they forget those images that contradict the message. This section of the book raises questions about the cost of pushing children into a disciplinary regime. Riboud recognized the advantages and disadvantages of China's efforts. His internal conflict of seeing such divergent representations of Chinese youth is represented in this particular ordering of images.

The relationship between work and travel becomes more prominent in the latter part of this section, and it reminds the reader of how Riboud ends the first section. Travel and work come together in a visually powerful image of a man working at a train factory (pp. 106–107). The trains are bright red, and they overwhelm a reader who has grown accustomed again to black-and-white photographs. It is the second series of photos taken with color film, although they do not all warrant color. Riboud returned to black and white after showing nine color photographs. In most cases, with the notable exception of the trains, the images are more effective in black and white, perhaps because the color is distracting. Riboud used color to grab the reader's attention, but he did so too much. The use of color could have been fewer and more selective.

The last image of the section shows a great number of people on a Shanghai street (p. 132). There is human congestion unimaginable to most Americans. The pedestrians cannot move in any direction without someone else moving first. Someone else must always move, and there is always someone who needs to move. Apparently a "Great Leap Forward" cannot happen without great coordination. This image becomes a metaphor for the problem. How do you get so many people to move or leap at once?

Section 3

The people trying to find the answer to the problem identified here are subjects in Section 3, "The General Party Line." This last section shows people who are trying to follow the party line in different ways, such as through work and celebrations. The first five photographs are in black-and-white, but the section goes back and forth between sets of black-and-white and color photographs. Most of the color photographs benefit from the use of color. The first color image is of a man writing with different colored chalk on a factory blackboard (p. 145). The colors attract the viewer's eye. For the person who does not read Chinese, the visual impact of the letters becomes greater than the linguistic significance. The following photographs also take advantage of the colors in the different scenes. One photograph shows the arrival of an important person (pp. 148–149). His open-top car is led by two motorcycles and followed by two additional motorcycles. Standing by the street are numerous people with colored flags. Girls are dressed in light-blue outfits waving red streamers. Both of these photos are examples of Riboud using color to bring out some of the liveliness of the party line support. The images no longer shock the reader, but instead celebrate the subject matter.

In contrast to the images of celebrations, Riboud has a black-and-white photograph of a woman in her early 20s knitting in a dorm room associated with a ball-bearing factory (p. 159). It is an image that appears often in Riboud's books—of peace, quiet, solitude, and serenity. There is something universal about this image. Its appeal may be that she seems so harmless and pleasant, which are qualities that do not strike fear in China's enemies. The reader can sense her loneliness as she knits alone in a simple, spartan room. The point of the photograph is that, in her own way, she is helping her country.

The rest of the section bounces back and forth between young people having fun and more militant images. This visual interplay becomes the dominant communication in the latter part of the section. This section lacks continuity, but this was probably on purpose. There is no simple description of China. It is too complex and broad for Riboud to present a unified response. Maybe this is why readers see the faces of young, innocent girls as they train with military rifles.

The missing continuity of the section is also indicative of the relatively weaker structuring of the book. *The Three Banners of China* lacks the more graceful flow of *Visions of China* and the more deliberate pairing of photographs in *In China*. *The Three Banners of China* is the only book of the three to regularly print more than one image per page. The excessive inclusion of photographs has a negative impact. The reader has a more difficult time discerning which image is the most important to look at when there is more than one on a page. The images must be smaller to fit, so it is more difficult to see the details in each photograph. Last, it breaks the flow of reading left to right. Too often the reader has to read left up to left down and then to the right. Riboud must be forgiven for being so overwhelmed by publishing this initial book on China. As Riboud gains more time and experience, his interpretation of China becomes better structured and decisive.

VISIONS OF CHINA

Riboud (1981), in his "Photographer's Note" to introduce *Visions of China*, said that the "photographs in this book are in no particular chronological or geographical order" because he "wanted them to confront and complete one another." He emphasized words like *understand* rather than *judge*. It would be naïve to think that the photographs do not reflect Riboud's view. They were not randomly selected or casually put in a careless order. His tentative wording defends any potential arguments that Riboud is criticizing China. A much more deliberate offensive is evident in the introduction written by Orville Schell. For example, the Introduction reads, "Mistakes, failures, wrong judgments were quickly obscured by a concealing web of official propaganda. . . ."

Riboud's personal introduction suggests that he was well aware of the changes that occurred in China over the decades. The change might have been especially noticeable for him because he was only able to visit the country occasionally. He was not able to sense change as a subtle, daily process. His comments also suggest that certain images became iconic representations of the state of affairs. The relationship between him and his images is not dependent on the image's aesthetic qualities or recognition in the photographic community. Instead the relationship is created by Riboud's experience in making the photographs.

Riboud reconciled his feelings in this book by including two types of photographs among the other images. First, a number of the images show changes. Second, there are a fair amount of photographs that have visual similarities. Together these two types of images overtake the various images of different subjects (snow, walking, eating, etc.). This book does not contain sections, so the system of representation previously seen in *The Three Banners of China* is not applicable to *Visions of China*. In addition, Riboud rarely has more than one photograph per page, unlike *The Three Banners of China*, which had numerous examples.

Two early photographs exemplify the changes he witnessed (Riboud, 1981, Plates 5 and 6). The first was taken in Peking during 1957. A person sits on personal belongings in front of a mural of a very large dove on a building. The caption in the back of the book reports, "Picasso's dove. China was part of the Peace Movement at the time." In contrast, the next photograph is of students marching in Peking's Tian'anmen Square during 1965. Riboud warned that the marchers "are a sign of the Red Guard fury to come." The pairing of these two photographs is rather evident. Riboud was not looking at these photographs from the point of view of 1957 and 1965, but from the time the book was being constructed, which was the late 1970s. There is a visual contrast between the dove and the marchers. One shows peace, whereas the other shows a possible threat. The possible threat becomes more explicit when contextualized by Riboud's caption. Even if the students are marching peacefully, the events that are sure to follow cause Riboud to reinterpret the nature of their marching. Riboud included a number of other contrasting photographs, some taken in the same year, and some of which are reinforced with a warning (see plates 15/16 and 39/40).

Figure 12.1. Photographs courtesy of Marc Riboud.

As well as contrasting social change, Riboud often used photographs to show how different scenes have visual similarities, the second manner in which Riboud quietly told the readers of change in China. This is noticeable in images on two facing pages that show people at work (plates 22/23). The first image shows the transplanting of rice by hand with mountains looming in the background, and the next shows mountain-like coolers in a heating plant at an iron factory. Both photographs were taken in 1965. Despite their initial differences, agrarian labor and industrial labor, there are a number of visual similarities. The rows of rice and trees in the background of the first image are transformed into railroad tracks and utility poles in the second image.

The placement of visually similar photographs continues on the next set of facing pages, and even throughout the book (plates 24/25). The first image contains a visual element similar to the one in the next shot. An umbrella in the first looks strikingly similar to the pagoda on the next page. A set of later photographs is almost a pun on this design structure (plates 33/34). The first image shows a man and a woman in Peking carrying a TV tied with rope in 1979. The next image is of a man and woman using rope and a rod to carry a sow to the market in Hunan during 1965 (Figure 12.1). Riboud tells us that the TV is costing the couple a year's worth of wages (see also plates 48/49, 88/89, and 90/91).

These examples demonstrate how Riboud's second book is able to reflect his additional visits to China and new experiences. Although the book is not broken into sections, it is the product of more critical thinking than

The Three Banners of China. The use of juxtaposing images becomes more prominent in *In China,* the next book. *In China* utilizes the basic concept of sections seen in *The Three Banners of China,* along with the pairing or juxtaposing of images to a greater degree.

MARC RIBOUD IN CHINA: FORTY YEARS OF PHOTOGRAPHY

Marc Riboud in China: Forty Years of Photography (1997) is the culmination of Riboud's experiences with China. It includes photographs from his recent visits, 1992 through 1995, as well as previously made images. *In China* represents a more refined structure than *The Three Banners of China* and *Visions of China,* although similar structural and rhetorical techniques are employed. The use of sections seen in *The Three Banners of China* is joined with the juxtapositions of photographs sometimes attempted in *Visions of China.*

The first section emphasizes the past as a context for the modernization visible later in the book. Additionally, numerous photographs tell the relationship between teamwork and labor, an important aspect in China's history. The second section uses juxtaposed images for comparison and explanation, and to address the life of women. The third section, with fewer juxtapositions, stresses the relationships between the wealthy couples and stylish women, the left-behind poor, and the changing environment.

Section 1

Riboud (1981) began Section 1 with a familiar image of two women turning the soil on a plot of land in Sichuan during 1965 (p. 11). The reader is given context for Riboud's idea of old China in this image. The women are largely alone, although in the distance there are a few others. This is an example of how Riboud returned to some familiar images that appeared in earlier books and ones that fit into the style of this book better. The latter are images taken during the 1950s and 1960s that show the Chinese people in their environment and often at work. These images now receive attention because the distance of time allowed Riboud to rethink how he wanted to portray the old China.

Many of the photographs in this section show Chinese teamwork and labor. The final image shows three children walking away from the photographer with their arms wrapped around each other (p. 38). It was taken sometime during 1957 in Beijing. It must be cold because the children are dressed very warmly as they stroll together, reminding readers that the Chinese are a friendly people who work well together. This image also demonstrates the experience Riboud had in China at this time. The section contains a balance

Figure 12.2. Photographs courtesy of Marc Riboud.

of images showing happy and industrious people. The fruitfulness of these early visits is also evident in an image that runs across two pages and is one of his most popular photographs (see Figure 12.2).[3]

Section 2

After going through the first few images, readers encounter juxtapositions of images arranged to alert the reader to the changes Riboud has seen in China. He created contrast by placing an older image on the left and a newer image on the right to show how China has changed. The style and importance of Riboud's juxtaposing is demonstrated by one set of images that contains the 1971 image of Mao's statue by smokestacks (pp. 48–49; Mao is on p. 48, Superman is on p. 49). The statue appears very large, and Mao seems to be signaling that industrialization is the future. To the right of this image is one taken in Beijing during 1994 (see Figure 12.3). A well-dressed woman sits with a box containing a new camera on her lap. She peacefully reads, while immediately behind her is a Superman figure that would be roughly real size. His right arm is raised as if he is flexing a muscle. There are signs located throughout the photograph offering different services and products.

---

3. I would like to add that this is one of the greatest documentary or journalistic photographs ever taken.

Figure 12.3. Photographs courtesy of Marc Riboud.

The image can be read by comparing Mao and Superman. Both are almost mythical figures because Mao served as a model character for others to emulate. Both figures have their right arm raised. Both look strong and brave, and both rise above people. Riboud argued that the Chinese are now revering more Western figures and commercial pursuits.

One of the greatest juxtapositions in the book is an image of a female worker facing the image of the actress Gong Li (see Figure 12.4). The 1965 image, taken in Shanxi, appeared previously. She is holding both a Chinese Youth newspaper and chopsticks while in front of a wall with lettering on it. The newspaper reads, "China explodes its second atom bomb" (p. 171). The 1993 image of Gong Li is somewhat similar. She, too, is facing right while in front of a wall with lettering on it. The second image shows the face much larger, and the actress is dressed stylishly.

The power of putting these two photographs together is their basic photographic similarity, while the lives of the women are so different. The images remind us of change, while reminding us that those pictured, in essence, have a similar national history. The image of the worker shows the woman as drab and conformist, especially when reading Riboud's caption that tells us she is wearing the common Mao garb. Gong Li, in comparison, looks like a star. Even if the reader does not know who she is, the reader will probably sense there is something different about her glowing presence.

Figure 12.4. Photographs courtesy of Marc Riboud.

This is a transition set because it also begins to direct the reader's attention to the condition of women.

Riboud began to actively compare women throughout this section. One set of photos shows a sophisticated older woman from 1957 along with a 1993 image of a young woman walking her bike in Shanghai (pp. 70-71). Riboud took notice of the young woman's "tiny shorts" and "confident stride," which is in stark contrast to the older woman's slower pace and long, cold weather coat. Another set shows an old, tired woman riding a train in 1956, while on the next page people work at a diner (pp. 86–87). Outside the diner is an advertisement for women's panties, with the obligatory beautiful woman wearing the product. Riboud remarked in the caption how modesty was one of the four traditional Chinese virtues. The last set of images shows a 1957 photograph of a sculptor who turns away from his nude female model while he sculpts, and the other photograph is of a soldier photographing a stylish woman on the sidewalk in 1985 (pp. 98–99). Riboud reminded the reader again of modesty in the caption for the first image. The modesty is in the sculptor turning his back on the nude model. These images serve as an introduction to modern Chinese women appearing in Section 3 of *In China*. They might be the most prominent symbol of

China's globally influenced modernization, which is why Riboud repeatedly reminded us of the new women.

Section 3

Section 3 opens with a 1993 image of a well-dressed couple walking hand-in-hand in Tian'anmen while an image of Mao looms over them in the background. Riboud asked in his caption, "What are the fruits of Mao's efforts today? . . . This couple have all the attributes of today's 'nouveau riches', all the new, flashy elements of the new ideal—plastic, fake leather, mini-skirt, dark glasses, sun hat . . ." (p. 111). This section is not just a representation of the new wealth of China, however. Riboud carefully compared the different lives of the Chinese through images of the rich and poor. This section basically shows wealthy couples and stylish women, the left-behind poor, and the changing environment.

The images are not always juxtaposed in a contrasting manner as in the previous section. Sometimes the images do contrast. One set from 1993 starts with a poor man walking past posters of a cute baby and a porn star taking off her shirt. The neighboring photograph shows a couple having lunch in Guangzhou in 1993. The man does business over a portable phone while the woman plays with a Game Boy (pp. 112–113). In another set, there is a stylish mother in skin-tight leggings walking with her son. The picture of the poor shows one man who Riboud thought is looking for work. He is dressed shabbily and looks bored as he supposedly waits for a job. Riboud asked, "What kind of future can this country expect when every leader is an only child?" (pp. 122–123). The idea or issue Riboud raised might be considered in the images of the newly poor, too. These are people left behind by changes in China's economic policies. Riboud scattered images of the poor throughout Section 3.

Other times Riboud's pairings reinforce each other more directly. One image shows a woman, likely a secretary, wearing a short dress in Shanghai during 1993. Riboud told his readers that the "Taiwanese invest a great deal in China and have a soft spot for pretty Chinese girls." To the right is a photograph of a rock band with posters on the wall showing their appreciation for Western "hair bands" of the 1980s (pp. 116–117).

Riboud became more adept at making strong arguments with single images. An example is an image of two young women in Shanghai coming from a "shopping spree" in 1992 (see Figure 12.5). They are wearing almost identical shoes, with short skirts of almost an exact length. The patterns and tops they are wearing are different, but the similarities are striking. This is

Figure 12.5. Photograph courtesy of Marc Riboud.

not merely a descriptive image. It is an explanatory photograph because Riboud showed how people still dress alike even with the differences that capitalist consumption allows. Riboud's interest in stylish women is evident in a number of photos (pp. 118–119). The stylish women represent the increasing influence of capitalism, individualism, and Westernization. The high hemlines are markers of a new freedom felt by younger women. Beauty and style are significant because they offer a new area of sales for business.

DISCUSSION

Marc Riboud's photographs make statements about China in the photographs, their placement in the books, and the captions that accompany them. Riboud's earliest book, *Three Banners of China*, showed some hope for the Chinese people. Riboud saw the poor conditions that people were living in, and he hoped that changes would benefit the people there. At the same time, you can witness his concern for the militancy of change. *Three Banners of China* can be described then as a statement in cautious hope.

Visions of China reflected his growing concern for the Chinese. His emphasis on change showed despair. This book is gray and, if it had a personality, it would be a sad one. He began to pair photographs that contain visual similarities, which is probably a device to reconcile his own feelings. This book communicates tenseness and uncertainty.

In *Visions of China*, Riboud described a photograph taken in 1957 and another one taken in 1965. For Riboud, the 1957 image of a broken-down rickshaw and the 1965 image of students doing rough, manual labor are representative of a prerevolution and a revolutionary era, respectively. In contrast, he said that the most recent photograph he took, which was in 1980, was of Chinese posed in front of a car in the heart of the Forbidden City. He was surprised not only by this change, but by the fact that Chinese were no longer posing in front of Mao's portrait. Riboud's concern with China's loss of culture has its seed in *Visions of China*, but it really does not fully emerge until *In China*.

In China deals with Riboud's mixed emotions. He saw that some people's lives were getting better, and that the growing role of capitalism made China seem more Western. One effect of this was the increasing loss of the Chinese identity. With billboards of women in lingerie and people visiting a McDonald's restaurant, it appeared to Riboud that the transformation had begun. This book seems to reflect the initial interest in trying to create a more egalitarian society, the problems created by a forceful government, and the increasing bland capitalist lifestyle appearing in the 1990s. The reader is given warning of Riboud's interpretation of China. He admires the ability of Chinese to grasp "money-making, commerce, speculation," but he fears that "the beauties of an ancient culture seem to be fading before our eyes." China is becoming an accelerated version of the West; it is moving quickly to catch up with other countries (p. 8).

The first photograph of Section 2 of *In China* shows Mao Zedong drinking from a small glass (p. 41). The reason for the photograph's inclusion is twofold. It allows the viewer to see the power in China, so that this photograph serves as descriptive context. In addition, there is a journalistic purpose. This photograph is a scoop, and its inclusion is a reminder that Riboud is a photojournalist. The caption tells us that Riboud, the only foreign photographer at this particular event with Mao, was forbidden to photograph him from the front (p. 170). Somehow Riboud was able to take this photograph, and he could not resist using the image. Riboud's photographs became less aesthetically complex during the last few decades. He seemed to be less concerned with form and more interested in symbolic content in his later work.

A few photographs that appear in all three books help show how Riboud's feelings have changed over time. Two examples help reinforce the idea that Riboud is concerned with or disillusioned by the changes in China. His famous 1965 photograph of a street scene taken from inside a store appears in *Visions of China* (see Figure 12.2). It contains a very short, neutral caption: ". . . the antique dealers' street, seen through the thoroughly Chinese doors and windows of a now-demolished shop" (Caption 91). Preceding and across from the photo is an image showing posters for "Chinese films and small businesses. They were prohibited during the Cultural Revolution but are making a comeback today (Caption 90). The street scene photograph appears again within *In China*. This time the photograph covers two pages. The caption reads, "In 1965 there were food shortages in Beijing and the inhabitants had to resort to selling their family heirlooms for the equivalent of a few pence" (pp. 20–21). The long caption is more reflective this time. It provides greater context for the reader and is more negative in tone than the one in *Visions of China*.

Riboud's photograph of a female peasant holding chopsticks and a newspaper appeared in all three books. In *Three Banners*, the photo appeared on a left-hand page. Riboud said the worker is leaving the canteen, and he explained that the newspaper headlines are about China exploding its second atomic bomb and a protest (pp. 50–51). The two photos to the right are of a peasant man and people learning to read and write. In *Visions of China*, the photo appeared on the right-hand page. This time the caption is shorter, but the content is similar. The photograph on the left is of a man in front of a wall belonging to the British Embassy. Attached to the wall are written protests of Anglo-French involvement in the Suez, according to Riboud (pp. 82–83). As stated earlier, the photograph appears to the left of an image of actress Gong Li in Riboud's last book, *In China* (see Figure 12.4). There are two changes in the photo's use in this book when comparing it to the versions in *Three Banners* and *Visions of China*. One change is that Riboud made a comment about the women's clothes. He said her hat is part of Mao's legacy. With more than a billion hats manufactured, "Mao must have been the envy of any fashion designer" (p. 68). The other change is the adjacent photograph. Gone are the images of peasants, which have been replaced by the image of a beautiful actress. The emphasis is now on the individual, particularly the celebrity, rather than the common person. Riboud is suggesting that China is becoming more interested in glitz and glamour than before, possibly to the detriment of the peasants, who might still need economic assistance.

In terms of lighting, Riboud's style was fairly consistent. His aesthetic constructions became more simplistic over time, however. Those images that could be described as the most artistic are earlier images, such as Figure 12.2. The later ones are shot more conventionally, and there are more street photographs, such as the women in Figures 12.3 and 12.5. Riboud might have avoided any excessive styling to emphasize what Terry Barrett (1990) called "ethically evaluative" photography. This kind of photography makes ethical judgments to "show how things ought or ought not to be" (p. 76). Ethically evaluative photographs might be as aesthetically compelling as those by Eugene Richards or as aesthetically mundane as those by Jacob Riis. Riboud was better able to show the differences between past and present by simplifying his compositions. His earlier photographs display his search to understand both China and his own work. The later images are devoid of much aesthetic self-awareness. The result is a more complex story told in an easy-to-consume fashion for readers. Taken individually, many of the later images are less visually gripping, however.

By identifying themes in Riboud's work, his perspective becomes clearer. This was not an exhaustive account of Riboud's style, but rather a study of the content he chose to include in his frames. His style was addressed as background, which could be described as a sort of interpretive and explanatory photojournalism. Riboud demonstrated that photography can be used to offer an opinion on changes within society.

REFERENCES

Barrett, T. (1990). *Criticizing photographs: An introduction to understanding images.* Mountain View, CA: Mayfield.

Cookman, C. (1999, August). *How Marc Riboud's photographic report from Hanoi argued the Vietnam War was unwinnable.* A paper presented to the Visual Communication Division at the annual conference of the Association for Education in Journalism and Mass Communication, New Orleans, LA.

Miller, R. (1999). *Magnum: Fifty years at the front line of history: The story of the legendary picture agency.* New York: Grove.

Mullarkey, K. (1988, January 25). Pictures within pictures. *Newsweek,* p. 71.

New York Times, June 11, 1996.

Riboud, M. (1966). *Three banners of China.* New York: Macmillan.

Riboud, M. (1981). *Visions of China.* New York: Patheon.

Riboud, M. (1997). *Marc Riboud in China: Forty years of photography.* New York: Harry N. Abrams.

Riding, A. (1996, June 11). Images of revolutions old and new. *The New York Times,* p. 15C.

Schoppa, K. (2000). *The Columbia guide to modern Chinese history.* New York: Columbia University Press.

CHAPTER THIRTEEN

Dashing Heroes and Eccentric Families in William Joyce's Picture Sagas of Our Common Culture

JOSEPH STANTON

UNIVERSITY OF HAWAI'I AT MĀNOA

WILLIAM JOYCE'S METICULOUSLY BEAUTIFUL PICTURE BOOKS have mul-tifarious popular-culture dimensions that are central to their vitality and their appeal to a broad audience of children and adults. Joyce has ex-plained that his books

> hearken back to the sort of shared popular culture that we all grew up with on television—Flash Gordon from the thirties, the Stooges from the forties, Bugs Bunny from the fifties. Growing up watching television, you would see this constant barrage of cool stuff . . . it's become a sort of shared sensibility. (cited in Telgen, 1993)

Joyce's achievement turns inside out the dire warnings that began in the 1950s and continue to this day. Joyce apparently spent a goodly portion of his 1960s childhood watching TV. Far from rotting his brain, this "vast wasteland" fueled his extraordinary picture book–making imagination. As this chapter proceeds, I argue that the shared sensibility he refers to contains (in addition to TV shows) classic picture books, series books, comic books, advertising art, toys, fashions, auto styles, and famous works of fine art. Tele-vision of the 1960s offered the young Joyce a compendium of inspirations; it seems to have served him as an easily available museum of popular culture.

Joyce's artistic means to the capturing of this shared sensibility is not, however, entirely popular in its approach. The striking beauty of Joyce's work—his knack for rising above the visual mediocrity of much popular cul-ture work—has much to do with his incorporation of fine arts influences and his overriding tendency toward elegant refinement of technique. Fine arts elements are much more important than Joyce ever admits to in his state-ments about his illustrations. His borrowings from the fine arts (as well as from popular works heavily influenced by the fine arts) are often what give his designs their compositional power. Meanwhile, his borrowings from the more disposable of the popular arts often supply much of his antic wit. At all times, it is difficult to sort his overlapping antecedents. As he put it in his *Scrapbook*, his ideas are "all smushed up inside [his] head" (Joyce, 1997b).

Ultimately, a definitive analysis of Joyce's influences is less important than grasping the joyousness that underlies his constructions. The vigorous delights of Joyce's illustrated world emerge as fortuitously playful gestures. While keeping his adult sophistication in charge of his technique, Joyce lets his inner child control his imagination. The "common culture" he wants us all to share has much to do with the sensibility he discovered for himself as a child. Joyce's embrace of the extravagant silliness of popular culture is crucial to the celebration of shared culture and sensibility that his work develops. His generous embrace of the popular provides him with a rich array of images and stylistic features without blocking him from giving his work sophistications of design derived from his training in artistic and cinematic modes.

Although Joyce rejoices in his role as the whimsical scribe and high priest for a shared nostalgic sensibility, his distillations both depend on and transcend the cultural elements he celebrates. His training as a fine artist and a filmmaker equip him with the means to create works that are often more beautiful and artistically interesting than the "cool stuff" that inspired them.

Joyce's strong grasp of principles of cinematic design was accentuated during his college days at Southern Methodist University when he switched his major from the studio art program to the filmmaking program. Images from the silver screen, which first became important to Joyce during his TV-obsessed childhood, have provided him with models for the melding of the popular and vigorously vulgar with the solidly crafted. Joyce understood that powerful visual composition in film contributed to the success, both artistic and financial, of both low- and high-brow classic films.

The strong compositions of still photos and painted posters used to promote movies also seem to have influenced Joyce both directly and through the intermediary of comic books, which were influenced by movie posters. Such influences are multiple in their effects, as film posters and stills were influenced by comic books and pulp novel illustrations, especially the sort used on covers. The circularity of such patterns of influence make them untidy and difficult to assess.

In this discussion, I focus on works for which Joyce produced both images and words. I examine the mix of popular and fine arts elements that are reflected in each work, but the organization of my survey of the Joycean world stress two major themes that have been prominent in all books of his published thus far. It is my contention that each of his self-authored picture books is organized around either the celebration of an eccentric family or the exposition of a tale of heroic action. The heroic actions are usually of a swashbuckling, cinematic sort. There is much overlap and interweaving of these two types of stories in the works discussed here: His eccentric family sagas always contain some elements of heroic endeavor, and his heroic adventures always have familial contexts or consequences.

For each work I discuss, I mention several of the major influences or echoes evident in the work. Because Joyce's pictures have influences that range from the grandest of Renaissance art to the most modest of comic strips, it is not easy to do justice to his antecedents. I endeavor, however, to give some sense of the common culture presented in his works.

HEROIC SAGAS

My examples of heroic sagas are *George Shrinks, Bently and Egg,* and *Santa Calls.*

George Shrinks (1985)

Joyce's first heroic adventure tale was also his first self-authored picture book (Plate 13.1, p. 283). Crucial to the excitement of *George Shrinks* is the boldly active and strikingly confident nature of George's attack on the tasks he performs despite the bizarre disadvantage of his reduced state. George's confidence and bravado bring to mind the heroic behaviors of silver-screen swashbucklers of the sort portrayed by such actors as Errol Flynn, but there is also a suggestion of the boyish straight-aheadness of the heroes of boy novels from Tom Sawyer through Tom Swift.

Although many commentators routinely assume that George is asleep and dreaming his adventures as a 3-inch-high boy (Cech, 1985), the text and pictures do not unambiguously support that view. In fact a case can be made, using evidence from the pictures, that he has been subject to a magical transformation in the *real* world, rather than a sleep-induced dream fantasy.[1] Readers do not need to resolve this question. No doubt Joyce wanted to leave the reality of the adventure unresolved. It seems likely that Joyce

---

1. Parallels to Maurice Sendak's *In the Night Kitchen* and Winsor McCay's *Little Nemo in Slumberland* might seem to indicate that George is dreaming, but parallels to fairy tales of tiny boys and the science fiction film *The Incredible Shrinking Man* suggest that George is strangely transformed in a *real* world. I asked Joyce

would lean toward the reality interpretation because to say an adventure is "just a dream" is to lessen its potency. As we see in his other works, Joyce clearly favors the empowerment of the fantastic.

Ultimately, it does not matter whether George is supposed to be literally asleep. The principle that controls his fantastic shrunken adventures is more cinematic than it is dreaming (of the nocturnal sort). Joyce's training as a filmmaker often seems to come to the fore as he conceptualizes his illustrations. He has commented that, "When I am working on a book, it plays as a movie in my head" (cited in Telgen, 1993). This filmic progression is especially clear in *George Shrinks*, where one image often anticipates and moves toward the next in ways that are suggestive of a storyboard for a film shoot. The most structurally cinematic parts are the bed scenes at the beginning and the end and the airplane scene that starts just past the middle of the book and carries on almost to the end.

As we move through the early to middle parts of the book, we are given one-page-per-adventure accounts of George's strange and wonderful exploits. Some scenes are hilarious, single-image tales that operate almost as film stills (which are complete narratives in the way history paintings are complete narratives), but even the largely self-contained scenes are played toward or against the image developed in its facing page. Double-page spreads always suggest a pairing of some sort and a flow of action from left to right.

The first bed sequence has a full-size George hugging his stuffed bear as the book begins. The next image in the sequence, showing a tiny George still asleep by his bear, was used as the frontispiece for the book and, thus, is out of sequence. The second captioned image offers a view down the pillow that shows George's waking to confront his reduced state, emphasized by the sudden hugeness of the toy bear; it provides a full view of the note from his parents, a towering paper tent toward which he is gazing. George then turns to face the vast landscape of his bedroom with a stance that expresses surprise and readiness for movement. His engaged posture suggests a heroic explorer facing a formidable landscape, which is really just a low-angle view of his bed and the doors of his closet and room. There is a sense that the "camera" has turned toward the direction he will need to move. The "camera" shifts again, and we see George and his bed in profile so that we can watch George pull up his blanket to begin his heroic fulfillment of his parents' in-

---

about this and he confirmed that, indeed, he wanted to leave the reader in some doubt with regard to the reality versus dream question, although he left small visual clues that George's shrinkage happened in reality. (Conversations) structions, starting with "Please make your bed." The ongoing carrying out of the parental directives provides the text and primary plot of the book.

In the next frame, George has left the bed behind as he gazes around the corner at his principal antagonist, his cat. We realize that George has ventured down from the relative safety of his bedtop to the edge of his room. This is the only image in the first half of the book that has no caption. It underscores the potential menace of the cat that will become an important part of the purely visual heroic plot, which operates parallel to the parental note-driven plot.

A strong pairing of actions occurs in the next double-page spread, where George sits on a bathtub faucet and brushes his teeth with a comically huge brush, followed by an image of George at sea in the tub firing his toy-boat cannon at his rubber ducky. George brushing with a brush twice his size is simply comical, but the nautical adventure in the tub is one of the most dramatic in the book. Our view, looking past the large foreshortened form of the duck toward George and his vigorous firing away from his boat in full sail, recalls similar compositions in nautical battle paintings and battleship comic books. The mock-heroic nature of this image and several others like it is what sets the tone for the book. Throughout the tale, George is undeterred by his absurd tininess and staunchly carries out his parents' directives. These tasks, which would be quite routine and easy if he were his normal size, are ridiculously glorious achievements for a 3-inch boy.

In the next pair of pictures, he cleans up his room (dragging huge toy soldiers) and then slides down the banister to get his "little" brother. The next spread gives us the kitchen scene, where George gorges himself on an immense cake and a towering soft drink, then does the dishes by skiing down them on a sponge. The next pair of images puts George and his brother at the edge of the house taking out the trash and then frightening the cat. Next, two "shots" give us a subtly interrelated wildlife sequence, where we first see a heroically caped George confronting a frog as big as he is followed by an inside-the-house scene of George feeding the goldfish while riding one of them. The rest of the book features the sequence of flying-the-toy-airplane scenes and the concluding parental return scenes.

George Shrinks refers to a wide range of movie genres and specific films. Among the horror-film influences, *The Incredible Shrinking Man* is the most vividly present, but images derived from *King Kong* peek through here and there. Direct references to famous paintings are not numerous in *George Shrinks*, which stays close to its overriding B-movie and picture-book origins, although there is the joking insertion of a print of Georges Seurat's

Sunday Afternoon on the Island of La Grande Jatte. This reduced version of a famous "Georges" painting hangs just above the shrunken version of George, the protagonist, as he slides down the bannister.

Picture-book traditions are key. Foremost among the picture-book influences is Maurice Sendak's *Where the Wild Things Are* and *In the Night Kitchen*. The unflappable courage George exhibits as he faces a monstrously large world suggests the similar pluckiness of Max as he faces down the wild things in their wild place and Mickey as he bravely rises up from his almost baking in the oven of the night kitchen. Furthermore, several of Joyce's airplane images in *George Shrinks* refer directly to the images of Mickey in flight over his night kitchen. Joyce also looks through Sendak toward Winsor McCay, whose Little Nemo's visits to dreamland are precursors to both Mickey's and George's antics. McCay's role as a pioneer in the development of film animation makes him an important ancestor for Joyce. We see further McKay echoes, especially in *Dinosaur Bob* and *Santa Calls*.

In this as well as other books, Joyce orchestrates a melange of elements he enjoys in the works of others. His books are not so much derivative as they are recombinative: He makes something strikingly original by eloquently reshuffling familiar motifs and enlivening the whole with his distinctively personal antic energy. One small, but interestingly clever, element in *George Shrinks* that shows Joyce's compositional and narrative ingenuity is his use of the eyes of toy figures to direct the gaze of the viewer. Compositional use of eyes is a standard device of the visual arts, of course, but Joyce gives it a new twist by arranging his scenes so that the eyes of the Teddy bear, the toy soldiers, and the other toy figures are always aimed toward George's activities. The lively dynamic of the watching toys is handled with versimilitude in each individual scene, so that the toys seem only accidentally to be providing meaningful glances. The consistently bemused witnessing by the toys contributes to the aliveness of each image without at any point seeming to violate our understanding that the toys are inanimate objects.

Bently & Egg (1992)

As we have seen, the heroic exploits and nonchalant courage of George are those of the staunch Sendakian child. In *Bently & Egg* (1992), however, we have a hero of another sort—a swashbuckling figure out of the old movies (Plate 13.2, p. 283). Curiously, the world this unlikely hero swashbuckles through seems derived from an uncinematic source—the books of Beatrix Potter. The dashing (and swinging-from-ropes-and-chandeliers) film hero—as exemplified by Douglas Fairbanks as Zorro and D'Artagnan or Errol Flynn as Robin Hood[2] and Captain Blood—is one sort of model for Bently's heroic rescue of Egg, but the visual vocabulary for such active heroics can be found in adventure films of every stripe, including cowboy flicks. The film *Around the World in Eighty Days* is evoked by Bently's gallant balloon-riding-rescue antics. The low-angle, dramatic compositions that image most of Bently's heroics bear resemblance to movie posters and comic-book images—in particular, Bently's scenes are suggestive of the high drama of comic-book covers, where striking compositions have always been greatly valued because hyperdramatic cover designs can arrest the attention of the potential purchaser.

The publication of *The World of William Joyce Scrapbook* in 1997 has made available to us an intimate view of Joyce's preoccupations and working methods. For instance, the *Scrapbook* shows us that the composition of one of the more striking pictures in *Bently & Egg*, the illustration of Bently lassoing Egg in cowboy fashion, is based on an arrangement of objects on Joyce's studio desktop. A photograph on page 26 of the *Scrapbook* shows us the objects posed for the picture; the three-monkey bookend, the books, the phone, the egg, and the chair are in the exact positions they occupy in the finished illustration. In the spot where we see Bently in the finished illustration, a toy cowboy with a lasso stands as the central figure. The juxtaposition of the illustration and its prototype photo shows that Joyce achieves striking toy's-eye-view compositions by providing himself with views from such positions. It is clear, too, that the careful use of models for objects plays a role in Joyce's production of images.

Bently & Egg demonstrates Joyce's artistic versatility. Painted just 2 years after *A Day with Wilbur Robinson*, it is handled in an entirely different style. The pale pastel colors and treatment of the animal characters suggest the influence of Beatrix Potter. In particular, the personality and the fastidious, gentlemanly manner of Bently recalls Potter's frog character Jeremy Fisher. With regard to the plot, there are other echoes. Bently's fearless wild rides recall Toad of *Wind in the Willows*, and the egg-minding plot of *Bently & Egg* is a familar one that looks back to the egg-sitting of a Margaret Wise Brown rabbit (in *The Golden Egg Book*, 1947) and Dr. Seuss' elephant-nesting (in *Horton Hatches the Egg*, 1948). There is also an abandoned-toy motif that recalls *The Velveteen Rabbit* and a use of poem composition as a means to comment on the moment that recalls a similar strategy used in the whimsical development of Winnie the Pooh's self-preoccupied escapades.

---

2. Joyce has mentioned in several places that he is a big fan of Robin Hood. He seems to have in mind classic illustrations by both N. C. Wyeth and Howard Pyle.

That *Bently & Egg* is a compendium of sources in no way diminishes the distinction of this lovely book; its originality lies in the way Joyce energizes variations on familiar plots and images by means of striking compositions, embedding all elements in a movie plot-derived, action-packed sequence of incidents. As Bently moves in a left-to-right, swashbuckling slash of movement, we are made to share his wild frame-by-frame progression. The willingness to try new styles and the care in composition evident in *Bently & Egg* signaled a new level of ambitious artistry that was to achieve further expression in *Santa Calls*. Joyce has said *Santa Calls* took 2 years.

Santa Calls (1993)

Art Aimesworth of *Santa Calls* resembles the heroes of series novels (Plate 13.3, p. 284). He is somewhat like a Hardy Boy or a Nancy Drew, but Art's preoccupation with inventions makes him, most of all, a hero in the mold of Tom Swift. On the surface, the plot follows a heroic, Tom Swift pattern, but underlying the young-inventor-as-crime-fighter tale is the family matter of his sister Esther's desire for respect. The heroic action is presented as a somewhat inflated and mock heroic chronicle, with the real tale involving Art's simple discovery of the value of his sister. The whole adventure is, in fact, Santa's present to Esther.

The most important single popular-culture influence is Winsor McCay's comic strip *Little Nemo in Slumberland*. McCay's classic strips from around 1905 to 1908 had been revived and partially republished by the time Joyce was working on *Santa Calls*. Some images in Joyce's North Pole resemble the images of two of the dream palaces lavishly depicted in McCay's strip—those of King Morpheus and Jack Frost. It is possible that Joyce sets his Santa tale in the year 1908 to underscore the connection with the strange dreams of Winsor McCay.[3] The Sendak inspiration also comes into play here because of the much-discussed influence of McCay's slumberland world on Sendak's *In The Night Kitchen*, which, as we saw earlier, was also a source of imagery for Joyce's *George Shrinks*. Joyce's use of high drama, night-time lighting, and the notion of a densely populated North Pole city probably owes something to Chris Van Allsburg's (1985) *Polar Express*, but Van Allsburg's austerely black-and-white, twilight-zone North Pole is very different in visual style and tone from Joyce's brightly colorful phantasma-

---

3. In 1976, Dover Publications reprinted a number of sequences of McCay's *Little Nemo in Slumberland* in full color. Included were episodes featuring the palaces of King Morpheus and Jack Frost.

goria. Film influences on *Santa Calls* include *Babes in Toyland* and Busby Berkeley musicals. Again there is much use of powerful low-angle shots of up-in-the-air heroics.

Some of the most spectacular scenes in *Santa Calls* seem inspired by Italian Renaissance art—especially the paintings of Venetian master Tintoretto, who was adept at dynamic images of bodies flying through space and elaborate scenes of assembly, presentation, and rescue. The central images in *Santa Calls*, in which the children are being presented toward raised platforms on which Santa and Mrs. Claus stand facing throngs of onlookers, recall such Tintoretto compositions as *St. Mark Rescuing a Slave*, *Presentation of the Virgin in the Temple*, and *Christ Before Pilate*. Regardless of whether Joyce was conscious of paralleling Tintoretto's heroic religious paintings, it is instructive to make the comparison to appreciate the visual grandeur of the images in this most epic of Joyce's books.

ECCENTRIC FAMILIES

The next four books under discussion reverse the pattern evident in the previous three. Whereas *George Shrinks*, *Bently & Egg*, and *Santa Calls* unfold their plots as heroic actions while presenting family feelings as underlying sentiments and punchlines, the next set—*Dinosaur Bob*, *A Day with Wilbur Robinson*, *Buddy*, and *The World of William Joyce Scrapbook*—are expositions of the antics of families with scattered instances of heroic or mock-heroic action serving as gags within the overall vaudeville of the eccentric household. Joyce's eccentric family books tend toward the variety-show structure. Although *Dinosaur Bob* and *Buddy* do have plots, after a fashion, the emphasis, even in those works, is more on the one-after-another staging of the antics than on structuring a narrative.

The culture of the family from the child's angle of vision is basic to Joyce's works. The kid's point of view is specifically that of a grown-up kid named William Joyce. Several of Joyce's books testify to the wonderful grandeur of families that can manage to be eccentric. Although one of the models for his use of the oddball family motif seems to be the penniless, goodhearted Sycamore family from *You Can't Take It with You*, the Frank Capra film based on the Kaufman and Hart play, pennilessness is not part of the context in any of Joyce's eccentric family pieces. In fact the odd behaviors of Joyce's lovable clans are often made possible by their riches. Joyce's eccentric families have the benign wealth of Daddy Warbucks of the *Little Orphan Annie* cartoons or of the Rich family of the *Richie Rich* comic books.

Dinosaur Bob and His Adventures With the Family Lazardo (1988)

Joyce's first eccentric family tale is in many respects his most remarkable (Plate 13.4, p. 284). *Dinosaur Bob and His Adventures With the Family Lazardo* gives us an elegantly mansion-ensconsed doctor, wife, son, and two daughters who make a habit of unusual vacations from which they bring back surprising things. Finding a brontosaurus during an expedition to Africa, they decide to adopt it as a pet and bring it home to their suburban estate in "Pimlico Hills."

Although some commentators have identified the setting of *Dinosaur Bob* as the 1930s—one critic calls it "an appealing homage to the 1930s" (Dirda, 1988, p. 10)—Joyce is quite specific about the year, declaring on the end-paper map illustration that, "This is 1929 ya know!" One can also note that a movie theater marquee in one of the Pimlico Hills images advertises a movie called *Girl Chasers of 1929*. It is important to the positive aura of the Lazardos that we see them as a fun family of the jazz age, rather than as an isolate moneybags clan of the Depression. The Roaring 20s connection is reinforced by the clothing, hairstyles, car designs, and names of two of the kids—who are dubbed Scotty and Zelda to remind us of jazz-age literary lights, F. Scott and Zelda Fitzgerald. The story is set at the last possible moment of the glorious 1920s when almost anything, including a dinosaur who can play "The Hokey Pokey" on a trumpet, still seems possible.

Between the lines of this bizarrely gorgeous book, Joyce presents a warmly affectionate view of a family unit. Here is a family whose vacations are a source of joy. They carry a globe with them and decide and revise their travel plans by happy impulse. So open to divergent changes in itinerary are the Lazardos that, once the redoubtable Bob makes his appearance, all plans reorganize around their newfound prehistoric pal. A voyage down the Nile on the back of Bob is followed by a Bob-centered, ocean-liner voyage home. The story that underlies this visual feast is slight, but at its heart resides a family ruled by the childish inclination to say yes to the most unlikely of possibilities. Among the factors that makes *Dinosaur Bob* such a kick for kids are the double satisfactions of eccentric impulse and complete confidence; the parental characters are as fully ruled by the childlike attitude as are their children, and the tale projects a strong confidence that the childlike attitude is absolutely the right approach. There is never any doubt that the ending will be happy and that the Lazardos' ridiculous willingness to adopt a pet larger than their mansion will work out well.

Influences on *Dinosaur Bob* obviously include the numerous books about dinosaurs that Joyce devoured as a boy and that he claims to have recycled in his elementary school drawings (*Scrapbook* 8). Old-fashioned dinosaur toys determine much of the look of this Brontosaurus-like animal. *King Kong* is the film of most important influence on this picture tale. The plot roughly parallels the capture-a-huge-creature-in-the-jungle-then-have-him-run-amuck-in-the-American-city motif made famous in *Kong* (*Scrapbook* 42). Joyce also points out that other great American legends of ridiculous heroic largeness, such as the Paul Bunyan tales, also contributed to his conception (*Scrapbook* 8). Other cinematic and historical references include tiny cameo appearances by figures that resemble such characters as Noel Coward, Otto Preminger, and Babe Ruth. The concluding events of Dinosaur Bob resemble the typical sports movie climax.

The influence of Winsor McCay on *Dinosaur Bob* can be assumed. McCay's pioneering animated film *Gertie the Dinosaur* featured an amiable Brontosaurus much like Joyce's Bob. Joyce makes an explicit connection to Harold Gray's *Little Orphan Annie* comic strip through the similar treatment of speechless turbaned helpers: Jumbu who works for the Lazardos is suggestive of Punjab, the loyal assistant of Daddy Warbucks. The visual arts influences include N. C. Wyeth and Maxfield Parrish. The striking use of color suggests both of these artists. The vivid blue skies with puffy white clouds seem particularly suggestive of Parrish. The look of the building-lined streets of the town bring to mind such Edward Hopper works as *Early Sunday Morning*, which was painted, appropriately enough, in the year 1930. Grant Wood is a key influence on the toylike depiction of human figures in many of Joyce's books, including this one, and the influence of Wood's swelling landscapes and bulbous trees can be seen in the scene where Dinosaur Bob rides a train.

Joyce's whimsicality has a friendliness to it that makes clear that this absurd world is not bent on the destruction of its inhabitants. The forms of his books are intentionally constructed to comfort. Joyce has confirmed that he prefers rounded forms because of the pleasures and comforts they offer his audiences (Conversations). The strong connection to Grant Wood serves a double purpose in *Dinosaur Bob*—evoking the feel of America in the late 1920s/early 1930s and providing the book's world with a pleasurable shapeliness.

A Day With Wilbur Robinson (1990)

The eccentric family motif receives expanded treatment in *A Day with Wilbur Robinson*, the next self-illustrated book Joyce did after *Dinosaur Bob* (Plate 13.5, p. 284). The styles of the two books are, indeed, quite similar.

Although the colors are somewhat more muted in *Wilbur Robinson*, compared with those of *Dinosaur Bob*, the stylistic resemblances are such that one could almost feel that the Lazardos and Robinsons might be neighbors. The historic period is vaguely treated, but it is made relatively clear in one view from the Robinson's backyard in which an automobile, identifiable as belonging to the late 40s or early 50s, is visible.

The ample visual wit of *A Day With Wilbur Robinson* more than makes up for the book's lack of plot. As with the best work of Randolph Caldecott, Joyce's *Wilbur Robinson* rewards the attentive reader with countless small visual delights. More often than not, the plain, understated text is counterpointed in bizarre ways by depicted absurdities. The words fall hilariously and intentionally short of doing justice to the events shown in the scenes. Many gags residing entirely in the images are not referred to directly in the words. The text is a bland first-person narration by a boy who has gone visiting at his friend Wilbur's house. It seems quite appropriate that the young man, who looks to be about 9 years old, is giving us so few words of description and commentary; the narration has a naturally boyish flavor, as if it were a brief account for a letter home or a school composition.

Starting with the arrival at the front door of the Robinson house, the narrator tells us that he has "said hello to the twin uncles, Dmitri and Spike," but gives us no explanation as to why the twins appear to be dwelling in large flower pots, one on each side of the door. We overhear Wilbur say that "Lefty will take your bag," but we must look carefully at this page and the one following to grasp that Lefty—who is never seen in his entirety anywhere in the book, despite the appearances of parts of him in almost every scene—is a gigantic octopus. Another silly subtlety observable at the front door are the tiny uniformed birds, never referred to in the text, but frequently seen throughout. These birds would seem to be the explanation of how Wilbur always knows of the narrator's arrival even before he knocks. (Yes, a little bird tells him.)

Our first glimpse of the inside of the house in the next image is accompanied by several exercises in understatement. We are told that, "Aunt Billie was playing with her train set, Cousin Pete was walking the cats, and Uncle Gaston sat comfortably in the family cannon." The words lack excitement, but the picture tells us that the "train set" is an enormous locomotive, "the cats" are three full-grown tigers, and "the family cannon" is a major piece of artillery.

The next image takes us into the backyard, where Wilbur's father is inexplicably using a metal detector to look for Grandfather's false teeth (and Grandfather). Mr. Robinson is assisted by Carl the robot, who is digging holes in the yard according to the dictates of the metal detector. The contents of these holes are presented as hilariously silly archaeological excavations; perhaps the funniest of these digs reveals a gigantic (presumably prehistoric) frog skull that is wearing a little top hat, which has to be a reference to the 1955 Warner Brothers' cartoon, *One Froggy Evening*, in which an infinitely excavated frog sings and dances to the ruination of the poor schmucks who dig him up. The play and counterplay of all this delightful goofiness makes this book a pleasure to reread. It is possible to see new things at every return visit to the Robinson mansion.

References to *King Kong* constitute a running gag in this and many of Joyce's other books. In one of the interior scenes, Wilbur's sister, Blanche, is seen "modeling her new prom dress," which is topped off with a hat that makes her look like a rendition of the Empire State Building with a tiny King Kong, assaulted by airplanes, climbing up the side. Joyce tells us that *King Kong* was his favorite movie when he was growing up (*Scrapbook* 42). Affection for this classic film ape has led Joyce to include Mr. Kong as an understated signature element in many of his books. Kong is not as relentlessly included as the bull terrier unfailingly repeated in Chris Van Allsburg's books, but Kong does often show up in Joyce's pictures.

A jacket cover comment on *A Day With Wilbur Robinson* describes it as "a thickly disguised" account of William Joyce's childhood. Joyce has mentioned that he derived the bizarre goings on at the Robinson mansion from memories of his childhood, combined with appealing bits and pieces of popular culture.

> *A Day With Wilbur Robinson* is about a lot of things that actually happened to me when I was a kid. My dad was always finding really cool stuff with his metal detector; my uncle told me he was from outer space; my grandfather had false teeth that were always getting lost; my sister paid me to feed her grapes while she talked to her boyfriend on the phone; and our dog was blind. (I gave her glasses in the book.) The kid down the street from me lived in a big grand house. . . . His house was really fun to visit. So I mixed all these things up with some of my favorite movies like *Tarzan* and *The Swiss Family Robinson* and *Bringing Up Baby* and *Earth vs. the Flying Saucers*, and what I ended up with was a book about a normal kid who spends the night at this amazing house filled with robots and animals and really interesting people. (*Scrapbook* 23)

Remarks of this sort in Joyce's *Scrapbook* reveal the extent to which he has consciously woven popular culture motifs into his books. He is, however, selective in the motifs he mentions, tending to accentuate what he sees as *fun* allusions.

Buddy: Based on the True Story of Gertrude Lintz (1997)

According to comments Joyce makes in the *Scrapbook*, it was a commission to "write" a movie that stimulated the creation of *Buddy*. He does not make clear the sequence of events, but it appears that he was a prime mover in the writing of the screenplay as well as the book (*Scrapbook* 42).

Although *Buddy* is based on "the true story of Gertrude Lintz," as narrated in her book *Animals Are My Hobby*, the way events unfold in the absurdly nonfictional *Buddy* resembles in many respects the way events unfold in the absurdly fictional *Dinosaur Bob*. In *Buddy*, Joyce deftly blends his impulse toward the fantastic with his re-invention of the life and times of the Lintz family.[4]

The Lintzs of the 1930s, like the Lazardos of 1929, are wealthy mansion dwellers. In both cases, the source of the fabulous wealth appears to be part inherited and part due to the success of the husband's medical practice. The Lintz household has the same sort of comaraderie and sense of fun as the Lazardo family, but the nature of the clan is quite different. The Lintz "family" is mostly animals—a gorilla, two chimpanzees, a leopard, a parrot, a komodo dragon, a dachshund, and two servants, in addition to the ostensible "parents," Gertie and Dr. Bill. The year in which Buddy begins is almost the same as the year of *Dinosaur Bob*, when we calculate that Buddy came to the Lintzs approximately 3 years before the 1933 World's Fair.

We can also find resemblance between the Lintz mansion and the eccentric big house of the Wilbur Robinson family. Each of the Lintz animals is an eccentric by its very nature, and these zoological oddities are seen to cavort on the croquet field in the early pages of the book in ways that somewhat suggest the hijinks we witnessed at the Robinson mansion. The odd similarities include the fact that both households have dogs that wear eyeglasses. A large pet gorilla may not be as bizarre as a gigantic pet octopus, but it is bizarre enough for a book that purports to be nonfictional.

---

4. Joyce adapts and condenses the Lintz material in numerous ways. In actuality, for instance, Gertrude Lintz had two gorillas. In addition to Buddy there was Masa, and some of the things that happened to Buddy in Joyce's book happened to Masa in the Lintz memoirs. Furthermore, Joyce's peaceable kingdomlike account of the Lintz menagerie does not include the more brutal behaviors and tendencies of certain of her animals—her leopard and her "Chinese dragon," for instance.

Despite its farcical elements, the story of Buddy's eccentricities goes beyond the comical. In the climax of the story, Buddy's hysterical fear of water revives the wild animal in him, and there is briefly a danger that he may seriously harm his adoptive human mother. This turn of events eventually leads to a satisfying conclusion, with Buddy loose in a large gorilla park at a zoo where the Lintz menagerie will be allowed to regularly visit him.

Buddy the book and *Buddy* the film have many striking differences. The opening segment of the film takes advantage of its visual medium to maximize the eccentricities of the animal household. The chimpanzees, in particular, get to do many silly and vivid things in the movie; in the book, they are largely helpful and benign—much like the lovingly good children of the Lazardo family. Also, despite the simplified nature of the storytelling in the book, the Gertrude Lintz we find there is more complex and satisfying than her film counterpart. For instance, in the book, Gertrude is the one who has the prudent doubts about the safety of taking Buddy to the World's Fair, but in the film it is always her doctor husband who provides the voice of caution. By keeping both the hopes about the apes and the fears about them as separate parts of Gertrude's attitude, Joyce makes Gertrude a more interesting and wiser person. The disadvantage is that the apparently mindless husband of Joyce's book seems to be as one dimensional as a cartoon character and rather unworthy of his dynamic wife.

I am probably not the only one who finds the stylish 1930s-era images and anecdotes of the book much more attractive work than the film's endless sequences of Hollywood-enhanced chimpanzee mischief. The chimps are funny, but the endless slapstick of their misbehaviors in the film distracts us from the ensemble of the Lintz household, which is orchestrated to such fine advantage in the book. It is, at any rate, to the book we must turn for Joyce's definitive version. The book is, in fact, more rich in cinematic possibilities than the current film version is able to realize. The look of the book is clearly influenced by films of the 20s, 30s, and 40s. It should also be noted that *Buddy* gave Joyce unusually rich opportunities to play with allusions to one of his favorite movies, *King Kong*. Perhaps Joyce will someday have an opportunity to do an animated version of *Buddy* that will bring this charming tale more fully to the screen. Although the interior illustrations of the book version of *Buddy* are in reddish monochrome pastels, rather than full-color paintings, the visual style is quite similar to that of *Dinosaur Bob* and, once again, owes much to the toylike and smoothly rounded world of the paintings of Grant Wood.

Joyce's childhood family life has obviously figured prominently in his books, but he has also written a book that devotes considerable attention to the eccentricities of his life as a parent. *The World of William Joyce Scrapbook* is a useful resource for background information about the artist's development, working methods, and attitudes toward the world and his art. It also devotes considerable space to the story of his life in the 1990s, as the father character in his very own eccentric family. In his *Scrapbook,* Joyce shows himself to be almost as zany as a dad as he is as an artist.

Joyce's playfulness emerges primarily in conjunction with holidays. For the Fourth of July, he organizes the neighborhood to set up fortresses constructed of styrofoam and other light materials; he furnishes these constructions with thousands of toy soldiers as well as innumerable flags, barricades, and so forth. When all is elaborately readied, implanted fireworks are set off to destroy the hapless toy armies.

Joyce's embrace of Halloween is equally enthusiastic and involves a makeover of the family home:

> Halloween is maybe my favorite holiday. I take the whole month of October off and decorate the house. Every year my next-door neighbors and I build some really spooky stuff—we've made 20-foot skeletons and a 30-foot spider. I've got over 100 skeletons in my closets, so we haul those all out, and paint the living-room walls with Halloween murals. (Joyce, 1997b)

Yet his head-over-heels involvement in Christmas is no less massive and involves a repainting of the interior of his house with snowflakes and other appropriate imagery. It goes without saying, of course, that Easter—with its opportunities for egg painting—is also a big event for the Joyce family. The egg-painting enthusiasm of the frog protagonist of *Bently & Egg* is one expression of Joyce's passion for that holiday.

While looking at Joyce family photos and reading Joyce's recountings of his holiday spiritedness, one wonders how he finds time amid his holiday preparations and heavy schedule of family activities to write his books. One suspects that he is a high-energy person who finds his work and his play to be two aspects of the same impulse. Looking at photos of Joyce cavorting with his kids at the beach, it is easy to see why the eccentric families of his books are not that difficult for him to imagine. One imagines that if Joyce and family encountered a real dinosaur, they would be just as ready as the Lazardos to adopt an unusually large pet (Joyce, 1997b).

The delight that Joyce takes in holidays brings us back to the concept of a common culture mentioned at the beginning of this chapter. Joyce's whole-hearted celebration of the pantheon of America's popular culture makes the whimsical faith that lies behind the famous slogan, "Yes, Virginia, there is a Santa Claus," into a "religion" that is always tongue-in-cheek, but never cynical. Joyce's attitude is childlike in the best sort of way. He revels in the play opportunities provided by America's adoration of the pseudo "dieties" that dominate our shared popular culture. His dashing hereos, like those of the silver screen, project an air of casual invulnerability—a godlike manner that has much in common with the attitude of the child at play. Neither Errol Flynn nor the American version of Robin Hood he portrays are godlike in any really religious way, but there is room in our world for adopting a playful wor-shipfulness toward what the actor and characters he acts combine to create.

In a not-yet-published series of books, described in the *Scrapbook,* Joyce promises to deliver a full pantheon of folk figures from the lore of bedtime tales. The Sandman, Jack Frost, the Man in the Moon, and the Tooth Fairy will all make appearances in books about "The Guardians of Childhood." He plans to establish a team of household gods that have some-thing to do with Mount Olympus, on the one hand, and DC Comics' Justice League, on the other.

It seems likely that Joyce's works will continue to carry on the hopeful playfulness that is crucial to the life of our common culture. It is a culture that does not segregate traditional folklore and mythology from the paral-lel concoctions of the various entertainment industries. Joyce's cheerfully postmodern common culture accepts it all—whether it comes by TV, movie screen, oil painting, comic book, dime novel, picture book, advertising slo-gan, or whatever. Because Joyce loves to be silly (but is nobody's fool) and because he has developed ways to capture the wonders of fantasy in glorious extravagances of illustration and wise minimalisms of wittily chosen words, he seems capable of becoming an artistic high priest (and low priest) of our common culture. He confirms for readers of all ages the value of the child-like view and seems to suggest, through the infusion of real bravery and antic swashbuckling into the midst of the family adventure, that having fun and being heroic have much in common with each other and mysteriously reinforce the affectionate loyalties that hold families together.

The value of Joyce's best work lies in the excellence of his art more than in the archaelogy of his images, but it is interesting and valuable that Joyce has found ways to make popular culture traditions count as traditions in exactly the same way as fine arts traditions. Because Joyce is so open and multifarious in his borrowings, he presents a valuable opportunity to witness how all sorts of traditions can flow together to invigorate the literary-visual forms of picture books.

REFERENCES

Bourne, G., & Cohen, M. (1975) *The Gentle Giants: The Gorilla Story*. New York: Putnam.

Brown, M. W. (1947). *The Golden Egg Book*. New York: Simon & Schuster.

Cech, J. (1985, November 10). A Palette of Picture Books. *The Washington Post Book World*, pp. 19, 22.

Dirda, M. (1988, October 9). Dinosaur Bob. *The Washington Post Book World*, pp. 10–11.

Geisel, T. [Dr. Seuss]. (1948). *Horton Hatches the Egg*. New York: Random House.

Grahame, K. (1908). *The Wind in the Willows*. London: Methuen.

Hart, M. & Kaufman, G. (1937). *You Can't Take it With You*. New York: Dramatist Play Service.

Joyce, W. (1985). *George Shrinks*. New York: Harper.

Joyce, W. (1988). *Dinosaur Bob and His Adventures with the Family Lazardo*. New York: Harper.

Joyce, W. (1990). *A Day with Wilbur Robinson*. New York: Harper.

Joyce, W. (1992). *Bently & Egg*. New York: Harper.

Joyce, W. (1993). *Santa Calls*. New York: Harper.

Joyce, W. (1997a). *Buddy: Based on the True Story of Gertrude Lintz*. New York: Harper.

Joyce, W. (1997b). *The World of William Joyce Scrapbook*. New York: Harper.

Joyce, W. (2002, June 13-14). Conversations with Joseph Stanton in Honolulu.

Lintz, G. (1942). *Animals Are My Hobby*. New York: McBride.

McCay, W (1976). *Little Nemo in the Palace of Ice and Further Adventures*. New York: Dover.

Potter, B. (1906). *Jeremy Fisher*. London: Frederick Warne.

Pyle, H. (1883). *The Merry Adventures of Robin Hood*. London: Sampson, Low, Marston, Searle and Rivington.

Sendak, M. (1970). *In the Night Kitchen*. New York: Harper.

Sendak, M. (1963). *Where the Wild Things Are*. New York: Harper.

Seuss, Dr. [Theodore Geisel]. (1940). *Horton Hatches the Egg*. New York: Random House.

Telgen, D. (Ed.). (1993). *Something About the Author*. Detroit: Gale Research.

Van Allsburg, C. (1985). *The Polar Express*. Boston: Houghton Mifflin.

Williams, M. (1922) *The Velveteen Rabbit or How Toys Become Real*. Illus. William Nicholson. London: Heinemann.

Contributors

Susan J. Balter-Reitz, Ph.D, is an Assistant Professor in the Department of Communication and Theatre at Montana State University–Billings. Her research interests include visual argument, argumentation theory, and the intersection of argumentation and the First Amendment. She has published in *Argumentation, Free Speech on Trial,* and *Free Speech Yearbook.* She received her Ph.D. from the University of Washington.

Ann Marie Barry, Ph.D., is the author of *Visual Intelligence* and *The Advertising Portfolio,* and numerous articles related to the neurology of image perception. She has been honored with the Distinguished Research Award of the International Visual Literacy Association, the National Communication Association Visual Commission Award for Excellence in Research, and an NBC/Carnegie Institute National Teacher's Award for work in media education. A Professor at Boston College, she teaches courses in visual communication theory, advanced visual theory and aesthetics, and visual design.

Susan B. Barnes, Ph.D., is an associate professor in the Department of Communication at the Rochester Institute of Technology (RIT). She is the author of *Online Connections: Internet Interpersonal Relationships, Web Research: Selecting, Evaluating, Citing* (with Marie Radford and Linda Barr), and *Computer-Mediated Communication.* She is the Associate Director of the Lab for Social Computing at the Rochester Institute of Technology.

Julie Borkin is a Ph.D. candidate in the Department of Communication at Wayne State University. Her dissertation project considers contemporary discourses in which social and institutional vitality is thought to depend on extravagant and sacrificial acts by ordinary subject citizens.

Kevin Michael DeLuca, Ph.D., is an associate professor at the University of Georgia. Author of the book *Image Politics: The New Rhetoric of Environmental Activism,* DeLuca explores humanity's relation to nature and how people's relationships to nature are mediated by technology. He has published essays on environmental politics, social movement practices, the rhetorics of violence and bodies, social theory, and media. Valuing nothing but time, DeLuca uses his privileged position to nurture his twin addictions to speed and images through world travel.

Diane S. Hope, Ph.D., is the William A. Kern Professor in Communications, Rochester Institute of Technology. Her work focuses on visual rhetoric, advertising, and the rhetoric of social change. A former editor of *Women's Studies Quarterly*, she has published book chapters in various collections and essays in *Communication Quarterly*, *Women's Studies Quarterly*, and the *Environmental Communication Yearbook*. She is currently working on a book on autobiographical rhetoric and women environmentalists.

Timothy R. Gleason, Ph.D., is an assistant professor of journalism at the University of Wisconsin-Oshkosh. He has published research in *Education About Asia*, *Journal of Asian Pacific Communication*, and *SIMILE*. His photography has appeared in a diverse group of publications including *Woman's World* magazine and the Welsh arts journal *Timbuktu*.

Lester C. Olson, Ph.D., is a Professor of Communication at the University of Pittsburgh. His scholarship concerning visual rhetoric concentrates on 18th-century visual culture. His award-winning books include *Emblems of American Community in the Revolutionary Era* and *Benjamin Franklin's Vision of American Community*. He has been researching visual communication for more than 25 years.

Leanne Stuart Pupcheck, Ph.D., is the Chair of the Department of Communication at Queens University of Charlotte, NC. She earned her Ph.D. from the University of South Florida, a Masters in Radio-Television-Film from Syracuse University, and a Bachelor of Journalism from Carleton University in Ottawa, Ontario. Her research interests include visual rhetoric, rhetorical history, and national identity.

Yana van der Meulen Rodgers, Ph.D., is Associate Professor of Women's and Gender Studies at Rutgers University. Her research interests lie in the economics of gender, the economics of children, and development economics. She has published in the *Journal of Labor Economics*, *Industrial and Labor Relations Review*, *Journal of Development Economics*, and *Economic Development and Cultural Change*. She received her B.A. from Cornell University in 1987 and her Ph.D. in economics from Harvard University in 1993.

Brian J. Snee, Ph.D. is Assistant Professor of Communication at the State University of New York, College at Potsdam. His research examines the intersection of communication and media and politics, and has appeared in such journals as *Communication Quarterly*, the *Journal of Media and Religion*, and the *Free Speech Yearbook*. Currently he is co-editing a book that examines the many political documentary films of the 2004 presidential campaign.

Joseph Stanton's books include *The Important Books: Children's Picture Books as Art and Literature, Cardinal Points: Poems on St. Louis Cardinals Baseball, Imaginary Museum: Poems on Art, A Hawai'i Anthology*, and *What the Kite Thinks*. He is at work on biographies of Winslow Homer and Stan Musial. He teaches art history and American studies at the University of Hawai'i at Manoa.

Karen Stewart is a doctoral student in the Hugh Downs School of Human Communication at Arizona State University. Her primary research focuses on the relationship between images and written/spoken texts, and methods for improving visual literacy. Her current work includes visually based performative narratives exploring discourse and visual culture.

Rick Williams has been a visual communications scholar and a documentary photographer for more than 30 years. His research explores visual communication and art as pedagogical tools that integrate rational and intuitive intelligences. His photographic work explores transitions in culture. His books include *Working Hands* and *Visual Communication: Integrating Media, Art and Science*. He is Chair of the Division of the Arts at Lane Community College in Eugene, Oregon.

Jing Ying (Sara) Zhang received her A.B. cum laude in economics and her M.P.P. from the College of William and Mary in Williamsburg, VA. Ms. Zhang worked for the Virginia Resources Authority, a provider of infrastructure financing for local governments. Ms. Zhang currently resides in Singapore.

Color Plates

Plate 4.1. Grand Central with Colorama. Courtesy of Eastman Kodak Company.

Plate 4.2. *Christmas Carolers,* 1961. Courtesy of Eastman Kodak Company.

Plate 4.3. *Farm Scene and Family Snapshots.* Courtesy of Eastman Kodak Company.

Plate 4.4. *Camping at Lake Placid, New York,* photographed by Herb Archer. Courtesy of Eastman Kodak Company.

Plate 4.5. *Monument Valley, Arizona,* Photographer, Peter Gales, 1962. Courtesy of Eastman Kodak Company.

Plate 8.1. Detail of Hecate, the literal and philosophical center of the storm surrounding fresco artist Ben Long's *Images at the Crossroads.* Photograph courtesy of Benjamin F. Long IV.

Plate 8.2. Ben Long's fresco *Images at the Crossroads* in Statesville, NC, depicts the frailty of Western humanity and the mythical strength of a woman protector of the crossroads against a backdrop of the local landscape. Photograph courtesy of Benjamin F. Long IV.

Plate 10.1. Moore's "Molotov cocktail." Courtesy Metro-Goldwyn-Mayer Inc.

Plate 10.2. Expository Mode. Courtesy Metro-Goldwyn-Mayer Inc.

Plate 10.3. Participatory Mode. Courtesy Metro-Goldwyn-Mayer Inc.

Plate 10.4. Fear in the News. Courtesy Metro-Goldwyn-Mayer Inc.

Plate 11.1. "Wash Day." REA Series 1 poster, 1937, Lester Beall. All images used with permission of the Lester Beall collection, Archives and Special Collections, RIT Libraries, Rochester Institute of Technology.

Plate 11.2. "Boy and Girl on Fence." REA Series 2 poster, 1939. In addition to the design, Beall also did the photography for this poster.

Plate 11.3. "A Better Home." REA Series 3 Poster, 1941., In this poster, Lester Beall depicted the benefits to farm women of having electricity in the home.

Plate 11.4. "Power for Defense." REA Series 3 Poster, 1941. In addition to a general message about electricity, Lester Beall communicated the idea that power was essential for the war effort.

Plate 13.1. Cover of *George Shrinks*. Copyright © 1985 by William Joyce. Used by permission of HarperCollins Publishers.

Plate 13.2. Cover of *Bently and Egg*. Copyright © 1992 by William Joyce. Used by permission of HarperCollins Publishers.

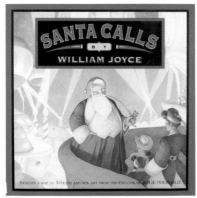

Plate 13.3. Cover of *Santa Calls*. Copyright © 1993 by William Joyce. Used by permission of HarperCollins Publishers.

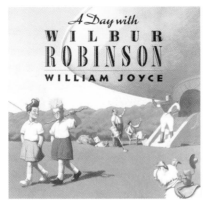

Plate 13.4. Cover of *Dinosaur Bob*. Copyright © 1988 by William Joyce. Used by permission of HarperCollins Publishers.

Plate 13.5. Cover of *A Day with Wilbur Robinson*. Copyright © 1990 by William Joyce. Used by permission of HarperCollins Publishers.

Index

Note: Page numbers with an *f* indicate figures; those with a *t* indicate tables; those with an *n* indicate footnotes; *pl.* refers to the color plates, which start on page 277.